# Object-Oriented Programming with Visual Basic .NET

## Related titles from O'Reilly

**In a Nutshell references**

C# in a Nutshell

ADO.NET in a Nutshell

ASP.NET in a Nutshell

.NET Windows Forms in a Nutshell

VB.NET Core Classes in a Nutshell

VB.NET Language in a Nutshell

**Pocket References**

C# Language Pocket Reference

C# and VB.NET Conversion Pocket Reference

VB.NET Language Pocket Reference

**Also available**

C# Essentials

COM and .NET Component Services

Learning C#

Learning Visual Basic .NET

Mastering Visual Studio .NET

.NET Framework Essentials

Programming ASP.NET

Programming C#

Programming .NET Web Services

# Object-Oriented Programming with Visual Basic .NET

*J.P. Hamilton*

O'REILLY®

Beijing · Cambridge · Farnham · Köln · Paris · Sebastopol · Taipei · Tokyo

**Object-Oriented Programming with Visual Basic .NET**
by J. P. Hamilton



Published by O'Reilly & Associates, Inc., 1005 Gravenstein Highway North, Sebastopol, CA 95472.

O'Reilly & Associates books may be purchased for educational, business, or sales promotional use. Online editions are also available for most titles (*safari.oreilly.com*). For more information, contact our corporate/institutional sales department: (800) 998-9938 or *corporate@oreilly.com*.

| | |
|---|---|
| **Editor:** | Ron Petrusha |
| **Production Editor:** | Brian Sawyer |
| **Cover Designer:** | Emma Colby |
| **Interior Designer:** | David Futato |

**Printing History:**

October 2002: First Edition.



ISBN: 0-596-00146-0
[M]

# Table of Contents

# Preface

This book is not a reference. That needs to be said right off the bat. It was written to be read cover to cover; it tells a story. It's an interwoven tale about object-oriented programming in the .NET world: building objects, moving them, and using them around the world. This is not just a how-to book; it's a why-to and a when-to book as well.

You will encounter many twists and turns ahead. Expect to learn the unexpected, but do not expect Visual Studio .NET. It didn't come out until a year after I got the .NET beta for the first time. Everything in this book is very hands-on, so if you're afraid you might chip a nail, turn back now. If you like being under the hood, though, you will feel right at home.

I started preparing for this book so long ago that it's not even funny. I actually have some old, crusty *.doc* files that refer to "Cool." That's what they were going to call C# before they called it C#. I'm not joking. This book began its life when most of the other .NET books began theirs—shortly after the Microsoft Professional Developer's Conference in 2000. Now, two years later, someone is finally reading it. Hopefully, you will see that it wasn't rushed to market. I have thought about everything in this book very carefully and have spent about a year and a half of my free time putting it together.

Why? I'm on a mission. Several, in fact. My main purpose is to provide an alternative to the big, fat reference book (especially the ones written by more than one author). I love reading books about programming—especially skinny books about computing that assume I am not an idiot. My goal is to write these kinds of books. I assume you know what HTTP, XML, and SOAP stand for. To me, that means something.

My second mission is to give all my readers a .NET epiphany. I remember talking to my editor Ron on the phone a couple of years ago. "Whaddya mean there's no COM?" I said. Shortly after the phone call, I received my first beta of .NET in the mail. The sheer size and depth of it stunned me. A super-secret, subterranean coding army must have been at work! I will never know how Microsoft managed to have something of this scope back then (that nobody knew about). My first goal was to "get it." I am still learning about .NET two years later, but now I "get it." I wasn't able to present everything under the sun in this book, but I think you'll also "get it" by the time you finish reading it.

My third mission is to make loads of cash. I remember a time when I sat around trying to think of how I could get a job that paid minimum wage in addition to all my contract work. I had too much of a social life back then, and all the time with my friends and family was really killing me. I found that I wasn't spending enough quality time in front of the computer. Then it hit me: "I'll write programming books!" I haven't slept since.

## Audience

Anyone can read a reference manual, but the reference often neglects the fundamental principals. I remember when I first started trying to learn Windows in 1991. I always ended up having more questions than answers at the end of the day (thank God for Charles Petzold!). My inexperience was partly to blame, but I have never forgotten those days, and I hope that beginners who read my book will learn from the lessons that I've managed to learn only with great pain. However, I also wrote this book for professional VB gunslingers who have been using the language for years to bring home the bacon. In some ways, VB.NET is a familiar friend. In others, it's an entirely new beast.

If you are looking for a language reference, this ain't it. If you are new to programming, though, you will need a reference. I suggest O'Reilly's *VB.NET Language in a Nutshell* by Steven Roman, Ron Petrusha, and Paul Lomax, which is concise and user friendly.

If you are not new to programming, a week and a help file is all you need to learn the language's syntax (OK, I am exaggerating a bit). Although this book is not a language reference, you can learn a lot from the example code; much of the VB.NET syntax is used within context.

## About This Book

This book primarily covers the topic of building objects. It discusses how they are designed, why they are designed that way, and how the design fits in with .NET. Here is a brief overview of what lies ahead.

Chapter 1, *Introduction*, is a high-level view of object-oriented programming and the key concepts of the .NET Framework. This chapter establishes key object-oriented terminology and shows how it applies to .NET.

Chapter 2, *Object Fundamentals*, discusses objects and the .NET world they live in. It includes discussions on compiling objects, namespaces, application domains, assemblies, intermediate language, and the .NET class library.

Chapter 3, *Class Anatomy*, shows how to build classes. Topics include member variables, methods, properties, access modifiers, and the use of access modifiers in class designs. The chapter also discusses passing parameters, the difference between reference types and value types, creating and destroying objects, the .NET garbage collector, events, and delegates.

Chapter 4, *Object-Orientation*, focuses on object-oriented programming (OOP). Topics include specialization and generalization, inheritance, and containment. The chapter also discusses polymorphism: substitution, method overloading and overriding, and shadowing. You will learn about using polymorphism, abstract base classes, and the Open-Closed Principle, which allows you to write flexible object hierarchies. Discussions of proper inheritance and the Liskov Substitution Principle are also included. The chapter ends with an in-depth look at interface-based programming and a few of the major interfaces you need to learn to make robust .NET objects.

Chapter 5, *Interfacing .NET*, discusses interface-based programming and how it fits into the world of OOP. The chapter also covers some of the most important .NET interfaces.

Chapter 6, *Exceptional Objects*, deals with exception handling within the .NET Framework. You will learn how and when to write your own exceptions, use the `AppDomain` unhandled exception handler, use a stack trace, resume and retry code, and use performance counters to profile application exceptions.

Chapter 7, *Object Inspection*, covers a powerful .NET technology called *reflection*, which allows you to query type information programmatically. The chapter discusses runtime type discovery, dynamic type inspection, and attributes. You will also learn how to build custom attributes by using them to provide behavior for VB.NET that mimics C# XML documentation comments.

Chapter 8, *Object In, Object Out*, deals with streams and serialization. Discussions include binary and XML serialization and the streams available in .NET, the Schema Definition Tool, and custom serialization. The chapter uses a TCP server and client to illustrate the use of network streams.

Chapter 9, *Object Remoting*, shows how to move objects into a distributed environment. It discusses channels, activation models, configuration, marshaling, lifetime leases, proxies, and other remoting fundamentals. The chapter uses a reusable Windows service to host remote objects and shows how to configure and use IIS to host remote objects. The chapter also demonstrates how to use object factories to build flexible, distributed systems.

Chapter 10, *Web Services*, describes how to write XML web services, host them from IIS, and make them available for .NET remoting. You will learn when to use web services and when to use remoting. The chapter also covers compatibility issues that affect consumption.

## Assumptions This Book Makes

At times, this book is ideal for beginners. At other times, it is for intermediate programmers. And sometimes, it is for advanced coders. Regardless of your skills, this book assumes three things: the .NET Framework is installed on a machine and under your control, you have access to a web server, and, when you get curious, you know how to look up whatever interests you in the documentation. .NET is massive. However, I wasn't able to cover every subject; I wanted the book to be manageable for the readers, fun, and informative.

This book was intended to leave you with some unanswered questions. By the end of it, you should have a better idea about which questions you need to ask. A good companion to this text, Dave Grundgeiger's *Programming Visual Basic .NET*, fills in a few gaps that I left out on purpose, particularly ADO.NET, Windows Forms, and ASP.NET. In this book, objects are objects. Whether they make a window on the screen or update a record in a database, you should follow fundamental rules when using them. That is one of the most important messages you'll learn from this book.

## Conventions Used in This Book

I use the following font conventions in this book:

*Italic* is used for:

- Unix pathnames, filenames, and program names
- Internet addresses, such as domain names and URLs
- New terms where they are defined

**Boldface** is used for:

- Names of GUI items: window names, buttons, and menu choices

`Constant width` is used for:

- Command lines and options that should be typed verbatim
- Names and keywords in programs, including method names, variable names, and class names
- XML element tags

## How to Contact Us

Please address comments and questions concerning this book to the publisher:

O'Reilly & Associates, Inc.
1005 Gravenstein Highway North
Sebastopol, CA 95472
1-800-998-9938 (in the United States or Canada)
1-707-829-0515 (international or local)
1-707-829-0104 (fax)

There is a web page for this book, which lists errata, examples, or any additional information. You can access this page at:

*http://www.oreilly.com/catalog/objectvbnet*

To comment or ask technical questions about this book, send email to:

*bookquestions@oreilly.com*

For more information about books, conferences, Resource Centers, and the O'Reilly Network, see the O'Reilly web site at:

*http://www.oreilly.com*

## Acknowledgments

First, I would like to thank my editor, Ron Petrusha, for all his help. Let it be known that I am probably not the easiest writer to work with, so his guidance was immensely appreciated. Why he decided to do a second book with me, I will never know. Of course, I must extend this gratitude to the rest of the O'Reilly gang: Tatiana Diaz, John Osborn, Glen Gillmore, Brian Sawyer, and Claire Cloutier.

Next, I'd like to thank my technical reviewers. I owe Robert C. Martin a very special thank you for reviewing the major OO portions of the book (Chapters 4 and 5). Having his input was an awesome experience because much of what I have learned about OOP comes from his writings. I would also like to thank Ingo Rammer for answering many of my remoting questions. Buy his book, *Advanced .NET Remoting* (APress). It's the best. And last but not least, thanks to Daniel Creeron for his thorough review of the entire book.

On a personal note, I don't think this book would have been possible without the many people who helped me this past year more than they will ever know: Natasha Deveraux, Kristen Guggenheim, Melinda Parmley, Marty Kelly, Michael Anderson, Joby Erickson, Kelly Christopher, Jon Polley, Joe Boley, Steve Myers, David Braddy, Robert Smith, and Ogre. God bless you all.

CHAPTER 1

# Introduction

To understand the world of object-oriented programming, look at the world around you for a moment. You might see vacuum cleaners, coffee makers, ceiling fans, and a host of other objects. Everywhere you look, objects surround you.

Some of these objects, such as cameras, operate independently. Some, such as telephones and answering machines, interact with one another. Some objects contain data that persists between uses, like the address book in a cell phone. Some objects contain other objects, like an icemaker inside of the freezer.

Many objects are similar in function but different in purpose. Bathtubs and kitchen sinks, for example, both provide water and are used for cleaning. But it is a rare occasion when you will take a bath in the kitchen sink or wash your dishes in the tub. However, the bathtub and the kitchen sink in your house probably share the same plumbing. Certainly, they share a common interface: hot and cold water knobs, a faucet, and a drain.

When you think about it, what is the difference between a sink and a bathtub? The location? The size of the basin? Their heights off the ground? How many more similarities are there than differences?

Sometimes the same action causes an object to do different things depending on the context of the situation. When you press Play on the remote, the DVD might play a movie on the television. But if a CD is in the player, it plays music out of the speakers. Same button, same action—different results. When you flip the switch on the back porch, the light comes on. But the switch in the kitchen turns on the garbage disposal. You use the same kind of switch, but obtain different results.

You can think about many objects around you in terms of *black boxes*. You comprehend the fundamentals of these objects and possess a basic understanding of what makes them work, but the specifics of their operation are unknown to you. And you like it that way. Do you really want to have to know the inner mechanisms of every object in your house in order to use it?

Consider that light bulb on the back porch. The filament in the bulb is nothing more than a simple resistor. When the 100-watt bulb is "on," the filament's temperature is about 2550 degrees Celsius. The resulting thermal radiation, which is proportional to the length of the filament (but not the diameter), produces about 1750 lumens worth of visible light at a wavelength of about 555 nanometers. And by the way, the filament is made out of tungsten.

Do you really want to know these minute details, or do you just want the light to come on when you flick the switch?

Any object has two inherent properties: *state* and *behavior*. The light bulb on the back porch has state. It can be on or off. It has a brand name and a life expectancy. It has been in use for a certain number of hours. It has a specified number of hours left before the irregular evaporation of its tungsten filament causes it to burn out. Behaviorally, it provides light; it shines.

But an object is rarely an island unto itself.

Many objects participate collectively in a system. The television and surrounding sound speakers are a part of a system called a home theater. The refrigerator and oven belong to a system called a kitchen. These systems, in turn, are a part of a larger system that is called an apartment. Collections of apartments make up a system known as a complex. Apartments and houses belong to neighborhoods and so on, ad infinitum.

In essence, this book discusses systems. Building and designing objects is one aspect of this process of building a system. Determining how these objects interact with one another is another. Understanding both phases of development is crucial when building any system that has more than a modicum of complexity.

Generally, you can think of this process of developing a system as object-oriented programming and object-oriented design. Specifically, though, you are really working toward an understanding of the objects you build and the system in which they participate. Component-based programming forms the basis of this system.

Programming objects in software doesn't require an object-oriented language, and just because you use an object-oriented programming language doesn't mean that your code is object-oriented. Languages can only assist the process; they can't make any guarantees. The ability to write object-oriented software was always available with VB. Writing it just hasn't always been easy because the language wasn't always oriented in that direction. Developing binary reusable components in VB has been possible for some time now, but using these components across languages used to be considered somewhat of a black art—until now.

Today, Visual Basic .NET is a cutting-edge, object-oriented language that runs inside of a state-of-the-art environment. It is feature-rich and designed to take advantage of the latest developments in object-oriented programming. Writing software and building components has never been easier.

# Visual Basic .NET and Object-Oriented Programming

Visual Basic .NET is a fully object-oriented programming language, which means it supports the four basic tenets of object-oriented programming: abstraction, encapsulation, inheritance, and polymorphism.

We have already conceptualized many of these object-oriented concepts by just looking at the objects that surround us in our everyday lives. Let's look more closely at these terms and see what they actually mean and what they do for developers of object-oriented software.

## Abstraction

A radio has a tuner, an antenna, a volume control, and an on/off switch. To use it, you don't need to know that the antenna captures radio frequency signals, converts them to electrical signals, and then boosts their strength via a high-frequency amplification circuit. Nor do you need to know how the resulting current is filtered, boosted, and finally converted into sound. You merely turn on the radio, tune in the desired station, and listen. The intrinsic details are invisible. This feature is great because now everyone can use a radio, not just people with technical know-how. Hiring a consultant to come to your home every time you wanted to listen to the radio would become awfully expensive. In other words, you can say that the radio is an object that was designed to hide its complexity.

If you write a piece of software to track payroll information, you would probably want to create an Employee object. People come in all shapes, sizes, and colors. They have different backgrounds, enjoy different hobbies, and have a multitude of beliefs. But perhaps, in terms of the payroll application, an employee is just a name, a rank, and a serial number, while the other qualities are not relevant to the application. Determining what something is, in terms of software, is *abstraction*.

In object-oriented software, complexity is managed by using abstraction. Abstraction is a process that involves identifying the crucial behavior of an object and eliminating irrelevant and tedious details. A well thought-out abstraction is usually simple, slanted toward the perspective of the user (the developer using your objects), and has probably gone through several iterations. Rarely is the initial attempt at an abstraction the best choice.

Remember that the abstraction process is context sensitive. In an application that will play music, the radio abstraction will be completely different from the radio abstraction in a program designed to teach basic electronics. The internal details of the latter would be much more important than the former.

## Encapsulation

Programming languages like C and Pascal can both produce object-like constructs. In C, this feature is called a *struct*; in Pascal, it is referred to as a *record*. Both are user-defined data types. In both languages, a function can operate on more than one data type. The inverse is also true: more than one function can operate on a single data type. The data is fully exposed and vulnerable to the whims of anyone who has an instance of the type because these languages do not explicitly tie together data and the functions that operate on that data.

In contrast, object-oriented programming is based on *encapsulation*. When an object's state and behavior are kept together, they are encapsulated. That is, the data that represents the state of the object and the methods (Functions and Subs) that manipulate that data are stored together as a cohesive unit.

Encapsulation is often referred to as *information hiding*. But although the two terms are often used interchangeably, information hiding is really the result of encapsulation, not a synonym for it. They are distinct concepts. Encapsulation makes it possible to separate an object's implementation from its behavior—to restrict access to its internal data. This restriction allows certain details of an object's behavior to be hidden. It allows us to create a "black box" and protects an object's internal state from corruption by its clients.

Encapsulation is also frequently confused with abstraction. Though the two concepts are closely related, they represent different ideas. Abstraction is a process. It is the act of identifying the relevant qualities and behaviors an object should possess. Encapsulation is the mechanism by which the abstraction is implemented. It is the result. The radio, for instance, is an object that encapsulates many technologies that might not be understood clearly by most people who benefit from it.

In Visual Basic .NET, the construct used to define an abstraction is called a *class*. The terms *class* and *object* are often used interchangeably, but an object is actually an instance of a class. A component is a collection of one or more object definitions, like a class library in a DLL.

## Inheritance

Inheritance is the ability to define a new class that inherits the behaviors (and code) of an existing class. The new class is called a *child* or *derived class*, while the original class is often referred to as the *parent* or *base class*.

*Inheritance* is used to express "is-a" or "kind-of" relationships. A car *is a* vehicle. A boat *is a* vehicle. A submarine *is a* vehicle. In OOP, the `Vehicle` *base class* would provide the common behaviors of all types of vehicles and perhaps delineate behaviors all vehicles must support. The particular *subclasses* (i.e., derived classes) of vehicles would implement behaviors specific to that type of vehicle. The main concepts behind inheritance are extensibility and code reuse.

In contrast to inheritance, there is also the notion of a "has-a" relationship. This relationship is created by using *composition*. Composition, which is sometimes referred to as aggregation, means that one object contains another object, rather than inheriting an object's attributes and behaviors. Naturally, a car *has an* engine, but it is not a *kind of* engine.

C++ supports a type of reuse called *multiple inheritance*. In this scenario, one class inherits from more than one base class. But many C++ programmers will tell you that using multiple inheritance can be tricky. Base classes with identical function names or common base classes can create nightmares for even the most experienced programmers.

VB.NET, like Java, avoids this problem altogether by providing support only for single inheritance. But don't worry, you aren't missing out on anything. Situations that seem ideal for multiple inheritance can usually be solved with composition or by rethinking the design.

When it comes to proper object-oriented design, a deep understanding of inheritance and its effects is crucial. Deriving new classes from existing classes is not always as straightforward as it might initially appear. Is a circle a kind of ellipse? Is a square a kind of rectangle? Mistakes in an inheritance hierarchy can cripple an object model.

## Polymorphism

*Polymorphism* refers to the ability to assume different forms. In OOP, it indicates a language's ability to handle objects differently based on their runtime type.

When objects communicate with one another, we say that they *send* and *receive* messages. The advantage of polymorphism is that the sender of a message doesn't need to know which class the receiver is a member of. It can be any arbitrary class. The sending object only needs to be aware that the receiving object can perform a particular behavior.

A classic example of polymorphism can be demonstrated with geometric shapes. Suppose we have a `Triangle`, a `Square`, and a `Circle`. Each class *is a* `Shape` and each has a method named `Draw` that is responsible for rendering the `Shape` to the screen.

With polymorphism, you can write a method that takes a `Shape` object or an array of `Shape` objects as a parameter (as opposed to a specific kind of `Shape`). We can pass `Triangles`, `Circles`, and `Squares` to these methods without any problems, because referring to a class through its parent is perfectly legal. In this instance, the receiver is only aware that it is getting a `Shape` that has a method named `Draw`, but it is ignorant of the specific kind of `Shape`. If the `Shape` were a `Triangle`, then `Triangle`'s version of `Draw` would be called. If it were a `Square`, then `Square`'s version would be called, and so on.

We can illustrate this concept with a simple example. Suppose we are working on a small graphics package and we need to draw several shapes on the screen at one time. To implement this functionality, we create a class called `Scene`. `Scene` has a method named `Render` that takes an array of `Shape` objects as a parameter. We can now create an array of different kinds of shapes and pass it to the `Render` method. `Render` can iterate through the array and call `Draw` for each element of the array, and the appropriate version of `Draw` will be called. `Render` has no idea what specific kind of `Shape` it is dealing with.

The big advantage to this implementation of the `Scene` class and its `Render` method is that two months from now, when you want to add an `Ellipse` class to your graphics package, you don't have to touch one line of code in the `Scene` class. The `Render` method can draw an `Ellipse` just like any other `Shape` because it deals with them generically. In this way, the `Shape` and `Scene` classes are *loosely coupled*, which is something you should strive for in a good object-oriented design.

This type of polymorphism is called *parametric polymorphism*, or *generics*. Another type of polymorphism is called *overloading*. Overloading occurs when an object has two or more behaviors that have the same name. The methods are distinguished only by the messages they receive (that is, by the parameters of the method).

Polymorphism is a very powerful concept that allows the design of amazingly flexible applications. Chapter 4 discusses polymorphism in more depth.

# The .NET Framework

The objects you construct with VB.NET will live out their lives within the .NET Framework, which is a platform used to develop applications. The platform was designed from the ground up by using open standards and protocols like XML, HTTP, and SOAP. It contains a rich standard library that provides services available to any language running under its protection.

The impetus behind its creation was the desire to develop a platform for building, deploying, and running web-based services. In spite of this goal, the framework is ideal for developing all types of applications, regardless of the design. The .NET Framework makes child's play of some of programming's most sophisticated concepts, giving you the ability to take advantage of today's cutting-edge architectures:

- Distributed computing using open Internet standards and protocols such as HTTP, XML, and SOAP
- Enterprise services such as object pooling, messaging, security, and transactions
- An infrastructure that simplifies the development of reusable cross-language compatible components that can be deployed over the Internet
- Simplified web development using open standards
- Full language integration that make it possible to inherit from classes, catch exceptions, and debug across different languages

Deployment is made simpler because settings are stored in XML-based configuration files that reside in the application directory; there is no need to go to the registry. Shared DLLs must have a unique hash value, locale, and version, so physical filenames are no longer important once these considerations are met. Not having physical filenames makes it possible to have several different versions of the same DLL in use at the same time, which is known as *side-by-side* execution. All dependencies and references are stored within the executable in a section called the *manifest*. In a sense, we're back to the days of DOS because to deploy an application, you only need to *xcopy* it from one directory to another.

This book explores many aspects of .NET in order to gain a complete understanding of the components you write and the world in which they live. Doing it any other way is impossible. The .NET Framework provides so many services your components will use that discussing one without referring to the other is literally impossible—they are that closely tied together.

Two major elements of the .NET Framework will be addressed repeatedly throughout this book. The first is the Common Language Runtime (CLR), which provides runtime services for components running under .NET.

The second element is the .NET class library, a vast toolbox containing classes for everything from data access, GUI design, and security to multithreading, networking, and messaging. The library also contains definitions for all primary data types, such as bytes, integers, and strings. All of these types are inherently derived from a base class called `System.Object`, which you can think of as a "universal" data type; there is no distinction between the types defined by the system and the types you create by writing classes or structures. Everything is an object!

The term .NET means many things to many different people. When the term is used in this book, it always refers to the .NET Framework—the Common Language Runtime and the .NET class library.

In the past, passing a string from a component written in VB to one written in C++ (or vice versa) could be frustrating. Strings in VB weren't the same as the strings in C++. In fact, under some circumstances, using a component written in C++ from VB was downright impossible because of issues involving data types. VB just doesn't know what to do with an `LPSTR`! Every language under .NET uses the same data types defined in the base class library, so interoperability problems of the past are no longer an issue.

This book touches on several major areas of the library and focuses on the development of components using VB.NET. However, if you follow the examples, you might be surprised at just how much you know.

## The Common Language Runtime

The CLR is the execution engine for the .NET Framework. This runtime manages all code compiled with VB.NET. In fact, code compiled to run under .NET is called *managed* code to distinguish it from code running outside of the framework.

Besides being responsible for application loading and execution, the CLR provides services that will benefit component developers:

- Invocation and termination of threads and processes
- Object lifetime and memory management
- Cross-language integration
- Code access and role-based security
- Exception handling (even across languages)
- Deployment and versioning
- Interoperation between managed and unmanaged code
- Debugging and profiling support (even across languages)

Runtimes are nothing new. Visual Basic has always had some form of a runtime. Visual C++ has a runtime called *MSVCRT.DLL*. Perl, Python, and SmallTalk also use runtimes. The difference between these runtimes and the CLR is that the CLR is designed to work with multiple programming languages. Every language whose compiler targets the .NET Framework benefits from the services of the CLR as much as any other language.

.NET is also similar to Java. Java uses a runtime called the Java Virtual Machine. It can run only with Java code, so it has the same limitations as the other languages mentioned previously. Another distinction is that the JVM is an interpreter. Although all languages in the .NET environment are initially compiled to a CPU-independent language called Intermediate Language (which is analogous to Java byte code), IL is not interpreted at runtime like Java. When code is initially executed, one of several just-in-time (JIT) compilers translate the IL to native code on a method-by-method basis.

Cross-language integration is one of the major benefits provided by the CLR. If a colleague has written a base class in C#, you can define a class in VB.NET that derives from it. This is known as *cross-language inheritance*. Also, objects written in different languages can easily interoperate. The two parts of the CLR that make this interoperation possible are the Common Type System and the Common Language Specification.

### Common Type System

The Common Type System (CTS) defines rules that a language must adhere to in order to participate in the .NET Framework. It also defines a set of common types and operations that exist across most programming languages and specifies how these types are used and managed within the CLR, how objects expose their functionality, and how they interoperate. The CTS forms the foundation that enables cross-language integration within .NET.

### Common Language Specification

The Common Language Specification (CLS) is a subset of the CTS that describes the basic qualities used by a wide variety of languages. Components that use only the features of the CLS are said to be CLS-compliant. As a result, these components are guaranteed to be accessible from any other programming language that targets .NET. Because VB.NET is a CLS-compliant language, any class, object, or component that you build will be available from any other CLS-compliant programming language in .NET.

## A First-Class Citizen

VB has always been easy to learn, but the power of simplicity came with a price. The language itself has never gotten the respect it deserves because it always hid so much from the developer; getting under the hood required a sledgehammer. This is no longer true. While VB is still a great language and is relatively painless to learn and use, you are no longer restricted in how "low you can go."

One of the most important concepts behind .NET is that all languages are on a level playing field; the choice of language should be determined more by your style than anything else. This is probably the reason why you prefer VB over other languages: you like the syntax of Visual Basic and appreciate its simplicity. No longer is choice of language a concern, because VB.NET is just as fast as C# and it does a few things, such as event declaration and conditional exception handling, better. But for the most part, any language that runs under .NET will provide you with the tools to develop cutting edge software. Thus, it truly is a matter of style. VB.NET is no more or no less of a language than any other in the .NET Framework.

# CHAPTER 2
# Object Fundamentals

Before designing and building objects for the .NET environment, understanding the environment itself is important. In this respect, a little bit of code goes a long way. This chapter deviates from the standard "Hello, world" application in favor of a "Hello, world" component. Then it builds a small client that uses the component to display a message to the console window.

## Creating and Compiling the Component

Example 2-1 contains the listing for our "Hello, world" component. It contains a single class named `Hello` with a single method named `Write`. Save the listing to a file named *hello.vb*. The rest of the chapter will use this listing as a foundation of discussion.

All Visual Basic source code should be saved to files with a *.vb* extension. One file can contain one class or several classes. How you organize the code is up to you.

*Example 2-1. The "Hello, world" component*

```
Option Strict On

Imports System

Namespace Greeting

Public Class Hello
    Public Sub Write(ByVal value As String)
        Console.WriteLine("Hello, {0}!", value)
    End Sub
End Class

End Namespace
```

The Visual Basic .NET command-line compiler is a program called *vbc.exe* that should be in your path once the .NET Framework is installed. All examples in this book assume that the example code exists in the root directory of your hard drive. This assumption is made to improve readability. If the code is not in your hard drive's root directory, you need to specify a fully qualified pathname to the compiled file or compile from the directory where the source code is located. With this in mind, you should be able to compile Example 2-1 to a dynamic link library (DLL) as follows:

```
C:\>vbc /t:library hello.vb
```

The `/t:` option is short for `target`, which can be one of the following values:

`exe`
: A console application. If the `/t` switch is omitted, this is the default value.

`winexe`
: A Windows executable.

`library`
: A DLL.

`module`
: A module. This value is similar to a *.lib* file in C++. It contains objects but is not an executable.

As a default, the compiler gives the output file the same name as the file being compiled. Here, a file named *hello.dll* is produced.

All examples in this book assume that `Option Strict` is turned on. `Option Strict` prevents the VB compiler from making implicit narrowing type conversions, which is often a source of errors. Implicit narrowing type conversion involves using one type where another type with a smaller range is expected. For example, the following code is illegal when `Option Strict` is turned on:

```
Dim x As Short = 5
Dim b As Byte = x
```

The code is illegal because `x` is a `Short`, a type whose range is `-32,768` through `32,767`. The code here assigns the value of this type to a `Byte`, an unsigned numeric type whose range is `0` to `255`. Since `Short` values from `-32,768` to `-1` and from `256` to `32,767` don't "fit" into a `Byte` variable, an implicit conversion could result in loss of data. Therefore, `Option Strict On` forbids the conversion; if you want to assign `x` to a `Byte` variable, you have to make the conversion explicit, as in the following code:

```
Dim x As Short = 5
Dim b As Byte = System.Convert.ToByte(x)
```

Or as in the following code, which uses an intrinsic Visual Basic function:

```
Dim x As Short = 5
Dim b As Byte = CByte(x)
```

You can put Option Strict On at the top of your source file to turn it on or specify /optionstrict+ from the command line when you compile. This is the recommended setting, but unfortunately, the default is Off.

Many examples in this book run in a console window. To compile them using Visual Studio .NET, change the Startup Object in the project properties dialog to "Sub Main."

# Namespaces

All classes are members of some namespace. You can think of a namespace as a user-defined scope—an organizational construct that allows you to group your classes in a meaningful way and uniquely identify your classes and their members in case of naming conflicts. The Hello class from Example 2-1 is a member of a namespace called Greeting denoted by the Namespace block surrounding its definition. Even if the namespace block were removed, the Hello class would still be considered a member of the *root namespace*, which is scoped to the executable.

## Imports

Every time anything is compiled with VB, two class libraries—*mscorlib.dll* and *Microsoft.VisualBasic.dll*—are referenced implicitly. The latter contains classes that provide backward compatibility to earlier versions of Visual Basic, while the former contains portions of the System and several other namespaces. Notice the second line of code in Example 2-1:

```
Imports System
```

This line brings the System namespace into the scope of the current file, *hello.vb*. This is done for the benefit of the call to Console.WriteLine, which writes a message to the console window. Without the Imports directive, the Console class could be referred to only through its namespace, which means the call would look like this:

```
Public Class Hello
    Public Sub Write(ByVal value As String)
        System.Console.WriteLine("Hello, {0}!", value)
    End Sub
End Class
```

This particular situation is not too bad, but if the file contained several calls to Console.WriteLine, things could get ugly. As most of the .NET class library is contained within the System namespace, importing it is usually your best option.

### Framework Organization

The `System` namespace is defined in *mscorlib.dll* and *System.dll*. Although *mscorlib.dll* is referenced by the compiler automatically, *System.dll* is not.

If you need to use a class from a namespace in *System.dll* (or any other portion of the .NET class library), you have to add a reference to it when you compile with the `/r` compiler option. For example:

```
vbc /t:exe /r:system.dll code.vb
```

Other major portions of .NET include:

- ASP.NET, which is mostly contained in *System.Web.dll*
- Windows Forms, which is mostly contained in *System.Windows.Forms.dll* and *System.Windows.Drawing.dll*
- Data and XML, which are contained in *System.Data.dll* and *System.XML.dll*

## Using a Component

Now that you have a component, you need a way to use it. Example 2-2 contains a listing for a simple client. Save it to a file named *hello-client.vb*. Let's see how everything fits together, and then you can compile it.

*Example 2-2. "Hello, world" client*

```
Imports System
Imports Greeting

Public Class Application

  Public Shared Sub Main()
    Dim hw As New Hello()
    hw.Write("World")
    Console.ReadLine()
  End Sub

End Class
```

The `Greeting` namespace defined in Example 2-1 was imported. Without it, every class in the `Greeting` namespace would have to be referenced directly, as in the following code:

```
Public Shared Sub Main()
  Dim hw As New Greeting.Hello()
  hw.Write("World")
End Sub
```

All standalone executables require an entry point with this signature:

```
Public Shared Sub Main()
```

This is where everything begins, but as you can see, not much is going on. The only thing the client does is declare an instance of the `Hello` class (which is defined in the component) and call its `Write` method.

When compiled, Example 2-2 must explicitly reference *hello.dll* for everything to compile. This can be accomplished with the `/r` compiler option. Assuming that the DLL lives in the same directory as the client code, this executable can be compiled as follows:

```
C:\>vbc /t:exe /r:hello.dll hello-client.vb
```

This compilation produces an executable named *hello-client.exe*. You can change the name of the output file by using the `/out` compiler option:

```
C:\>vbc /t:exe /r:hello.dll /out:hello.exe hello-client.vb
```

When the executable runs, the following code is dumped to the console:

```
Hello, World!
```

# Application Domains

In an unmanaged Windows environment, applications are isolated from one another by process boundaries. As shown in Figure 2-1, each Win32 program is given its own process and a 4 GB virtual address space to go along with it. Additional libraries or components share this address space with their client. The operating system handles all the work associated with mapping the virtual address space to an actual address in memory. The advantage of this isolation is that if a program crashes, it won't take the entire system down—just the current process.

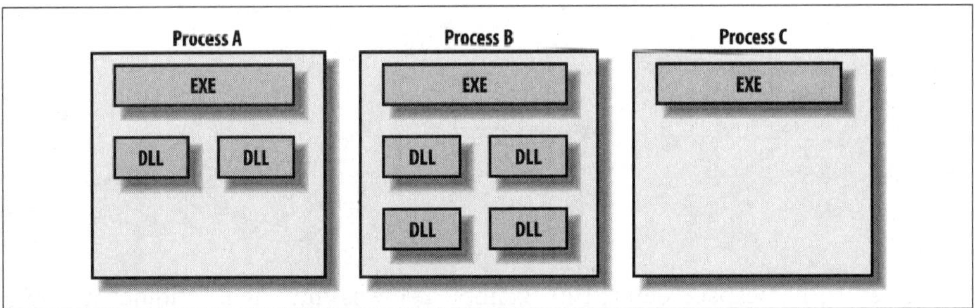


*Figure 2-1. The Win32 process boundary*

Under .NET, the CLR manages the memory; Windows doesn't give it to you directly. One reason for this is garbage collection. The CLR needs to know where memory is located to free it or determine if it is in use at all, which is why no pointers are allowed in managed code. This level of indirection, in regard to memory, allows the CLR to provide application isolation with more granularity. In .NET, an entity called an *application domain* determines isolation.

> **Managed Versus Unmanaged Code**
>
> The term *managed code* refers to code compiled under the .NET Framework. The framework automatically manages the lifetime of an object, hence the term. *Unmanaged code* is simply all other code running outside of the bounds of .NET.

As shown in Figure 2-2, several application domains can exist within the same process and still remain isolated from one another. They can also be loaded and unloaded independently of the process, which means that if a crash occurs, the offending application domain can be unloaded without affecting the entire process. This is highly efficient, considering the amount of overhead involved in creating a process.

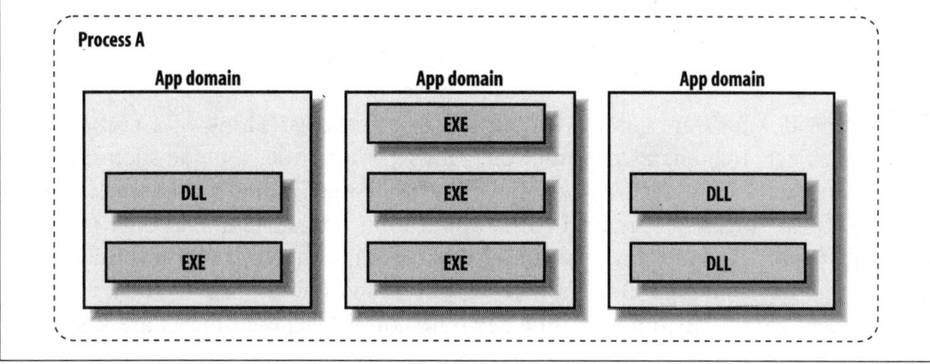


*Figure 2-2. Application domains provide isolation for .NET applications within a process.*

Application domains do not share the same restrictions as a process. They can contain any number of EXEs or DLLs in several combinations. Typically, though, an application is loaded into one application domain. This is the case with *hello-client.exe* and *hello.dll*. In fact, you can verify this yourself with the CLR shell debugger. In a console window, run *hello-client.exe*. Spawn a second console and start up the debugger from the command line like this:

```
C:>cordbg
```

Once the debugger is running, you can issue a `pro` command to get information on all managed .NET applications that are running on the system. It will look similar to this:

```
C:\>cordbg
Microsoft (R) Common Language Runtime Test Debugger Shell
Version 1.0.3705.0 Copyright (C) Microsoft Corporation 1998-2001.
All rights reserved.

(cordbg) pro
```

```
PID=0x818 (2072)  Name=C:\hello-client.exe
        ID=1  AppDomainName= hello-client.exe

PID=0x6c0 (1728)  Name=C:\WINNT\Microsoft.NET\Framework\v1.0.3705\aspnet_wp.exe
        ID=8  AppDomainName=/LM/w3svc/1/root/eyeofnet-7-126592112951200512
        ID=7  AppDomainName=/LM/W3SVC/1/ROOT-6-126592112840541392
        ID=6  AppDomainName=/LM/W3SVC/1/Root/oowd-5-126591711176576976
        ID=5  AppDomainName=/LM/w3svc/3/root/eyeofnet-4-126591677652271392
        ID=4  AppDomainName=/LM/W3SVC/3/Root-3-126591677517878144
        ID=1  AppDomainName=DefaultDomain
```

Loading *hello-client.exe* and *hello.dll* into two different application domains is possible. But exotic configurations such as this require additional code. The hello client would have to create the assembly dynamically and load the hello component into it. Calls between the two executables would require remoting across the application domain boundaries, which is very similar to the behavior of an out-of-process COM server.

## Contexts

Application domains are subdivided further into *contexts*. Think of a context as a group of objects that share the same rules of use. These rules include such things as just-in-time activation, security, synchronization, thread affinity, transactions, and security. Under ordinary circumstances, application domains contain only one context: the *default context*. However, in some situations, the application domain contains additional contexts. Objects that support transactions (provided by COM+), for instance, would be contained in a separate context. These objects are known as *context-bound objects*.

Now that you better understand the execution environment of a .NET executable, let's look at the executable itself.

## Assemblies

When you have an instance of a class, you are said to have an *object*. A collection of object definitions comprises a *component*. For instance, *msado15.dll* is a COM component that contains the `Connection`, `Command`, and `Recordset` objects (among others) found in ADO. In .NET, the concept of an *assembly* is roughly analogous to that of a component, but you can think of it as more of a "super component."

In addition to your program's code, assemblies contain a *manifest*, which is a block of metadata that describes everything in the assembly and how it relates to everything else. As shown in Figure 2-3, it contains references to other assemblies that the current assembly might need, as well as a description of the types contained within the assembly. These references make the assembly self-describing, alleviating the need for type libraries and IDL files. In Visual Basic, assemblies can be a single executable with a `Sub Main` entry point or a class library in a DLL.

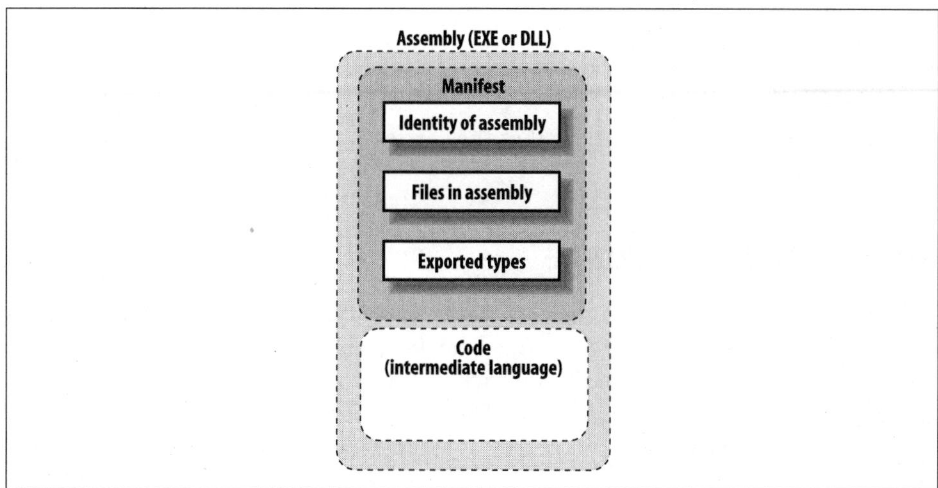


*Figure 2-3. Structure of an assembly*

Assemblies can also contain nonexecutable files of any type, similar to a resource file in a traditional Windows executable. The difference is that these additional files do not have to exist as binary information that is part of the executable. Every file that comprises an assembly can retain its individual identity within the filesystem. However, as far as the runtime is concerned, they are a single, cohesive unit. Multimodule assemblies, which contain resources in addition to code, are built using the Assembly Linker utility (*al.exe*) that is part of the .NET Framework SDK. The VB compiler only emits single module assemblies containing code.

Assemblies are the fundamental units in which code is deployed, version information is specified, and security permissions are defined. An assembly also represents a boundary for the identity of a type. If two different assemblies contain the same type definition, the runtime considers each a different type. This happens irrespective of the namespace the two types are defined within. Remember that namespaces are just mechanisms for organizing type information; the CLR resolves type names through namespaces.

## Modules

*hello-client.exe* and *hello.dll* are two distinct assemblies. They can be deployed and versioned independently of each other, and each can maintain a different level of security. Instead of compiling *hello.vb* to a DLL, you can compile it into a *module* as follows:

```
C:\>vbc /t:module hello.vb
```

This compilation produces a file named *hello.netmodule*.

A module is similar to an assembly, but it is nonexecutable and does not have any of the attributes associated with an executable. It does not maintain a version, for instance. You can recompile the hello client and link the module by using the */addmodule* compiler option:

```
C:\>vbc /addmodule:hello.netmodule hello-client.vb
```

One advantage to using modules is that they are compiled and can be distributed in place of source code.

## Intermediate Language

VB is not compiled directly into machine code. It is first compiled to a CPU-independent language called Microsoft Intermediate Language (MSIL, or simply IL). You might think this compilation is a throwback to VB's early years as an interpreted language, but the situation is not so grim. The code is not interpreted; eventually, it is converted to machine code at runtime by a just-in-time (JIT) compiler. This happens during execution, as code is needed. Then it is cached as machine code until the process terminates.

The .NET Framework SDK ships with an IL disassembler called ILDASM, which allows you to view the IL produced by the VB compiler (or any .NET compiler, for that matter). This feature can be very useful if you want to see how something in the .NET class library was implemented or to determine what classes are available in a particular library. The *hello.dll* assembly can be examined by running the IL Disassembler (*ildasm.exe*) from the command line:

```
C:\>ildasm hello.dll
```

From the ILDASM dialog, you can view the manifest and navigate every namespace within the given assembly. As shown in Figure 2-4, ILDASM presents a tree view that allows inspection of the manifest, the various namespaces, classes, and methods contained within the assembly. Example 2-3 contains the entire IL listing for *hello.dll*, which was produced by selecting File/Dump from the menu.

*Figure 2-4. The ILDASM dialog*

*Example 2-3. The IL dump of hello.dll*

```
//  Microsoft (R) .NET Framework IL Disassembler.  Version 1.0.3705.0
//  Copyright (C) Microsoft Corporation 1998-2001. All rights reserved.

.assembly extern mscorlib
{
  .publickeytoken = (B7 7A 5C 56 19 34 E0 89 )
  .ver 1:0:3300:0
}
.assembly extern Microsoft.VisualBasic
{
  .publickeytoken = (B0 3F 5F 7F 11 D5 0A 3A )
  .ver 7:0:3300:0
}
.assembly hello
{
  .hash algorithm 0x00008004
  .ver 0:0:0:0
}
.module hello.dll
// MVID: {8A2071A6-F906-43C1-B6DB-CA5058F54BC4}
.imagebase 0x00400000
.subsystem 0x00000002
.file alignment 512
.corflags 0x00000001
// Image base: 0x03090000
//
// ============== CLASS STRUCTURE DECLARATION ==================
//
.namespace Greeting
{
  .class public auto ansi Hello
         extends [mscorlib]System.Object
  {
  } // end of class Hello

} // end of namespace Greeting

// =============================================================

// =============== GLOBAL FIELDS AND METHODS ===================

// =============================================================

// =============== CLASS MEMBERS DECLARATION ===================
//   note that class flags, 'extends' and 'implements' clauses
//          are provided here for information only

.namespace Greeting
{
  .class public auto ansi Hello
         extends [mscorlib]System.Object
  {
```

*Example 2-3. The IL dump of hello.dll (continued)*

```
    .method public specialname rtspecialname
            instance void  .ctor() cil managed
    {
      // Code size       7 (0x7)
      .maxstack  8
      IL_0000:  ldarg.0
      IL_0001:  call       instance void [mscorlib]System.Object::.ctor()
      IL_0006:  ret
    } // end of method Hello::.ctor

    .method public instance void  Write(string 'value') cil managed
    {
      // Code size       12 (0xc)
      .maxstack  8
      IL_0000:  ldstr      "Hello, {0}!"
      IL_0005:  ldarg.1
      IL_0006:  call       void [mscorlib]System.Console::WriteLine(string,
                                                                    object)
      IL_000b:  ret
    } // end of method Hello::Write

  } // end of class Hello

// =============================================================

} // end of namespace Greeting

//*********** DISASSEMBLY COMPLETE ***********************
// WARNING: Created Win32 resource file C:\hello.res
```

Do not listen to those who tell you that learning IL is a waste of time. It is simply not true. You should develop at least a basic understanding of the language because it gives you an edge over those who do not know it. After all, every single .NET language compiles to IL. Once you know IL, you will really know .NET.

Some things can be done in VB that can't be done in C#, and vice versa. Other things can be done only in IL. Arrays with arbitrary bounds, for instance, cannot be declared in any .NET language; IL, however, does support them.

One way to start learning the language is by disassembling your own programs. Once you see how an assembly is laid out (which we'll go over momentarily), understanding it will be much easier. The .NET Framework SDK ships with two documents: the *MSIL Instruction Set* specification and the *IL Assembly Language Programmer's Reference*. Peek at both every once in a while—learn a command here and there. Before you know it, listings like Example 2-3 will become quite readable.

The .NET Framework also supplies an IL assembler called ILASM (*ilasm.exe*). Assuming that Example 2-3 is saved to a file named *hello.il*, you could compile it back to a DLL like this:

```
C:\>ilasm /DLL hello.il
```

### ILDASM

To get a better idea of the functionality provided by `System` and `Microsoft.VisualBasic`, examine them with ILDASM. Remember, `System` is contained primarily in *mscorlib.dll*, but parts of it reside in *System.dll*. `Microsoft.VisualBasic` is located in *Microsoft.VisualBasic.dll*.

Both DLLs are located in the .NET Framework directory, which is usually located here: *<%windir%>\Microsoft.NET\Framework\(version number)*

The following registry script adds an "Open with ILDASM" option to the context menu associated with EXEs and DLLs. This menu is available by right-clicking on these types of files in Explorer. Save the script to a file called *ildasm.reg* and double-click the file to execute it. If you type in this listing, everything between square brackets [ ] needs to be on the same line.

Before running this script, make sure that the *bin* directory for the .NET SDK is in your path. The directory should be similar to *C:\Program Files\Microsoft Visual Studio .NET\FrameworkSDK\Bin*. Locating the *bin* directory allows you to run all .NET Framework SDK utilities from the command line without having to worry about the path. Otherwise, you have to modify the script to include the full path to *ildasm.exe*:

```
REGEDIT4

[HKEY_CLASSES_ROOT\.dll]
@="dllfile"

[HKEY_CLASSES_ROOT\dllfile\shell\
Open With ILDASM\command]
@="ildasm \"%L\""

[HKEY_CLASSES_ROOT\.exe]
@="exefile"

[HKEY_CLASSES_ROOT\exefile\shell\
Open With ILDASM\command]
@="ildasm \"%L\""
```

## Assembly Internals

Let's examine the individual elements of Example 2-3 to get a better idea of how an assembly is put together. The first thing to look at is the manifest, which starts at the top of the listing and continues to the beginning of the `Greeting` namespace block.

The listing begins with two references to external assemblies that *hello.dll* needs to run properly—*mscorlib.dll* and *Microsoft.VisualBasic.dll*:

```
.assembly extern mscorlib
{
    .publickeytoken = (B7 7A 5C 56 19 34 E0 89 )
    .ver 1:0:2411:0
```

```
}
.assembly extern Microsoft.VisualBasic
{
    .publickeytoken = (B0 3F 5F 7F 11 D5 0A 3A )
    .ver 7:0:0:0
}
```

The VB compiler references these two assemblies automatically; there is nothing you can do to change this fact. Each reference contains a `publickeytoken` that contains the low 8 bytes of the SHA1 hash of the originator's public key. The CLR uses this public key token to verify that an external assembly is valid. You can find out the public key token in your own code by using the .NET Framework Strong Name tool from the command line:

```
C:\>sn -t hello.dll

Microsoft (R) .NET Framework Strong Name Utility  Version 1.0.2914.16
Copyright (C) Microsoft Corp. 1998-2001. All rights reserved.

Public key token is f45b0326d39e29a9
```

In addition to a public key token, all references must have a version number, which is built using four 32-bit integers.

The assembly definition for *hello.dll* follows the external assembly references:

```
.assembly hello
{
  .hash algorithm 0x00008004
  .ver 0:0:0:0
}
```

It contains a version number, too, but as you can see, it has not been defined, so it consists of four `0`s. You also see the `hash algorithm` key here that denotes the use of the SHA1 algorithm, used to generate the cryptographic hash of the file's contents (the public key token for *hello.dll*).

The rest of the manifest consists of the following:

```
.module hello.dll
// MVID: {EE8D826F-18C1-4317-82C5-74209B06C55E}
.imagebase 0x00400000
.subsystem 0x00000002
.file alignment 512
.corflags 0x00000001
// Image base: 0x03080000
```

Modules (in this context, the EXEs or DLLs) are not referred to by filename, but are referenced logically by the runtime. Here, the `module` key is the same as the filename, but it doesn't necessarily have to be that way. If you examine the manifest for *mscorlib.dll*, for instance, you will see that the actual name of the module is `CommonLanguageRuntimeLibrary`.

The `imagebase` entry contains the preferred address of the image (EXE or DLL) when it is loaded into memory. `File alignment` is the alignment of the raw data in the image. Neither key is metadata related. Executables in .NET are still in the Windows PE format. These settings relate to the PE header for the file.

The `subsystem` key contains one of two values: `2` or `3`. A `2` means that the program should run using whatever standards are necessary for a program that has a graphical user interface. If the value is a `3`, the program is console-based.

The `corflags` key is a reserved metadata field. It does not tell you anything about the current assembly.

Rather than get into the actual code portion of *hello.dll*, look at Example 2-4, which contains a listing for a standard "Hello, world" application in IL. It is not as jumbled as the IL dump from Example 2-3, and it is pretty readable, even if you don't know the language.

*Example 2-4. Simple "Hello, world" in IL*

```
.assembly extern mscorlib {}
.assembly HelloWorld {}
.class Hello {
  .method static void Main() {
    .entrypoint
    ldstr      "Hello, World!"
    call       void [mscorlib]System.Console::WriteLine(string)
    ret
  }
}
```

Save it to a file named *hello-world.il* and compile it:

```
C:\>ilasm hello-world.il
```

## The Global Assembly Cache

If you use an object from the .NET class library in your own code, you have to reference the assembly in which it is defined at compile time. For instance, if you want to use the `MessageBox` class in one of your applications, you need to make sure that the *System.Windows.Forms* assembly is made available to the compiler. This assembly contains the `System.Windows.Forms` namespace, which in turn contains the `MessageBox` class. The command-line statement needed to compile your source code is:

```
vbc /t:winexe /r:System.Windows.Forms.dll mycode.vb
```

Referencing one of your own assemblies is no different, but a full path to the assembly is expected. For example:

```
vbc /t:library /r:<path>\mylib.dll mycode.vb
```

A path is not necessary for *System.Windows.Forms.dll* because like all .NET class library assemblies, it lives in the *global assembly cache* (GAC). The GAC is a directory, shown in Figure 2-5, that contains assemblies that are meant to be shared by several applications on a single machine. The actual path to the GAC is *<%windir%>/assembly*.

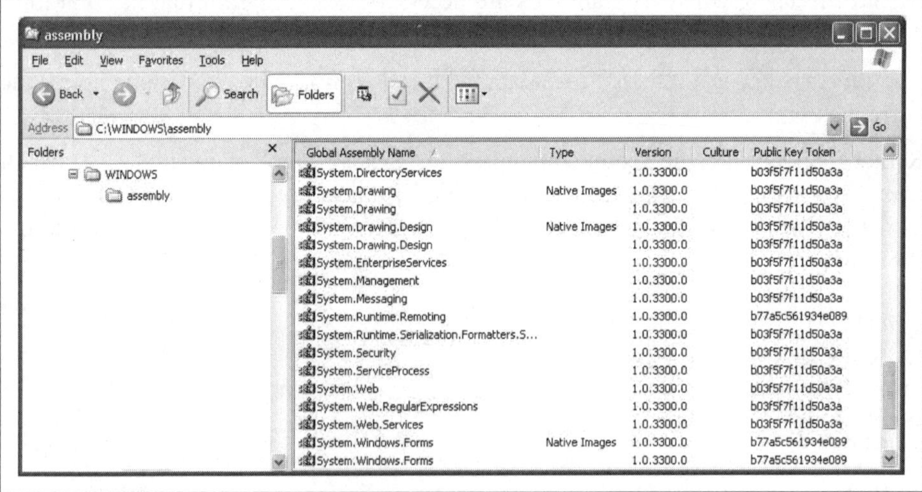


*Figure 2-5. The GAC in an Explorer list pane*

## Strong Names

If you want to share an assembly by putting it in the GAC, it must have a *strong name*. A strong name defines the assembly's identity: its name, version number, and culture information (if it exists), a public key, and a digital signature.

### Strong Name utility

The first step toward giving an assembly a strong name is creating a key pair file that contains the public/private keys used to sign the assembly. To create the key pair file, use the Strong Name tool from the command line:

```
sn -k hello.snk
```

Doing so creates a key pair file named *hello.snk*.

### Assembly Linker

Next, you need to use the Assembly Linker (AL) to sign the assembly with the key pair file. This utility is not specific to any language, so you can't feed it source code. You do need to compile your library to a module first, using a command line like the following:

```
vbc /t:module hello.vb
```

Compiling your library produces a module called *hello.netmodule*. Now you can use AL to create a signed assembly like this:

```
al /out:hello.dll hello.netmodule /keyfile:hello.snk
```

The result is a signed assembly with the name *hello.dll*.

### Gacutil

Now that you have a signed assembly, you can use the Global Assembly Cache tool, *gacutil.exe*, to install it to the GAC, as shown in the following command:

```
gacutil /i hello.dll
```

## System Namespace

Every time you compile anything in Visual Basic, the compiler automatically references two assemblies: *mscorlib.dll* and *Microsoft.VisualBasic.dll*. These two components contain the `System` and `Microsoft.VisualBasic` namespaces, respectively (a small portion of the `System` namespace is also contained in *System.dll*).

The `System` namespace is the root namespace of primary types in .NET and contains the base data types used by all languages in the framework. When you declare a primitive data type in VB, it is actually mapped to a type defined in this namespace. Table 2-1 provides a list of the types in `System` and how they relate to Visual Basic.

*Table 2-1. Data type mappings from System to VB*

| System | Visual Basic | Description |
|---|---|---|
| `Byte` | `Byte` | 8-bit unsigned integer |
| `Int16` | `Short` | 16-bit signed integer |
| `Int32` | `Integer` | 32-bit signed integer |
| `Int64` | `Long` | 64-bit signed integer |
| `Single` | `Single` | 32-bit floating point |
| `Double` | `Double` | 64-bit floating point |
| `Boolean` | `Boolean` | `True` or `False` |
| `Char` | `Char` | Unicode character |
| `Decimal` | `Decimal` | 96-bit decimal value |
| `String` | `String` | Unicode character string |
| `Object` | `Object` | Base of all objects |

How you declare variables in your code doesn't matter. Each represents a functional equivalent:

```
Dim x As System.Int32
'Is the same as
Dim x As Integer
```

If you examine Table 2-1 you will see that the Byte is the only unsigned data type supported by VB. All other integer types are signed. The Common Language Specification doesn't support unsigned integers larger than 8 bits, but they do exist in the framework (see Table 2-2). They can be used freely, provided you understand that the code you write might not be CLS-compliant.

*Table 2-2. Non–CLS-compliant types*

| Class | Description |
|---|---|
| SByte | 8-bit signed integer |
| UInt16 | 16-bit unsigned integer |
| UInt32 | 32-bit unsigned integer |
| UInt64 | 64-bit unsigned integer |

You can always call GetType to get the underlying type:

```
Console.WriteLine(GetType(Integer))
```

This code returns "System.Int32".

It is OK to use non–CLS-compliant types internally within your classes and still produce CLS-compliant objects. However, methods that are exposed to the outside world should not contain non–CLS-compliant types as parameters. Keep this in mind if it is important for your objects to be accessible to everyone.

In addition to defining core data types, the System namespace contains classes that provide a wide variety of services:

- Data type conversion
- Mathematical functionality
- Exception handling
- Remote and local program invocation
- Garbage collection

It also contains secondary and tertiary namespaces that compose the rest of the .NET class library.

## The Microsoft.VisualBasic Namespace

The Microsoft.VisualBasic namespace contains all that can be considered *classic* Visual Basic. It contains all the functionality that has been with the language before its evolution into object orientation.

String functions such as Left, Right, and Mid are in this namespace. They are members of the Strings class. The FileSystem class makes traditional file I/O using Open, Input, and Write available. Array validation functions like LBound and UBound are available through the Information class. Notification functions like MsgBox, InputBox, and even Beep are available via the Interaction class.

These methods are all defined with Public Shared access, which means you don't need specific instances of Strings, Information, or Interaction to call these functions. Public Shared access is similar to declarations using the static keyword in C++, C#, and Java. You can access the members of these classes directly, so your code still has the look and feel of traditional Visual Basic (which looks more procedural).

Example 2-5 shows a simple Visual Basic program that takes a phone number as a command-line argument. The program adds up the digits that correspond to the phone number and returns the value in the console window. The example uses functionality strictly found in the Microsoft.VisualBasic namespace. Examine the code carefully. In a moment, we'll look at the same program rewritten using only classes from the System namespace.

*Example 2-5. A phone in VB*

```
Option Strict On

Imports System
Imports Microsoft.VisualBasic

Public Class Application

  Public Shared Sub Main()

    Dim i As Integer
    Dim digit As String
    Dim total As Double

    'Get phone number from command line
    Dim phoneNumber As String = Command()

    If Len(phoneNumber) > 0 Then
      For i = 1 To Len(phoneNumber)
        'Get each digit
        digit = Mid(phoneNumber, i, 1)
        If IsNumeric(digit) Then
          total += Val(digit)
        End If
      Next i
      Console.WriteLine("Your phone number totals: " & total)
    End If

    Console.WriteLine("Press ENTER to continue...")
    Console.ReadLine()

  End Sub

End Class
```

In Example 2-5, the phone number is retrieved using `Command`, which retrieves command-line arguments, but unfortunately does not provide us with a means to specify which argument we are interested in. Fortunately, there is only one argument in this example (assuming that there are no spaces in the input). The string representing the phone number is then searched, one character at a time, by using `Mid`. If a character represents a numerical value, then it is converted to a `Byte` by calling `Val`, and the result is added to the total. The total is then displayed in the console window.

If you save Example 2-5 to a file named *phone.vb*, you can compile it into an executable using the `/t:exe` compiler option as follows:

```
C:>vbc /t:exe /optionstrict+ phone.vb
```

This compilation produces an executable named *phone.exe*, which you can run from the command line like this:

```
C:>phone (713)555-1212
Your phone number totals: 32
```

You can replace the `Console.WriteLine` call in Example 2-5 with a call to `MsgBox` to display the result in a message box:

```
MsgBox("Your phone number totals: " & total)
```

However, you need to compile the example to a Windows executable by using the `winexe` target option:

```
C:>vbc /t:winexe phone.vb
```

## The .NET Class Library

It could be argued that much of the functionality that exists in `Microsoft.VisualBasic` is not a part of the Visual Basic language, but merely tied to it by heritage.

Consider the C runtime library. It contains functions that have been used by C programmers for years. The function used to output a message to the console, `printf`, has been used in millions of lines of code since the dawn of time, which we all know began on January 1, 1970. However, this function is not part of the C language proper. It is defined in a file called *stdio.h*. As a C programmer, you could write your own `printf` function to replace the one in the runtime library. Doing so is not practical, but you can still do it because it is not a part of the language specification.

Most, if not all, functionality provided by `Microsoft.VisualBasic` is available through the .NET class library. An argument that can be made against using `Microsoft.VisualBasic` is that programmers using other languages will have a difficult time understanding this code. People using other languages to develop for the .NET platform will use the .NET class library extensively and will probably not use anything from `Microsoft.VisualBasic`. It sounds strange to say this in a book about Visual Basic, but if you are a newcomer to VB, this is something you might want to consider.

Learning everything in both namespaces will be like learning two languages at once instead of one—a daunting task, to say the least.

Conversely, if you have experience with Visual Basic, this issue will not affect you. The `Microsoft.VisualBasic` namespace is targeted toward you, and its primary purpose is to provide the functionality that was part of the language since its inception. You can use what you know and love and get all the benefits of the .NET platform. However, you should still learn as much as you can about the .NET class library and start incorporating that knowledge into your future projects.

To get another perspective on this issue, look at Example 2-5, which is rewritten in Example 2-6 to use only the .NET class library. Note that the code's atmosphere is completely different. Using classes from the `Microsoft.VisualBasic` namespace will give your code an almost procedural look at times. In contrast, using functionality from the other namespaces of the .NET class library results in code that is less procedural and more object-oriented. "Is it Visual Basic?" you ask. The answer to this question is simple. Yes, of course it is.

*Example 2-6. Phone in .NET*

```
Imports System

Public Class Application

  Public Shared Sub Main(ByVal args() As String)

    Dim c As Char
    Dim total As Integer

    If args.Length = 0 Then
      Return
    End If

    'Get phone number from command line
    Dim digits() As Char = args(0).ToCharArray()

    For Each c In digits
      If Char.IsDigit(c) Then
        total += Convert.ToInt32(c.ToString())
      End If
    Next c

    Console.WriteLine("Your phone number totals: {0}", _
                      total.ToString())
    Console.WriteLine("Press ENTER to continue...")
    Console.ReadLine()
  End Sub

End Class
```

Examples 2-5 and 2-6 do exactly the same thing. They are both Visual Basic, but stylistically they are completely different. Save this code to *phone.net.vb* and compile it.

In this example, you get the digits of the phone number from the command line through the `Environment` class instead of the `Command` method. In this case, you can specify which argument you want and convert the result directly to an array of characters. Then you can traverse the array easily by using the `For...Each` language syntax. The `Char` data type provides a shared method called `IsDigit` that lets you determine whether you are dealing with a numeric value. If so, the `Convert` class converts the character to a `Byte`, and the result is added to the total.

Almost everything in the two listings is completely different. Even the seemingly innocuous call to `Console.WriteLine` was modified. In Example 2-5, it looked like this:

```
Console.WriteLine("Your phone number totals: " & total)
```

Here, `total` is implicitly converted to a string and then concatenated to the output message.

In Example 2-6, the call looks like this:

```
Console.WriteLine("Your phone number totals: {0}", total.ToString())
```

In this case, a format specification `{0}` is replaced with the value of `total` when the output message is displayed. Also, `total` is explicitly converted to a `String`.

After comparing Examples 2-5 and 2-6 side by side, can you say that one method is better than the other? No, not really. It's all a matter of preference and style. Aspects of each listing are appealing. As a Visual Basic programmer, you will probably initially use functionality from both `System` and `Microsoft.VisualBasic`. It won't be an either-or situation.

# CHAPTER 3
# Class Anatomy

*Encapsulation* is the idea that data and the functions that manipulate that data are kept together. In Visual Basic .NET, encapsulation is achieved with the *class*, which can be thought of as the blueprint of an object. Classes contain *member variables* that are used to hold the state of an object—brightness, contrast, hue—and *member functions* (also known as methods) that describe the behavior or operations that can be performed on the object: turn on, turn off, or change the channel. They also are a source of *events*, which notify clients on the current affairs of the object.

Figure 3-1 illustrates the basic structure of a class, which contains four primary entities: member variables, methods (or member functions), properties, and events. As Example 3-1 shows, the class can exist as part of a namespace (or not).

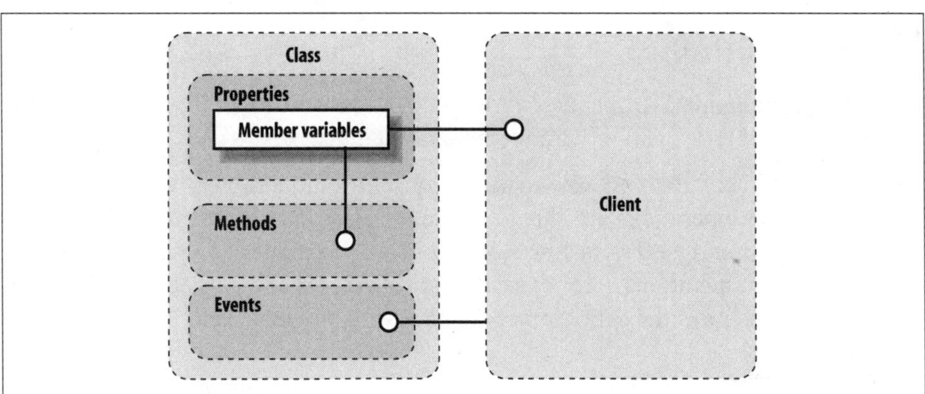


*Figure 3-1. Class overview*

*Example 3-1. Structure of a class block*

```
Namespace [Namespace Name]

Public Class [Class Name]

    'Member variables
```

*Example 3-1. Structure of a class block (continued)*

```
    'Methods

    'Properties

    'Events

End Class

End Namespace
```

Each class entity (with the exception of events) comes in two distinct flavors, *instance* or *shared*. Instance variables, methods, and properties operate on a specific instance of a class. When an object is created (instantiated), it receives its own copy of all the member data defined by the class. All method (and property) calls are made through that specific instance.

Example 3-2 contains a shared method named Hello. Shared entities are mutual across all class instances, so you don't need an actual instance of the class to call the method:

```
Console.WriteLine(World.Hello())
```

In addition to being associated with a data type, all class entities (events included), and the class itself, are associated with an *access modifier*. These modifiers determine whether a client can access the entity or if the entity is available only internally within the object, in its descendents, or in the executable in which it is defined.

## Member Variables

As shown in Example 3-1, member variables of a class are typically declared at the top of the class block (with or without an initial state).

The term "member variables" also includes constants and enumerations. By default, constants and enumerations are shared, so an instance of the class is not necessary; these values pertain to every instance of an object. Constants can refer to any data type, while enumerations are restricted to Byte, Short, Integer, and Long. Example 3-2 illustrates the definition of member variables in a class.

*Example 3-2. Member variables*

```
Public Class World

    'Member data represents state
    Private age As Double

    'Constants
    Public Const AverageDensity As Single = 5515  '(kg/m3)
    Public Const PolarRadius = 6356.8             'In km
    Public Const SatelliteCount As Byte = 1       'The Moon
```

*Example 3-2. Member variables (continued)*

```
    'Enums
    Public Enum Continents
        Africa = 1
        Antarctica = 2
        Asia = 3
        Australia = 4
        Europe = 5
        NorthAmerica = 6
        SouthAmerica = 7
    End Enum

    Public Shared Sub Hello()
        Console.WriteLine("Hello, World!")
    End Sub

End Class
```

### Variable Names

When naming classes or constant values, by convention PascalCasing should be used. With PascalCasing, each word comprising the variable name should start with an uppercase letter. Conversely, instance variables use camelCasing, which always makes the first word lowercase.

In all cases, Hungarian notation is avoided. Rather than naming your variables based on a type, you should use a meaningful name instead. The .NET Framework Design Guidelines contains a complete description of the naming conventions used within the framework.

Many of you will no doubt give up on using Hungarian notation when it's pried from your cold, dead fingers (regardless of what some specification has to say about it). How about a compromise? Try to use it only internally and make your public interfaces follow convention. Think about how your public interfaces look to the people who use your code. The era of IntelliSense has arrived!

VB.NET also supports named arguments, which means you can refer to a parameter during the method call. Which is easier to remember?

```
car.Display(Name:="Rolls-Royce")
```

or

```
car.Display(strCarName:="Bentley")
```

## Properties

In traditional OOP languages like C++, it is considered good practice to provide accessor methods to manipulate an object's state. For instance, if an object has a member variable named weight, a programmer often writes two functions. One function is used to get the value of weight, and another to set the value—something akin to get_Weight and set_Weight. To provide read-only access, the programmer would forego the get_ method.

Properties in VB.NET are merely a language construct used to provide this frequently used functionality and enforce good programming practice through the language.

Whenever you create a property, VB.NET automatically generates a get_ and set_ method behind the scenes. Essentially, a property is nothing more than language convenience. Check it out with ILDASM.

Properties can be ReadOnly, WriteOnly, or both. Read-only properties contain a Get block that allows retrieval of a value, but prevents it from being changed:

```
Public ReadOnly Property Age() As Double
    Get
        Return Me.age
    End Get
End Property
```

Write-only properties use a Set block, which allows values to be initialized but not retrieved:

```
Public WriteOnly Property Age() As Double
    Set
        'age is a Private member variable
        Me.age = value
    End Set
End Property
```

Properties that provide both read and write access must specify only an access modifier:

```
Public Property Age() As Double
    Get
        Return Me.age
    End Get
    Set (ByVal value As Double)
        Me.age = value
    End Set
End Property
```

In the Set block, you can specify the name and type of the incoming value. If you choose not to, the compiler uses "value" as the placeholder for the property value.

### Read-only fields

The ReadOnly keyword can also be applied to member data. These fields can be initialized during object construction, but not after. Usually, member data, like the private member age from Example 3-2, is accessed through a property. But access to it can be tedious when you just want to provide access to a read-only value that does not need processing before you return it to the caller.

```
Public Class World

     Public ReadOnly age As Double

End Class
```

### Default properties

Default properties allow array-like access to a class. These properties are also known as *indexers* and are very useful for implementing collections. In Example 3-3, a collection of `Planet` objects is created and then iterated. You do not need to refer to the default property (`Item`) by name. The collection class can be used like an array. You can see its use in the `For...Next` loop at the bottom of Example 3-3.

*Example 3-3. Default properties*

```
Imports System
Imports System.Collections

Public Class Planet
  Public ReadOnly Name As String

  Public Sub New(ByVal name As String)
    Me.Name = name
  End Sub

End Class

Public Class Planets

  Private myPlanets As New ArrayList()

  Default Public ReadOnly Property Item(ByVal idx As Integer) As Planet
    Get
      'Convert object in array list to Car and return
      Return CType(myPlanets.Item(idx), Planet)
    End Get
  End Property

  Public ReadOnly Property Count() As Integer
    Get
      Return myPlanets.Count
    End Get
  End Property

  Public Sub Add(ByVal value As Planet)
    myPlanets.Add(value)
  End Sub

End Class
```

*Example 3-3. Default properties (continued)*

```
Public Class App

  Public Shared Sub Main()

    Dim i As Integer

    Dim myPlanets As New Planets()

    Dim p1 As New Planet("Neptune")
    Dim p2 As New Planet("Venus")
    Dim p3 As New Planet("Pluto")

    'Add 3 planets to collection
    myPlanets.Add(p1)
    myPlanets.Add(p2)
    myPlanets.Add(p3)


    For i = 0 To myPlanets.Count - 1
      Console.WriteLine(myPlanets(i).Name)
    Next i

  End Sub

End Class
```

# Methods

In VB.NET, methods come in three varieties: functions, subroutines, and properties.

Functions allow you to return a value resulting from an operation. They are defined with the `Function` keyword and can contain any number of parameters. They can also return a result to the caller with the `Return` keyword:

```
Public Class SpaceTime

    'In meters per second
    Private Const LightSpeed As Double = 299792458

    Private Function Energy(mass As Double) As Double
       'Same as LightSpeed * LightSpeed * mass
       Return LightSpeed *= LightSpeed * mass
    End Function

    'Really technical stuff goes here
End Class
```

Subroutines perform tasks that do not require a return value and are declared just like functions, except they are defined using the `Sub` keyword:

```
Public Class SpaceTime

    Public Sub FoldSpace()
```

```
        'Suprisingly simple
    End Sub

End Class
```

You might think that using subroutines is a bad idea because they don't allow you to return the status of an operation, such as an error code or a flag indicating whether the operation was successful. Well, never fear. Error codes usually are not passed around in .NET as they are in more traditional programming languages because the CLR provides structured exception handling (SEH) for this purpose. Using SEH alleviates the need for writing statements that check return values of functions for success or failure.

A class should represent one and only one abstraction. The methods of a class should use most of the member data within the class most of the time. This means that if you find that half of the class methods operate on half of the data members, but the other methods use the remaining half, there is an implied division within the class. You probably have two classes instead of one.

To formulate this concept as a general principle, make sure there are no broken lines of communication within a class.

## Access Modifiers

Everything that comprises a class is associated with an access modifier that determines the scope or visibility of the entity in question. This is where the art of object design lies. Beyond the semantics of declaring member data and methods, an understanding of these access modifiers is crucial. Each modifier has a few basic guidelines geared toward designing robust, object-oriented code. Figure 3-2 shows the relationships between the four basic modifiers: `Public`, `Private`, `Protected`, and `Friend`.

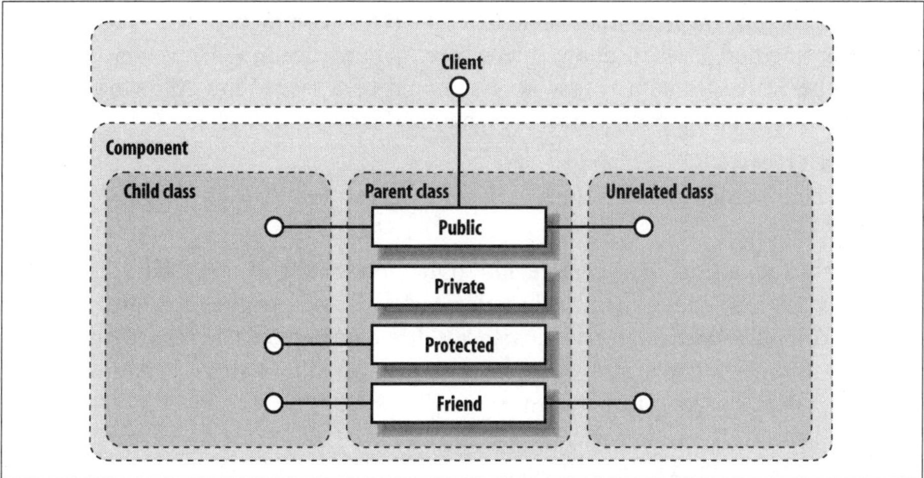


*Figure 3-2. Access modifier relationships*

`Public`
: `Public` classes are visible to everyone and not restricted in any way. `Public` members are visible inside and outside the class in which they were declared.

  Member variables are not typically defined with public scope because this definition would allow unrestricted access to an object's state. In solid OO designs, member variables are kept private.

`Private`
: `Private` classes can only be nested within another class and are completely restricted outside of that scope; it is not possible to declare a standalone class with this modifier. `Private` classes encapsulate functionality that is specific to the class where they were declared.

  `Private` member variables are accessible only within the current class where they were declared. Even derived classes *do not* have access to `Private` members; they can be accessed through properties.

  `Private` is the most restrictive modifier.

`Protected`
: `Protected` access is similar to `Private`. Like private classes, protected classes can be nested only within another class. Unlike private classes, protected classes are accessible from derived classes.

  `Protected` member variables are also accessible from derived classes. Think of protected member data as "private within the inheritance tree." This modifier should be used only in rare circumstances when it is applied to member data.

`Friend`
: `Friend` classes are available only within the scope of the program where they are defined. They are suitable for encapsulating functionality that is shared across an assembly.

  `Friend` variables and methods are available from all classes defined in the same assembly, but they are not visible externally. It is common to use `Friend` access at the method level to allow inter-object communication. However, declaring member variables with `Friend` access should be a rare event. Allowing another class to have such intimate access to member data is not advised.

`Protected Friend`
: This modifier has the attributes of both `Protected` and `Friend`.

`Shared`
: `Shared` is an access modifier specific to member data and methods; classes cannot be shared. `Shared` member function methods and member data are not associated with a particular class instance (although they can be called through a class instance). The `String` class, for instance, contains a shared method named `Format` that is used to format strings:

```
Dim newString As String
newString = String.Format("Formatted Number: {0}", num.ToString())
```

Shared has the same meaning as *static* in C#, C++, and Java.

When using access modifiers, you should treat member data differently than member functions. Visual Basic, like all languages, gives developers a certain amount of rope to hang themselves. For instance, member data can be declared with all the access modifiers that were discussed (such as `Public`, `Private`, `Protected`, and `Friend`). These modifiers have their place when it comes to class and method declarations; however, *member data for classes should always be private.*

Remember that this rule does not apply to constants or enumerations belonging to a class. These constants and enumerations are public and shared by default and define qualities that apply to every class instance.

## Public Methods

`Public` methods and properties define your object's interface—i.e., how users will interact with your object. It designates unrestricted access. With that said, this modifier should be used as little as possible. Public interfaces should be minimal to allow flexible class designs.* This means using the fewest number of public methods (with the fewest number of parameters) required to meet the object's design goals.

Hiding as much information as possible should be a paramount concern when designing a class, because hidden information can be changed easily without affecting the clients of the class. OOP emphasizes the idea of separating the interface from the implementation. Public interfaces are one way to express an implementation, so take care when determining what the outside world will see.

For instance, exposing a `ConnectToDatabase` method on an object would not be a good idea. A client should not be concerned with the fact that a database even exists; this behavior should be abstracted away in the application's data services tier. If the data source becomes an XML file at a later date, this method would have no meaning in the new context. Simply removing the method definition could render derived classes useless.

Before making a method public, determine if the class can handle the work instead. If a class requires the client to make a sequence of calls to accomplish a task, the abstraction is probably flawed. A method should not be made public simply because "it makes things easier." It can be a short-term solution like duct tape, but in the long run, the object hierarchy ends up having more holes in it than a piece of Swiss cheese.

* In this context, the term "interface" refers to the public methods and properties exposed by a class.

Public interfaces represent a contract of sorts. Remember that once code that uses the public interface of an object is written, that interface should be considered *published*. What happens to all objects that rely on the existence of a published interface when that interface is changed, a parameter is added, or the return type is changed? The relationship is destroyed. Code won't compile, and many classes need to be rewritten as a result.

Don't change published interfaces.

## Private Methods

`Private` methods are used for behaviors that should not be exposed outside of the class. They usually handle details that clients should not have to worry about. They simplify an abstraction, which is the primary goal of any class design.

Take a hypothetical `CreditCard` object. This object contains data that not everyone in the company should see, so before the object persists itself to the database, it must encrypt all of its member data. However, a developer should not have to know this detail. What if the `Encrypt` method is not called before the call `Save`? The data would be unencrypted when it was written to the database, available to all prying eyes.

The appropriate way to handle this situation is to have a private method that is called from `Save` and handles the encryption, as shown in the following code:

```
Public Class CreditCard

    Private ccNumber As String

    Private Sub Encrypt()
      'Secret algorthim
    End Function

    Public Function Save() As Boolean
      Encrypt()
      '
      'Persist to database here
      '
    End Function

    Public ReadOnly Property CardNumber() As String
      Get
        Return ccNumber
      End Get
    End Property

End Class
```

This solution frees the developer from one more implementation detail. Breaking the encryption routine out into a private method, rather than doing it right from `Save`, is good modular design. It allows you to substitute new encryption routines without having to rewrite any code. Remember, the more you can hide from the users of your objects, the better (even if that user is you).

## Protected Methods

`Protected` methods are available from the class where they are declared, as well as from any derived classes. In terms of visibility, protected methods lie somewhere between public and private. They aren't as restrictive as private methods, but they aren't quite as open as public methods. Like the `Public` modifier, `Protected` should be used with caution. Does a child class definitely need access to the parent implementation? Nine times out of ten, the answer is No.

However, the best reason to use a protected method is when a child class needs to do the same thing as a parent class, but in a different way. Consider the `CreditCard` class. As with the `Encrypt` routine, there is also a routine that validates the card number. Like `Encrypt`, the validation routine will be called within the class, perhaps when the class is created:

```
Public Class CreditCard

  Private ccNumber As String

  Private Sub Encrypt()
    'Secret algorthim
  End Sub

  Public Function Save() As Boolean
    Encrypt()
    '
    'Persist to database here
    '
  End Function

  Public ReadOnly Property CardNumber() As String
    Get
      Return ccNumber
    End Get
  End Property

  Protected Overridable Function Validate() As Boolean
    'Validate number here
  End Function

End Class
```

> Ignore the `Overridable` keyword until the next chapter. For now, just understand that it means a derived class has permission to rewrite the method.

Derived classes want to validate a credit card in different ways. Visa, for instance, has components that can be used to verify their cards. A `Visa` card class might call these routines during `Validate`, but a `MasterCard` object would not. Because the method is protected and overridable, a derived class can write its own version. The `Validate` routine remains hidden outside of the class hierarchy, but the `ccNumber` data member remains private. Derived classes use the public `CardNumber` property to access the number.

## Friend Methods

Friend access provides a way for classes to communicate with one another on an assembly-wide basis. This communication is usually necessary when you don't want to expose a relationship through a public class interface. It is not uncommon for the `Friend` modifier to be discussed in terms of family secrets. Everyone in the assembly knows, but client code doesn't—much as the whole family knows that dad has a new toupee, but not everyone in the outside world knows (because it's a really well-made toupee from Hong Kong).

One scenario involves two classes: `ShoppingCart` and `Order`. These classes run the shopping cart and order processing portions of an Internet commerce site. Both `ShoppingCart` and `Order` need to access the items they contain: a collection of `Item` objects.

Suppose you always want an `Item` to be associated with either a `ShoppingCart` or an `Order`. That is, it can't exist by itself; it has to have a relation to either an order or the shopping cart. You can create this association by giving the item class constructor (see "Creation and Destruction" later in this chapter) `Friend` access:

```
Public Class Item

    Friend Sub New(...)

        'Initialize object here

    End Sub

End Class
```

This access prevents code outside the assembly from creating an `Item`. However, orders and shopping carts can create items all day long. The item class might also have several methods with friend-level access that could be called between `ShoppingCart` and `Order`. `Friend` access is similar to `Protected` access between two unrelated classes.

You should watch out for some things in this situation. Classes that participate in relationships like these are known as *cliques* and should be kept to a minimum to prevent dependencies. Each new relationship adds complexity to the overall system.

## Protected Friend Methods

The `Protected Friend` modifier provides both protected and friend visibility. It is almost like a union of the two. As shown in Figure 3-3, nonderived classes in another assembly have friend access; however, in the declaring assembly, derived classes have protected access.

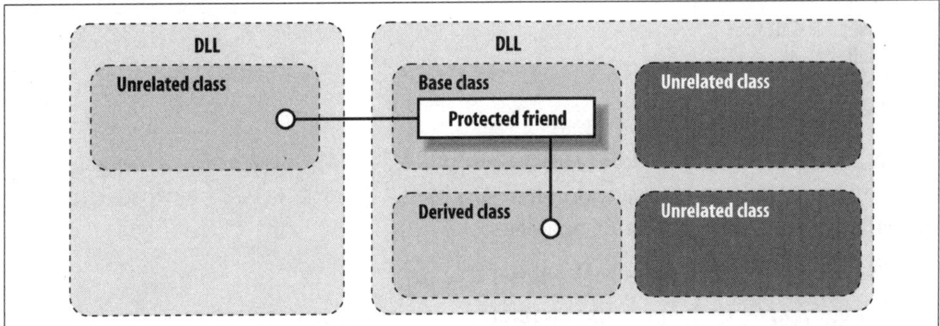


*Figure 3-3. Protected Friend access*

# Passing Parameters

Data types fall into two categories: values types and reference types. Examples of value types include the built-in data types like `Short`, `Integer`, and `Long` (`System.Int16`, `System.Int32`, and `System.Int64`). Value types are created on the stack, which is the area of memory that is local to a method. When the location is destroyed, the value type is destroyed—the garbage collector does not manage the stack.

Reference types are defined using classes and created on the heap, which is available for the lifetime of the object. The garbage collector manages this area of memory.

By default, both types are passed by value; a copy of the value is placed on the stack. Therefore, any changes made to a variable are local to the method. Example 3-4 demonstrates this concept.

*Example 3-4. Passing parameters ByVal*

```
Imports System

Public Class App

  Private Class Counter

    Public Sub Increment(ByVal x As Integer)
      x += 1
    End Sub

  End Class
```

*Example 3-4. Passing parameters ByVal (continued)*

```
  Public Shared Sub Main()
    Dim cc As New Counter()
    Dim x As Integer = 1
    cc.Increment(x)
    Console.WriteLine(x.ToString())
    Console.WriteLine()
    Console.WriteLine("Hit ENTER to continue.")
    Console.ReadLine()
  End Sub

End Class
```

When Example 3-4 is executed, the output will be `1` because a copy of `x` was passed to the `Counter.Increment` method. It is useful to use the `ByVal` keyword explicitly instead of relying on the default behavior:

```
Public Sub Increment(ByVal x As Integer)
```

Replacing `ByVal` with `ByRef` causes a reference to be passed instead of a copy. A reference is similar to a pointer. However, a reference should be thought of as an alias of a data type, not some arbitrary location in memory.

```
Public Sub Increment(ByRef x As Integer)
```

The output resulting from this change will be `2`.

## A Word on Reference Types

Here is where things might get a little confusing. The previous example used a value type (an `Integer`), and we saw that it was not modified after returning from the call to `Counter.Increment`. A reference type—i.e., a type defined by a class—is also passed as `ByVal` by default. What this means is that the actual reference is passed by value. The contents of the object can be changed, but as Example 3-5 shows, changing the reference to point to a different object instance has only a local effect.

*Example 3-5. Passing references by value*

```
Imports System

Public Class Message
  Private myText As String
  Public Property Text() As String
    Get
      Return myText
    End Get
    Set(ByVal Value As String)
      myText = value
    End Set
  End Property
End Class

Public Class ReferenceTest
```

*Example 3-5. Passing references by value (continued)*

```
  Public Sub New()
    Dim A As New Message()
    A.Text = "I am object A"

    Dim B As New Message()
    B.Text = "I am object B"

    SwitchRef(A, B)

    Console.WriteLine(A.Text)
    Console.WriteLine(B.Text)
  End Sub

  Private Sub SwitchRef(ByVal A As Message, _
                        ByVal B As Message)
    A = B
    A.Text = "I am still object B but changed"
  End Sub

End Class

Public Class App
  Public Shared Sub Main()
    Dim refTest As New ReferenceTest()
  End Sub
End Class
```

Here's what is going on. In `ReferenceTest`, two distinct objects, `A` and `B`, are passed to the `SwitchRef` method. Inside this method, `A` is aliased to object `B`. When `A.Text` is called, the text for object `B` is actually being changed. This process is verified upon return when the text for object `A` and `B` is written to the console. The output looks like this:

```
I am object A
I am still object B but changed
```

More confusing still are strings. Strings are reference types, but because strings are immutable, strings passed `ByVal` behave as value types and strings passed `ByRef`, when modified, actually return a different object instance.

## Value Types

Reference types and value types are both derived from `System.Object`. However, value types are treated differently in terms of allocation. When a value type is passed to a `ByVal` method, the actual value is copied. Also, assigning a value type to another instance of that type causes the value to be copied. The exception occurs when a value type is a reference type's data member; then it is heap allocated right along with the rest of the class.

In the following code fragment, number1 and number2 are two distinct locations in memory that each contain the value 5:

```
Dim number1 As Integer = 5
Dim number2 As Integer = number1
```

This contrasts with reference types (classes). Consider the following fragment, in which two objects are instantiated and then one is assigned to the other:

```
Dim object1 As New Object()
Dim object2 As New Object()

object2 = object1
```

After the assignment, there are no longer two objects; object2 is now a reference to object1. The location in memory formerly associated with object2 is now sitting around waiting to be garbage collected.

Sometimes defining a value type is beneficial—especially when you have small amounts of related data (that consist of value types). A perfect example is the Point structure:

```
Public Structure Point
    Public x As Integer
    Public y As Integer
End Structure
```

Value types always contain known values. The compiler automatically generates a default constructor that is used to initialize all the values of the structure to a known value.

Once a Point is declared, it can be used just like any other value type. There is no need to use the New operator because the default constructor is called automatically:

```
'After assignment p1 and p2 are two different points

Dim p1 As Point
Dim p2 As Point

p1.x = 10
p1.y = 10

p2 = p1
```

Structures have many of the same features as classes—like constructors, for instance. While the use of a default constructor is restricted (no arguments), it is legal to define a constructor that contains parameters:

```
Public Structure Point
    Dim x As Integer
    Dim y As Integer

    Public Sub New (x As Integer, y As Integer)
        Me.x = x
        Me.y = y
```

```
    End Sub
End Structure
```

However, the New operator must be used to initialize a structure through a non-default constructor:

```
'Still have two different points

Dim p1 As New Point(10,20)
Dim p2 = p1
```

Structures have other similarities to classes (they can have methods and events), but there are other limitations besides not being able to define a default constructor:

- Structures implicitly inherit from System.ValueType, but the buck stops there. It is not possible to inherit from a structure.
- Finalize methods are not allowed.
- Protected members cannot be used.
- It is impossible to use the New keyword to initialize member data at the time of declaration.
- Array sizes cannot be specified at the time of declaration.

Structures are best used to group small pieces of related data that do not require additional functionality. It's recommended that the instance size of a structure does not exceed 16 bytes. The Point structure is a perfect example that meets both of these criteria.

The data members of Point are value types, which means that both x and y are allocated inline within the structure. If the structure contained a reference object like a String, the String would be allocated on the heap just like any other reference type. However, the reference to that String object would be allocated inline in the structure. If the String object in question were a member of another class, then both the object and the reference would be heap allocated. Thus, even if a structure contains a reference type member, theoretically, there is one less level of indirection. Whether there is a noticeable difference (performance-wise) in a practical situation remains to be seen.

Ideally, a structure should contain only value type members so that everything is stack-allocated. This situation works especially well when you deal with arrays:

```
Public Sub LotsOfPoints()
    Dim points(1000) As Point

    'Use points
End Sub
```

Here, the overhead of calling the constructor is avoided and, likewise, the garbage collector does not have to free 1,000 objects. The stack is destroyed when the method returns.

Value types can be used where an object is expected. For example, Console.WriteLine expects an Object as a parameter, but it easily accommodates a Point:

```
Dim p As New Point(11,6)
Console.WriteLine(p)
```

When a value type is used where an object is expected, an object wrapper is allocated on the heap, and the actual value is copied into it. This wrapper makes it appear as if the value type is a reference type. This process is called *boxing*, and you should obtain a minimal understanding of the process to avoid potential performance problems. Boxing operations aren't cheap.

The various collection classes in the framework expect objects. Adding 1,000 Points to a collection could result in 1,000 boxing operations, not to mention the fact that 1,000 objects are now in line for garbage collection.

# Creation and Destruction

The lifetime of an object running under .NET is not as straightforward as it is in other languages like C++ or managed VB.

In these languages, when an object is created, its constructor is called, which allows the object to be initialized. When the object goes out of scope, its destructor is called, providing a convenient place to free resources; this is usually the point at which database connections are closed, file handles are freed, and memory allocated during the object's lifetime is released. The object has a practical, convenient mechanism for cleanup. But as you will see, .NET handles things differently.

## Constructors

VB.NET does provide the means to declare a constructor similar to that of Java, C++, and most other OO languages. In this respect, VB.NET is similar to these languages. However, in VB.NET, the declaration of a constructor is a little more intuitive. The constructor for an object is a method named New, which makes perfect sense because this is what is called when you declare a new instance of an object. The following fragment calls the *default constructor* for the Hello class:

```
Dim hello As New Hello()    'Calls Hello.New()
```

The default constructor does not have any arguments, and, like all constructors, it does not return a value:

```
Public Class Hello
    Public Sub New()
        Console.WriteLine("Hello, World!")
    End Sub
End Class
```

In addition to a default constructor, you can define New so it takes any number of arguments. In fact, you can define as many different versions of New as you want for the same object, as long as each has a different function signature. This process is called overloading, and it looks like this:

```
Public Class New

    Public Sub New()
        Console.WriteLine("Hello, World!")
    End Sub

    Public Sub New (name As String)
        Console.WriteLine("Hello, {0}", name)
    End Sub

End Class
```

### Instances versus references

Creating an instance of an object is different from declaring a reference to an object, which can be confusing to beginning programmers.

Object instances are created with the New operator, as in "gimme a new one of those." An instance of an object has methods that can be called and properties that can be accessed:

```
Dim myLunch As New Donut() ''Creates an instance of Donut
myLunch.Eat()              'that can be used
```

Object references, on the other hand, *refer* to other objects. By themselves, they do nothing. In fact, if you try to use an uninitialized reference, an exception will be thrown by the runtime:

```
'No New here
Dim lasso As Rope   'This is a reference to a Rope object
lasso.Twirl()       'Error, lasso does not refer to anything
```

References must be assigned to an existing instance before they can be used. Think of an object reference as an alias:

```
Dim chevy As New Car()      'Create a new car
Dim superSport As Car       'This is only a reference to the chevy

superSport = chevy          'Now superSport refers to chevy
superSport.Drive()          'Calls chevy.Drive() really
```

In the previous fragment, there is only one object: chevy. The superSport reference is only an alias.

## Destructors

VB.NET does not provide a destructor that is called when an object goes out of scope. Instead, the lifespan of a VB.NET object is *nondeterministic*. This means you don't know when an object will be freed. You can't rely on this to happen when the object goes out of scope (although it often does) because, like Java, memory is managed for you. The runtime provides a garbage collector that handles the memory associated with an object.

The runtime provides a way to release resources when objects are freed. It's called *finalization*. Because every object in .NET ultimately derives itself from `System.Object`, all objects inherit a method named `Finalize`. The implementation of this method, by default, is just an empty function—it doesn't do anything. However, it can be overridden.

If the `Finalize` method was overridden, when the garbage collector decides that our object is trash, it will be called. Then the memory used by the object will be reclaimed and made available once again. This process is similar to a traditional destructor, except `Finalize` is not called when the object goes out of scope. It's called after the object is no longer referenced anywhere in the program, and even then only when the garbage collector gets around to calling it.

Example 3-6 uses a class named `Hello` to display a message to the console. When the class constructor is called, the console displays "Hello, so and so!" When the garbage collector decides to free the object, `Finalize` is called, causing "Goodbye, so and so!" to be displayed in the console. Ignore the semantics of `Finalize` for now. It will become much clearer after you read about function overriding in the next chapter.

*Example 3-6. Goodbye, World!*

```
'finalize.vb

Imports System

Public Class Hello

  Private myName As String

  Public Sub New(ByVal name As String)
    myName = name
    Console.WriteLine("Hello, {0}!", name)
  End Sub

  Protected Overrides Sub Finalize()
    Console.WriteLine("Goodbye, {0}!", myName)
  End Sub

End Class

Public Class Application

  Public Shared Sub Main()
    Dim hello As New hello("Mom")
  End Sub

End Class
```

Save this example to *finalize.vb* and compile it to a standard executable. When you run it, you see the following output:

```
C:>goodbye
Hello, Mom!
Goodbye, Mom!
```

This code appears to work just like a C++ program. You created an instance of `Hello` that caused "Hello, Mom!" to be displayed to the console. `Hello` goes out of scope and is garbage collected, and the `Finalize` method is called. "Goodbye, Mom!" is then displayed to the console.

This process is mostly correct. `Finalize` was not called because `hello` went out of scope, but because the application shut down. The only time when you can count on finalization to occur is when an application terminates, but only if the application terminates normally. Add the following line of code to the previous example. Place it right after the declaration of `Hello`:

```
Public Shared Sub Main()
    Dim hello As New Hello("Mom")
    Dim x As Integer = 31 / x
End Sub
```

Running this code generates an unhandled overflow exception. If the CLR jumps in and asks if you would like to debug the executable, just say no. Control will return to the console window, and you will see that the object is never finalized (you won't see a goodbye message).

### System.GC

Finalization can be forced using the `System.GC` class (for garbage collection), which provides limited access to the garbage collector. The class contains a method named `GC.Collect` that forces a garbage collection to occur when it is called. To better understand this, modify `Main` from the previous example to look like this:

```
Public Shared Sub Main()
    Dim i As Integer
    For i = 1 to 5
        Dim hello As New Hello(i.ToString())
    Next i
End Sub
```

The output should look like this:

```
C:\>finalize
Hello, 1!
Hello, 2!
Hello, 3!
Hello, 4!
Hello, 5!
Goodbye, 5!
Goodbye, 4!
Goodbye, 3!
```

```
Goodbye, 2!
Goodbye, 1!
```

The objects seem to be freed in the reverse order from which they were created, implying insertion into a stack-like structure. This is, in fact, what happens. Now, add a call to `GC.Collect` in Example 3-5:

```
For i = 1 to 5
    Dim hello As New Hello(i.ToString())
    GC.Collect()
Next i
```

Now the objects are freed after each iteration of the loop:

```
C:\>finalize
Hello, 1!
Goodbye, 1!
Hello, 2!
Goodbye, 2!
Hello, 3!
Goodbye, 3!
Hello, 4!
Goodbye, 4!
Hello, 5!
Goodbye, 5!
```

When an object is created, if it contains a `Finalize` method, a pointer to the object is placed in the *finalization queue*. This pointer is an internal data structure maintained by the garbage collector that contains a list of objects that can be finalized—in other words, objects that implemented a `Finalize` method.

During garbage collection, this queue is traversed and all pointers found in it are placed in the `freachable` queue. Objects that do not have `Finalize` methods are freed at this point. Objects with a `Finalize` method are not (objects implementing `Finalize` are freed last).

A special runtime thread is dedicated to calling `Finalize` methods. When objects appear in the `freachable` queue, the thread is awakened, and `Finalize` is called for every object in the queue. Thus, just because you call `GC.Collect` doesn't mean that the object will be freed immediately. After all, the call occurs on a different thread. More often than not, you should avoid making calls to `GC.Collect` because of the overhead associated with the call; it's an application-wide call.

When a .NET process (think application domain) is initialized, the CLR allocates a contiguous block of memory called the managed heap. When objects are created, they are allocated from this heap until there is no more room left. When this happens (and when an application shuts down), a garbage collection is performed.

To make the garbage collector earn its money, modify Example 3-5 to create 10,000 instances of `Hello`:

```
Dim i As Integer
For i = 1 to 10000
```

```
        Dim hello As New Hello(i.ToString())
    Next i
```

The GC is optimized to work with small objects like `Hello` in its sleep, so add the following member variable:

```
    Public Class Hello

        Private bigChunkOMemory(10000) As Byte
```

Now when you run the example, you create 10,000 objects that are over 10,000 bytes in size. This should cause the GC to start pumping. Recompile the example and run it, but redirect the output to a text file instead of the console; otherwise the output won't fit:

```
    C:\>finalize > test.txt
```

Run this code several times and examine the output each time. You should notice that the output is different almost every time you run the program. If there is one thing to learn from this example, it is that you should not count on objects being freed in the order they were created. They are freed in order in small examples that use a few very small objects. In real-world scenarios, though, objects can contain references to other objects, so the garbage collector cannot determine an order to perform finalization.

## Close and Dispose

You should avoid using a `Finalize` method for several reasons. One reason is that objects with `Finalize` methods take longer to allocate. This book has shown how a pointer to the object must be stored in the finalization queue and later added to the `freachable` queue. This is no big deal in a simple program, but what about the example that allocates 10,000 objects? This scenario could add significant overhead, not to mention the overhead involving the garbage collector calling `Finalize` 10,000 times. In this situation, freeing an object takes longer as well. Also, objects that have a `Finalize` method are freed after everything else, so they could have a longer than necessary lifespan.

The best solution is to design your objects so they don't need cleaning up in the first place. But when it is necessary, you can solve this problem by implementing your own cleanup method. Then you can free resources explicitly whenever you want. The only foreseeable problem with implementing your own method is making sure that the people who will use your objects know about the method in the first place. However, some methods are specifically used for this purpose.

Classes in the .NET library follow the convention of using a `Close` or `Dispose` method. Typically, `Close` is used in situations when an object could be reopened at a later time; `Dispose` is used in situations when the object should not be used again.

Example 3-7 shows a simple example that uses the `Timer` class. Before the program terminates, the timer is closed and its resources are freed.

*Example 3-7. Close method*

```
'references: system.dll
'compile: vbc /t:exe /r:system.dll timer.vb

Option Strict On

Imports System
Imports System.Timers

Public Class Application

  Private Const EnterKey As Integer = 10

  Public Shared Sub Main()

    'Create a Timer that fires every 2 seconds.
    Dim myTimer As Timer = New Timer(2000)

    'Specify Timer event
    AddHandler myTimer.Elapsed, AddressOf OnTimerEvent

    'Turn on the Timer
    myTimer.Enabled = True

    Console.WriteLine("Press ENTER to quit")

    'Wait for ENTER key
    Console.ReadLine()

    'Free resources associated with the Timer
    myTimer.Close()

  End Sub

  'The timer event
  Public Shared Sub OnTimerEvent(ByVal source As Object, _
    ByVal e As ElapsedEventArgs)
    Console.WriteLine("Hello, World!")
  End Sub

End Class
```

As you can see in Example 3-7, the `timer` implements a `Close` method. If you examine the class in ILDASM (it's located in *system.dll*), you won't be able to tell that the timer class also implements a `Finalize` method; it's inherited from `System.ComponentModel.Component`. If `Close` is called, `Finalize` is not called for the timer object and the overhead penalty of finalization is not incurred. If `Close` is not called (say, someone forgets to call it), the inherited `Finalize` method calls `Close` for you, so the resources allocated by the timer are eventually freed. `Finalize` is present only to act as a safety net.

## Delegates and Events

You have seen several ways that classes can establish a rapport with one another. A derived class can converse with its parent through `Protected` methods and a non-derived class can use the `Public` or `Friend` (if in the same assembly) methods.

You might have noticed that this level of communication implies a priori knowledge of the classes involved; all classes and their methods are known at compile time. Therefore the lines of communication are drawn, hardcoded into the mix.

Consider the following piece of code:

```
Public Class Log

    Public Sub Write(ByVal msg As String)
        #If Debug Then
        Console.WriteLine(msg)
        #End If
    End Sub

End Class
```

You can imagine that this simple class provides basic debugging capabilities for some application. As you can see, it is wired to write a message to the console. Not very accommodating, is it? What if you wanted to write the message to a text file or database or send it to a remote debugging console? Or worse yet, what if you moved the class to a Windows executable? There wouldn't be a console window anymore.

You could go into the class and add new methods for each scenario, but that wouldn't help much if calls to `Log.Write` were already scattered throughout your object model. You could always rewrite `Log.Write` every time you wanted to send the message to a different location, but that's not too practical either. OOP involves code reuse, not code rewrite. That wouldn't exactly lead to a class that you could share with your friends and neighbors.

It would be nice to tell the `Log` class which method to call in order to do the logging. Then you could switch methods at runtime—perhaps even incorporating several different logging methods: logging to a local text file or sending debug messages to a remote debug window.

For years, C/C++ programmers used callbacks to achieve this capability. In a callback situation, one function receives a pointer to another function through its argument list. The function can then use this pointer to send a notification to the callback. If you could use the pointer in this way with the `Log` class, you could tell it which function you wanted it to use to handle the writing.

The C/C++ callback method has some drawbacks. First, it is not typesafe. There is no way to ensure that the pointer actually refers to a function with the appropriate signature—that it has the same parameters *and* return type. Second, there is no way to extend the callback to use more than one function without rewriting the method to accommodate the change. What if you wanted to log to the console *and* the database?

## Delegates

VB.NET has the function pointer you need, but without the drawbacks just discussed. The pointer is called a *delegate*. As shown in Example 3-8, it is declared much like a `Sub` or a `Function`, except it doesn't have a body. It just defines a function signature.

You can think of a delegate as a typesafe function pointer, but it is really much more. A delegate can be associated with one method, or it can refer to several methods, as long as the methods have the same signature and return value. It can also refer to an instance method or a class method. Try that in C++!

*Example 3-8. Using delegates, Part I*

```
Imports System
Imports System.IO

Public Class Log

  Public Delegate Sub Writer(ByVal msg As String)
  Private myWriter As Writer

  Public Sub New(ByVal writeMethod As Writer)
    myWriter = writeMethod
  End Sub

  Public Sub Write(ByVal msg As String)
    myWriter(msg)
  End Sub

End Class
```

Notice that once you define a delegate, you can declare a variable that holds that type. This is the case with `myWriter`, which is declared immediately after the delegate declaration. The constructor for the class is then used to specify which method `Log` should use to perform its duties. The method is saved in `myWriter` to be used later during the call to `Write`.

When you declare a delegate, you actually derive a class from `System.MulticastDelegate`, which itself is derived from the `Delegate` class.

This class contains three methods that are used to handle the callbacks internally: `Invoke`, `BeginInvoke`, and `EndInvoke`.

`Invoke` is used for synchronous callbacks such as the example in this chapter; `BeginInvoke` and `EndInvoke` are used for asynchronous callbacks that are typically found in a remoting scenario.

Supplying the Log class with a Write method is simple, as Example 3-9 illustrates. You can provide your own version of Write, which outputs to a text file by using the AddressOf operator. This operator returns a delegate that can be passed to the Log class.

*Example 3-9. Using delegates, Part II*

```
Imports System
Imports System.IO

Public Class Log

  Public Delegate Sub Writer(ByVal msg As String)
  Private myWriter As Writer

  Public Sub New(ByVal writeMethod As Writer)
    myWriter = writeMethod
  End Sub

  Public Sub Write(ByVal msg As String)
    myWriter(msg)
  End Sub

End Class

Friend Class Test

  Public Shared Sub Write(ByVal msg As String)

    Dim file As New FileStream("debug.log", _
                               FileMode.OpenOrCreate, _
                               FileAccess.Write)

    Dim stream As New StreamWriter(file)

    'Write date/time and message
    stream.Write("{0} - {1}", DateTime.Now, msg)

    'Close the stream (and the file, too)
    stream.Close()

  End Sub

  Public Shared Sub Main()
    Dim debugLog As New Log(AddressOf Write)
    debugLog.Write("Welcome to Visual Basic!")
  End Sub

End Class
```

Try using AddressOf with a method that has a mismatched signature. You won't get far. The compiler checks the signatures, sees that they don't match, and gives you an error.

A delegate can refer to more than one method. You can do this with the `Delegate.Combine` method, which lets you chain any number of methods together using the same delegate. Let's put a new method in `Log` to house this functionality:

```
Public Class Log

    Public Sub Add(ByVal writeMethod As Writer)
        myWriter = myWriter.Combine(myWriter, writeMethod)
    End Sub
```

If you want to add another method to the delegate, you can do so. Verify this behavior by adding another method to the `Test` class from Example 3-9:

```
Friend Class Test

    Public Shared Sub SimpleWrite(ByVal msg As String)
        Console.WriteLine(msg)
    End Sub
```

Now you only need to modify `Main` to add `SimpleWrite` to the delegate chain:

```
    Public Shared Sub Main()
        Dim debugLog As New Log(AddressOf Write)
        debugLog.Add(AddressOf SimpleWrite)
        debugLog.Write("Welcome to Visual Basic!")
    End Sub
```

When `Write` is called, the message is displayed to the console window *and* written to *debug.log*.

As the laws of symmetry demand, you should also provide the functionality to remove a method from a delegate. This can be accomplished by wrapping a call to `Delegate.Remove` in the `Log` class:

```
Public Class Log

    Public Sub Remove(ByVal writeMethod As Writer)
        myWriter.Remove(myWriter, writeMethod)
    End Sub
```

Delegates are much more powerful than traditional function pointers. They can permit sophisticated interactions between the objects in the libraries or frameworks that you write.

The end of this chapter lists the source code for a simple remote debugging console. A class called `RemoteDebug` is also listed to send messages to the remote console. These listings are provided as an exercise for you. See if you can add the Write method of `RemoteDebug` to the delegate example you worked with in this section.

## Events

Events allow an object to broadcast a message without knowing who will receive the notification. For instance, an `AlarmClock` object might fire an `Alarm` event at a designated time, allowing anyone using the object to receive the event and execute code based on the event. AlarmClock just sends a message. It has no idea who will get it. The recipient could be one or 100 objects. It all depends on how many objects subscribed to the event.

Example 3-10 shows a class that could simulate your odds of winning the Texas Lottery. The constructor of the class takes an array of 6 numbers, each between 1 and 54. When the Play method is called, the class randomly generates 6 numbers. If all 6 numbers match, you win! If not, it tries again for 10,000 more attempts (each play costs a dollar). If 3 or more numbers match, a Match event is raised. The example is big, despite the fact that it contains no error handling whatsoever. It is worth stepping through, as you can glean quite a few language features from the code.

*Example 3-10. Texas Lottery simulation class*

```
Option Strict On

Imports System
Imports System.Text

Public Class TexasLottery

  Public Event Match(ByVal msg As String)

  Private numbers() As Byte
  Private attempts As Integer

  Public Sub New(ByVal numbers() As Byte)
    Array.Sort(numbers)
    Me.numbers = numbers
  End Sub

  Public Sub Play()
    'Get random number class
    Dim rnd As New Random()
    'Declare 3 Integers
    Dim i, randomNumber, matches As Integer

    Do While attempts < 10000
      matches = 0
      For i = 1 To 6
        'Get random number 1-54
        randomNumber = rnd.Next(1, 54)
        'Search array for number
        If Array.BinarySearch(numbers, randomNumber) > 0 Then
          matches += 1
        End If
      Next i

      If (matches > 2) Then

        RaiseEvent Match( _
```

*Example 3-10. Texas Lottery simulation class (continued)*

```
          String.Format("{0} matches on attempt {1}", _
              matches.ToString(), attempts.ToString()))

        If (matches = 6) Then
          Dim msg As String
          msg.Format("You won the lottery on attempt {0}", _
                     attempts.ToString())
          RaiseEvent Match(msg)
          Exit Do
        End If

      End If

      attempts += 1 'Increment attempts

    Loop

  End Sub

End Class
```

Now that you have a class that generates events, you need a class that can receive them. Several options are available to you at this point. You can subscribe to events at design time or wait until runtime. Example 3-11 demonstrates the former option by using the `WithEvents` and `Handles` keywords to connect to an event source.

*Example 3-11. WithEvents and Handles*

```
Imports System

Friend Class Test

  Private Class LottoTest

    Private WithEvents lottery As TexasLottery

    Public Sub New()
      Dim myNumbers() As Byte = {6, 11, 23, 31, 32, 44}
      lottery = New TexasLottery(myNumbers)
    End Sub

    Public Sub Play()
      lottery.Play()
    End Sub

    Private Sub OnMatch(ByVal msg As String) Handles lottery.Match
      Console.WriteLine(msg)
    End Sub

  End Class

  Public Shared Sub Main()
```

*Example 3-11. WithEvents and Handles (continued)*

```
    Dim test As New LottoTest()
    test.Play()
  End Sub

End Class
```

If you find it necessary, you could use the same event handler to handle multiple events:

```
Private WithEvents lottery1 As TexasLottery
Private WithEvents lottery2 As TexasLottery

Private Sub OnMatch(msg As String) _
    Handles lottery1.Match, lottery2.Match
    Console.WriteLine(msg)
End Sub
```

## Dynamic Event Handling

Example 3-12 shows how to dynamically bind to an event source at runtime rather than at compile time. You do not have to use `WithEvents` when declaring the `TexasLottery` object.

*Example 3-12. Dynamic event handling*

```
Imports System

Friend Class Test

  Public Class LottoTest2

    Private lottery As TexasLottery

    Public Sub New()
      Dim myNumbers() As Byte = {6, 11, 23, 31, 32, 44}
      lottery = New TexasLottery(myNumbers)
      AddHandler lottery.Match, AddressOf Me.OnMatch
    End Sub

    Public Sub Play()
      lottery.Play()
      RemoveHandler lottery.Match, AddressOf Me.OnMatch
    End Sub

    Private Sub OnMatch(ByVal msg As String)
      Console.WriteLine(msg)
    End Sub
  End Class

  Public Shared Sub Main()
```

*Example 3-12. Dynamic event handling (continued)*

```
    Dim test As New LottoTest2()
    test.Play()
  End Sub

End Class
```

AddHandler connects to the event source, while RemoveHandler handler disconnects from it. The arguments for both are the same. The first is the event you wish to address, and the second is a delegate pointing to the event handler. You can connect to more than one event by using AddHandler. This process is similar to what you did with the log class using Delegate.Combine and Delegate.Remove.

## Delegates Versus Events

At this point, you might wonder what the differences between delegates and events are. After all, Example 3-10 could be rewritten to use delegates in a manner similar to Example 3-8. There really isn't a difference between the two. Internally, events are built with delegates. The various event keywords merely instruct the compiler to inject additional code into a class definition where the events are wired up behind the scenes.

Example 3-13 shows two simple classes that contain minimal event code. Class A exposes a public event called Notify that is raised in the Raise method. Class B contains a private instance of class A and a method that handles the raised event.

*Example 3-13. Examining events*

```
Imports System

Public Class A

  Public Event Notify(ByVal msg As String)

  Public Sub Raise()
    RaiseEvent Notify("Notifying")
  End Sub

End Class

Public Class B

  Public WithEvents myClassA As A

  Public Sub New()
    myClassA = New A()
    myClassA.Raise()
  End Sub

  Sub NotifyMessage(ByVal msg As String) Handles myClassA.Notify
```

*Example 3-13. Examining events (continued)*

```
    Console.WriteLine("Notified")
  End Sub

End Class
```

When the compiler sees an Event declared, several things happen. First, the event declaration is replaced with a multicast delegate and a reference to that delegate is added. The names are then generated from the event's original name:

```
Public Class A

    Public Delegate Sub NotifyEventHandler(msg As String)
    Private NotifyEvent As NotifyEventHandler
```

Next, two methods are added to the class, which simply wrap calls to `Delegate.Combine` and `Delegate.Remove`. They are used by whatever class decides to consume the event.

```
    Public Sub add_Notify(obj As NotifyEventHandler)
        NotifyEvent = NotifyEvent.Combine(NotifyEvent,obj)
    End Sub

    Public Sub remove_Notify(obj As NotifyEventHandler)
        NotifyEvent = NotifyEvent.Remove(NotifyEvent,obj)
    End Sub
```

Finally, any instance of RaiseEvent is replaced with a small block of code that makes the call through the delegate.

```
    Public Sub Raise()
        If Not NotifyEvent Is Nothing Then
            NotifyEvent.Invoke("Notifying")
        End If
    End Sub
```

Example 3-14 contains the entire listing of class A. If you compile it, the IL produced will be identical to the IL produced from Example 3-13.

*Example 3-14. Setting up an event from scratch*

```
Public Class A

  Public Delegate Sub NotifyEventHandler(ByVal msg As String)
  Private NotifyEvent As NotifyEventHandler

  Public Sub Raise()
    If Not NotifyEvent Is Nothing Then
      NotifyEvent.Invoke("Notifying")
    End If
  End Sub

  Public Sub add_Notify(ByVal obj As NotifyEventHandler)
    NotifyEvent = NotifyEvent.Combine(NotifyEvent, obj)
```

*Example 3-14. Setting up an event from scratch (continued)*

```
  End Sub

  Public Sub remove_Notify(ByVal obj As NotifyEventHandler)
    NotifyEvent = NotifyEvent.Remove(NotifyEvent, obj)
  End Sub

End Class
```

Like Event, when the compiler sees the WithEvents keyword, things start to happen. The instance variable declared with the WithEvents keyword is replaced by an ordinary definition of the class. The variable name is then prefixed with an underscore:

```
Public Class B

    Private _myClassA As A
```

Next, a property is added to the class that has the same name as the variable. This property is where the event target and event source are bound. A check is made to ensure that the event has not already been consumed. Then the event handler's address is passed to the add_Notify method in the event source:

```
Public Sub NotifyMessage(msg As String)
    Console.WriteLine("Notified")
End Sub

Private Property MyClassA() As A
        Get
            Return _myClassC
        End Get
        Set
            If Not _myClassA Is Nothing Then
                _myClassA.remove_Notify(AddressOf NotifyMessage)
            End If
            _myClassA = Value
            If Not _myClassA Is Nothing Then
                _myClassA.add_Notify(AddressOf NotifyMessage)
            End If
        End Set
End Property
```

The compiler then modifies the event target's constructor. The event source's private instance is attached to the event handler through the property that was added by the compiler:

```
Public Class B

    Private _myClassA As ClassA

    Public Sub New()
        MyClassA = New C()
        MyClassA.Raise()
    End Sub
```

The entire listing for class B is shown in Example 3-15.

*Example 3-15. Consuming an event from scratch*

```
Imports System

Public Class B

  Private _myClassA As A

  Public Sub New()
    MyClassA = New A()
    MyClassA.Raise()
  End Sub

  Public Sub NotifyMessage(ByVal msg As String)
    Console.WriteLine("Notified")
  End Sub

  Private Property MyClassA() As A
    Get
      Return _myClassA
    End Get
    Set(ByVal Value As A)
      If Not _myClassA Is Nothing Then
        _myClassA.remove_Notify(AddressOf NotifyMessage)
      End If
      _myClassA = Value
      If Not _myClassA Is Nothing Then
        _myClassA.add_Notify(AddressOf NotifyMessage)
      End If
    End Set
  End Property

End Class
```

## Event Arguments

Forget everything you have seen about event arguments. Although you can define an event with any number of arguments, the .NET framework uses the following convention (and you should, too):

```
Public Event EventName(ByVal sender As Object, ByVal e As System.EventArgs)
```

The first parameter is the object that raised the event, and the second contains the arguments to the event. If the event does not send data, using `System.EventArgs` is acceptable; if it does, you should derive a class from `EventArgs` and provide additional members to describe the event. In the lottery example, for instance, it would be nice to know which numbers have matched. You can create a new event class `LotteryEventArgs` (all derived classes should end with "`EventArgs`") that provides this information:

```
Public Class LotteryEventArgs : Inherits EventArgs

    Public ReadOnly Matches() As Byte

    Public Sub New(ByVal matches() As Byte)
        Me.Matches = maches
    End Sub

End Class
```

## Design Considerations

Many books that cover object-oriented design do not focus on any particular language. Some don't even contain one line of code, which shows that knowledge of object design can transcend whatever language you work with.

This chapter mentions several good and not-so-good programming practices, but this discussion is only an introduction to the topic. You should remember a few general rules that will get you started on the right track:

- Design a class from the user's perspective, not yours. Keep it as simple as possible.
- Limit scope as much as possible when dealing with classes, methods, and member data. Classes should expose as little as possible through their public interface. `Public` interfaces should have as few parameters as they can. Member data should always be `Private`. If it is not, think long and hard about why it isn't. Remember, changes to a class are easier to accommodate if information is hidden.
- Classes are nouns; methods are verbs. If you find yourself writing a class named `Wash`, you really might be writing a method that should be in `Car`.
- Methods imply behavior; properties imply state. Don't confuse the two concepts.
- Minimize interactions among classes to reduce complexity in the system.
- The first abstraction you come up with is probably not the best. If you get an abstraction wrong, you might end up coding yourself into a corner later on and be forced to punch holes in your once-beautiful object hierarchy.
- Whatever you do, be consistent. A lack of consistency is a lack of style. Develop your style. The people who have to look at your code when you leave will thank you instead of curse you.

## An Exercise

The chapter is "officially" over (wink, wink). The following two listings are only an exercise. Example 3-16 contains a remote debugging console. This console window can run on any computer on your network (or it can run on your only computer if you are processor-challenged). It just sits there, waiting for messages from the RemoteDebug class, which is shown in Example 3-17. To run the remote debug console, compile Example 3-16 and type the following code on the command line:

```
C:\>listener 1969
```

This line causes the remote console to wait for messages on port 1969.

Example 3-16 can be compiled from the command line as follows:

```
vbc /t:exe /r:system.dll listener.vb
```

Example 3-17 contains the listing for the RemoteDebug class, which sends messages to the remote debug console. It also contains a small test class so you can compile the class to an executable and test it. Once the remote debug console is started, you have to open up a second console window to run the executable containing the RemoteDebug class (assuming you are testing and listening on the same machine).

Example 3-17, however, wires the remote debug class into the Log example from Example 3-9 earlier in the chapter. It can be compiled the same way as Example 3-16.

*Example 3-16. Remote debug console*

```
'references: system.dll

Imports System
Imports System.Net
Imports System.Net.Sockets
Imports System.Text

Public Class Listener
  Implements IDisposable

  Private port As Integer
  Private myListener As TcpListener
  Private mySocket As Socket
  Private disposed As Boolean

  Public Sub New(ByVal port As Integer)
    Me.port = port
    myListener = New TcpListener(port)
  End Sub

  Public Sub Listen()

    Dim buffer(1024) As Byte

    Dim bytes As Integer
    Dim ASCII As Encoding = Encoding.ASCII

    'Start the listener
    myListener.Start()

    'Wait for a connection
```

*Example 3-16. Remote debug console (continued)*

```
    mySocket = myListener.AcceptSocket()

    myListener.Stop()

    'Read incoming bytes and convert to an ASCII
    'string
    bytes = mySocket.Receive(buffer, buffer.Length, 0)

    Do While (bytes > 0)
      Dim msg As String
      msg = ASCII.GetString(buffer, 0, bytes)
      Console.WriteLine(msg)
      bytes = mySocket.Receive(buffer, buffer.Length, 0)
    Loop

    mySocket.Close()

  End Sub

  Protected Overridable Sub DoDispose()
    mySocket.Close()
    MyListener.Stop()
    GC.SuppressFinalize(Me)
  End Sub

  Public Sub Dispose() Implements IDisposable.Dispose
    Dispose(True)
    GC.SuppressFinalize(Me)
  End Sub

  Protected Sub CheckDispose()
    If (disposed) Then
      Throw New ObjectDisposedException( _
          "RemoteDebug has been disposed.")
    End If
  End Sub

  Protected Sub Dispose(ByVal disposing As Boolean)
    If Not disposed Then
      disposed = True
      If (disposing) Then
        DoDispose()
      End If
    End If
  End Sub

  Public Sub Close()
    Dispose()
  End Sub

  Protected Overrides Sub Finalize()
    Close()
  End Sub
```

*Example 3-16. Remote debug console (continued)*

```
End Class

Public Class Application

  Public Shared Sub Main(ByVal args() As String)
    If args.Length > 1 Then
      Dim port As Integer = Convert.ToInt32(args(1))
      Console.WriteLine("Listening on port {0}", port.ToString())
      Dim myListener As New Listener(port)
      While (True)
        myListener.Listen()
      End While
    Else
      Console.WriteLine("USAGE: listen <port number>")
    End If
  End Sub

End Class
```

*Example 3-17. RemoteDebug class*

```
'references: system.dll

Imports System
Imports System.Net
Imports System.Net.Sockets
Imports System.Text

Public Class RemoteDebug
  Implements IDisposable

  Private remoteServer As IPAddress
  Private endPoint As IPEndPoint
  Private sock As Socket
  Private ASCII As Encoding
  Private disposed As Boolean

  Public Sub New(ByVal server As String, ByVal port As Integer)
    ASCII = Encoding.ASCII
    remoteServer = Dns.Resolve(server).AddressList(0)
    EndPoint = New IPEndPoint(remoteServer, port)
    'Create the Socket for sending data over TCP
    sock = New Socket(AddressFamily.InterNetwork, _
                      SocketType.Stream, _
                      ProtocolType.Tcp)
    sock.Connect(EndPoint)
  End Sub

  Public Sub Write(ByVal msg As String)
    CheckDispose()
    If sock.Connected Then
      Dim buffer() As Byte = ASCII.GetBytes(msg)
      sock.Send(buffer, buffer.Length, 0)
    End If
```

*Example 3-17. RemoteDebug class (continued)*

```
  End Sub

  Public Sub Dispose() Implements IDisposable.Dispose
    Dispose(True)
    GC.SuppressFinalize(Me)
  End Sub

  Protected Overridable Sub DoDispose()
    sock.Shutdown(SocketShutdown.Send)
    sock.Close()
    GC.SuppressFinalize(Me)
  End Sub

  Protected Sub CheckDispose()
    If (disposed) Then
      Throw New ObjectDisposedException( _
          "RemoteDebug has been disposed.")
    End If
  End Sub

  Protected Sub Dispose(ByVal disposing As Boolean)
    If Not disposed Then
      disposed = True
      If (disposing) Then
        DoDispose()
      End If
    End If
  End Sub

  Public Sub Close()
    Dispose()
  End Sub

  Protected Overrides Sub Finalize()
    Close()
  End Sub

End Class

Public Class Test

  Public Shared Sub Main()
    Dim dbg As New RemoteDebug("localhost", 1969)
    dbg.Write("This is a test")
    dbg.Close()
  End Sub

End Class
```

# CHAPTER 4
# Object-Orientation

Several different mechanisms of reuse are available in Visual Basic. *Implementation inheritance* allows you to derive a child class from a parent class. The behaviors of the parent class are inherited by the child and possibly extended. The parent class typically contains general operations (if any), while the child class contains more specialized behaviors. The relationship is known as an *is-a* relationship (i.e., a `Car` *is a* `Vehicle`).

The second type of reuse, which is often confusing to beginning programmers, is *containment*. In containment, one class contains another, representing a *has-a* relationship. For instance, a `Vehicle` *has a* `Motor`.

Finally, in Chapter 5, you will learn about *interface-based programming*. Interfaces represent services that don't necessarily conform to class boundaries. The relationship could be described as a *provides-a* relationship. A `Vehicle`, for example, can be painted, but so can a `House`. These two objects are completely different, unrelated in almost every way. Although painting either object would involve vastly different work, a common description of the process (characterized by a common verb, such as "to paint") is possible.

While the syntax of each type of reuse is simple, the when and the why require more of an explanation. For instance, not all relationships defined in terms of *is-a* are appropriate for inheritance. Improper modeling of these relationships accounts for many of the design errors in an object-oriented system ("too much" design actually causes most design errors). Therefore, it is worth discussing their proper use. Inheritance is one of the most fundamental aspects of object-oriented programming. A thorough understanding of both how it works and when you should use it is essential to a successful object-oriented system.

## Generalization and Specialization

If you are lucky, you are part of a programming team that places a premium on design. You know that a good design results in lower software development costs over time, which ultimately means a paycheck for you. Good programmers know that the cost of writing software cannot outweigh the benefit it yields; you must be profitable. A good design is critical. Fortunately, a perfect initial design is not critical. In fact, perfection rarely occurs, if it happens at all. A good design is arrived at over time.

Usually, after running headfirst into the code and writing several classes, you begin to see patterns. You might notice that several classes share the same kind of data and exhibit the same behavior. You might find that you can group this data and behavior into one class. This scenario is called *generalization*. Usually, generalizations are discovered after the fact—the derived classes are written first and the base class is determined last. You can think of this process, *refactoring*, as retroactive OOP.

Refactoring is somewhat contrary to the idea of *specialization*, in which class hierarchies are derived over several versions of an application to handle special cases. For example, in Version 1.0 of your application, `Employee` might have been sufficient to handle all company employees. Over time, though, it became necessary to create derived classes based on `Employee` to handle the following new situations that did not exist when the application was first written:

- `ContractorThatGetsNoRespect`
- `WeirdGuysOnTheThirdFloor`
- `TheLoneUnixAdmin`

Rather than use a contrived example involving geometry seen in most OOP books, we instead will use a contrived example involving payments in an Internet commerce setting (which is much cooler than squares and circles). And if you squint, the examples will almost seem like real-life code. But just in case you are one of those people that think real OOP books must use examples with shapes, you will find such an example at the end of the chapter.

## Inheritance

Once upon a time, in a dimly lit cube...

After writing `CreditCard`, `GiftCertificate`, and `Check` classes, a self-realization occurs: "Self, I see that I can group all of the common behavior from these classes into a base class called `Payment`." This realization usually happens when you start to see that many classes you work with have the same method names (meaning that they exhibit the same behavior).

This general payment class (shown in Example 4-1) might contain methods to authorize, credit, and bill for a specific amount, as well as associate the payment with an account number. The general rules of the class are that all payments are authorized first, then they are billed. A billed payment may also be credited.

*Example 4-1. General Payment class*

```
Imports System

Public Class Payment

  Private account As String
  Private amount As Double
  Private authorized As Boolean
  Private billed As Boolean

  Public Sub New(ByVal account As String)
    Me.account = account
    authorized = False
    billed = False
    amount = 0
  End Sub

  Protected ReadOnly Property AccountNumber() As String
    Get
      Return Me.account
    End Get
  End Property

  Public Function Authorize(ByVal amount As Double) As Boolean
    If authorized Then
      Console.WriteLine("Payment is already authorized")
    Else
      Me.amount = amount
      Console.WriteLine("Authorizing payment for {0:c}", _
        amount)
      authorized = True
    End If
    Return authorized
  End Function

  Public Function Bill() As Boolean
    If authorized Then
      Console.WriteLine("Billing payment for {0:c}", _
        amount)
      billed = True
    Else
      Console.WriteLine("Payment is not authorized")
    End If
    Return billed
  End Function

  Public Function Credit() As Boolean
    If billed Then
      Console.WriteLine("Crediting payment for {0:c}", _
      amount)
      billed = False
      Return True
    Else
```

*Example 4-1. General Payment class (continued)*

```
      Console.WriteLine("Payment has not been billed")
    End If
    Return False
  End Function

End Class
```

Account information is considered sensitive. This information would probably be stored in a database somewhere in an encrypted state. When the payment information is retrieved, the account number can be unencrypted and used by the object itself. It never needs to be seen by human eyes. It makes sense, then, that `AccountNumber` should be a protected property, since derived classes would need access to account information as well. The remaining methods of the class are public.

After grouping this behavior in a base class, you can now extend it through inheritance. As shown in Example 4-2, a specialized class—perhaps a credit card—might need to verify the account number. Also, making the account number readily available outside of the class is unwise. However, in terms of credit card numbers, it is often necessary to display a portion of the number on an invoice. To make this display possible, you can add a `DisplayNumber` property to the class that returns the account number but hides most significant digits (i.e., `4XXXXXXXXXXX1234`).

Using the `Inherits` keyword, you can create a `CreditCard` class that includes all the public methods from `Payment`. Additional methods can then be added to the derived class, as shown in Example 4-2.

*Example 4-2. Derived CreditCard class*

```
Imports System
Imports System.Text

Public Class CreditCard

  Inherits Payment

  Public Sub New(ByVal account As String)
    MyBase.New(account)
  End Sub

  Public Sub Verify()
    Console.WriteLine("Verifying...")
  End Sub

  Public ReadOnly Property DisplayNumber() As String
    Get
      'Faster than concatenating normal strings
      Dim sb As New StringBuilder()
      Dim account As String = Me.AccountNumber
      Dim len As Integer = account.Length
      sb.Append(account.SubString(0, 1))
```

*Example 4-2. Derived CreditCard class (continued)*

```
      sb.Append(New String("X"c, len - 5))
      sb.Append(account.SubString(len - 4, 4))
      Return sb.ToString()
    End Get
  End Property

End Class
```

Alternatively, inheritance can be declared like this:

```
Public Class CreditCard : Inherits Payment

  'Methods here

End Class
```

Here, the colon signifies a new line of code in VB and mimics the inheritance declaration of C#, C++, and Java. Both definitions are equivalent, and using either is a matter of style. The latter will be used throughout the book, but only for readability—not to garner the respect of C++ programmers.

However, there is a problem. Constructors are *not* inherited, so every class must provide one. Otherwise, the compiler will create an empty one. In fact, if the base class has parameterized constructors but does not have a parameterless constructor, a constructor must be defined explicitly. If it is not, the VB.NET compiler will generate an error.

Before an instance of `CreditCard` is created, a constructor that passes the account number to the base class must be provided. The `MyBase` keyword allows a base class method to be called from a derived class, so the task is trivial:

```
Public Class CreditCard : Inherits Payment

  Public Sub New(ByVal account As String)
    MyBase.New(account)
  End Sub

  Public Sub Verify()
    Console.WriteLine("Verifying {0}", Me.AccountNumber)
  End Sub

  'Other methods here
End Class
```

Now that an appropriate constructor is in place, you can create an instance of `CreditCard` that can use all the public methods from `Payment`:

```
Dim cc As New CreditCard("4111111111111111")
cc.Verify()
If cc.Authorize(3.33) Then
  If cc.Bill() Then
    cc.Credit()
  End If
End If
```

Remember that everything that is protected in Payment is not available from outside the class:

```
'Error - internal use only
Dim visa As New CreditCard("4111111111111111")
Dim accountNumber As String = visa.AccountNumber
But it is available within the derived class:
Public Class CreditCard : Inherits Payment

  Public Sub Verify()
    Console.WriteLine("Verifying {0}", Me.AccountNumber)
  End Sub

End Class
```

Everything that is private in the Payment class is just that. You can do nothing about it. Private data is not directly accessible outside of the scope where it was declared, regardless of whether it is a derived class or not. And to reiterate (and probably not for the last time), all member data for *any* class should always be private.[*]

Base classes should represent a general concept. Therefore, a good rule is to always make your base classes abstract.

### Strings Are Immutable

Be careful and considerate when using strings. Strings in .NET are immutable, meaning they cannot be changed. There really is no such thing as appending one string to another, although the following code fragment mistakenly suggests otherwise:

```
Dim msg As String = "Hello"
msg += ", World!"
```

Actually, when two strings are concatenated like this, a third string is created. The string "Hello" is then marked for finalization.

You will often need to compose a string within a loop by appending a value to a master string on each iteration. This is the case with Example 4-2. Do *not* use String for this purpose. Instead, use the StringBuilder class in System.Text.

## Inheritance from System.Object

The Payment class implicitly derives from System.Object, as does CreditCard. This is done automatically; nothing special has to be done because the compiler handles it all.

[*] It should be private—at least initially. Relaxing restrictions is easier than enforcing them. Working from a totally public class interface would be more difficult than working from a more restricted one because of interdependencies that could occur during the development cycle.

Inheritance from `System.Object` provides a common set of functionality for all objects running under .NET. Therefore, each object will have the following standard set of behaviors associated with it:

`Equals`
: This behavior compares objects. You can override this method and make your own determinations about when one of your objects is considered equal to another.

`ReferenceEquals`
: This behavior determines whether two objects share the same reference.

`Finalize`
: This method is called before the garbage collector frees the memory associated with the object. It is not called when the object goes out of scope; rather, it is called whenever the garbage collector deems it necessary. Therefore, you should not rely on this method to free any limited resources that might be associated with your object.

`GetHashCode`
: This method generates a number that represents the object's value. It allows all objects to participate in the hash table implementations provided by .NET.

`GetType`
: This behavior returns an instance of `System.Type`, which is used heavily in reflection (see Chapter 7). A Type object can be used to find class-related information about an object, such as the methods it has, whether the class is abstract, and the events it publishes.

`ToString`
: This method describes an object by returning a meaningful text string. By default, it returns the name of the class, but it can be overridden. When an object is used in a place that requires a string, this method is called automatically. For example, `Console.WriteLine(myObject)` results in a call to `myObject.ToString`.

## NotInheritable

VB does not support multiple inheritance; a class cannot be derived from more than one class *at the same time*. A single inheritance hierarchy can be sustained indefinitely, though, as the following code suggests:

```
Public Class Visa : Inherits CreditCard

End Class
```

Here, we've defined a `Visa` class, which inherits from the `CreditCard` class, which in turn inherits from the `Payment` class. The `Payment` class in turn implicitly inherits from the framework's `System.Object` class.

Eventually, your hierarchies will become very specific, and at some point you may want to prevent further derivation. You can use the NotInheritable modifier to accomplish this goal. This modifier is mutually exclusive with MustInherit, the Visual Basic keyword discussed in the next section:

```
Public Class NotInheritable DebitCard : Inherits Visa
    'Can no longer inherit
End Class
```

## Abstract Base Classes

Considering that there is no generic way to authorize, bill, and credit the various payment types, you should probably make Payment an *abstract base class* (ABC). An ABC usually contains minimal functionality that can be used by all derivatives, but its main purpose is to serve as a template of sorts. It defines the methods a subclass needs to support to be considered a kind of the base class.

To make Payment an abstract base class, add the MustInherit keyword to the class declaration from Example 4-1. The class declaration then appears as follows:

```
Public MustInherit Class Payment
```

The derived CreditCard class still functions as it did before, but the ABC cannot be instantiated:

```
Dim myPayment As New Payment()    'Error
```

Preventing instances of a base class is usually preferable because it represents an idea more than a specific "thing." The specifics are left to the *concrete* classes that are derived from the base class, such as CreditCard, GiftCertificate, and Check.

# Containment

Containment indicates that one object contains another. Example 4-3 shows a hierarchy of contained classes, each nested within the other; the CreditCard object contains a BillingInfo object, which in turn contains an Address object.

The contained object, if it is used only within the parent object, can be declared as Private. Being restrictive (in terms of scope) at the class level is as important as being restrictive within the class itself. Don't make the class available if it is not needed. Here, Address is an object that could be used by several other classes, such as Order, ShippingInfo, or Invoice. BillingInfo is restricted to the payment and should not exist outside of it.

*Example 4-3. Containment relationships*

```
Public MustInherit Class Payment
  'Payment data
End Class
```

*Example 4-3. Containment relationships (continued)*

```
Public Class Address
  'Address1, Address2
  'City, ST, Zip
End Class

Public Class CreditCard : Inherits Payment

  Private Class BillingInfo
    Private myAddress As Address
    'Methods to get to address here
  End Class

  Private myBillingInfo As BillingInfo

End Class
```

Remember that the classes represent a *has-a* relationship between the parent class and the child class or classes.

The exception to this rule is the various collection classes that contain a type of an object. In this case, the container's primary behavior is to insert, remove, and maintain the objects it contains.

The same rule regarding accessibility that applies to member data also applies to a contained class; it should be private. The outer class uses the inner class, but the relationship between the two classes should be exposed only through a property.

The containing class *should* know what it contains, but a contained class *should not* know what contains it; the contained class should not use the container class in a way that exposes the type of container. Doing so could create a dependency between the two classes and possibly prevent them from being reused.

Many classes in .NET are sealed; they have been declared `NotInheritable`. They are declared `NotInheritable` because of performance considerations; it is not a diabolical plot to prevent reuse in the .NET library. In many cases, if a class is sealed, methods that would normally be virtual (determined at runtime) can be inlined by the compiler. In situations like this, containment allows the features of a class to be extended.

To see how this works, consider strings. If you have used VB for any considerable amount of time, you probably have a few string functions from ancient times, before strings were object-oriented. Supposed you'd like to modify the `String` class to include your old favorites. Guess what? The `String` class is final, so you're out of luck.

Almost.

Containment is a viable alternative to inheritance in this circumstance. You probably don't need every single public method available from a String, so wrap the ones you do need and delegate to the contained String. This concept is illustrated in Example 4-4, which defines a class called XString that contains a String. The class provides a method called WrapTag, which wraps the string in an XML tag and returns the result. It also provides a Length property that delegates to the internal String class' Length property.

*Example 4-4. Using containment for final .NET classes*

```
Imports System

Public Class XString

  Private myString As String

  Public Sub New(value As String)
    Me.myString = value
  End Sub

  'New proprietary string function
  Public Function WrapTag(ByVal tagName As String) As String
    Return String.Format("<{0}>{1}</{2}>", _
                         tagName, _
                         Me.myString, _
                         tagName)
  End Function

  'Wrap Length property of String
  Public ReadOnly Property Length() As Integer
    Get
      Return myString.Length
    End Get
  End Property

End Class

Friend Class Test
  Public Shared Sub Main()
    Dim t As New XString("test")
    Console.WriteLine(t.WrapTag("center"))
  End Sub
End Class
```

Contained objects that share the same scope should never be in a *uses* relationship with one another.

## Polymorphism

You may also want to change how a behavior in the base class works by redefining it in your derived class. Authorizing, billing, and crediting are very different processes, depending on what type of payment you are talking about.

While the `Payment` class can provide minimal functionality that is common across all of the various payment types, a derived class still needs to redefine or most likely extend the base class implementation. This process is called *overriding*.

You might also want to provide another way to initialize the object. Currently, the account number is passed directly to `New`. In the real world, the constructor would probably take a customer ID and a payment ID of some kind, and the card number would be retrieved from a database (where it was stored encrypted). You could add an additional constructor to do this. Providing more than one way to do the same thing with an object is called *overloading*. Overloaded functions have the same name but different arguments to distinguish them from one another.

The power of inheritance is not apparent until polymorphism is brought into the picture. In fact, the two concepts go hand in hand, so much so that discussing one without the other is very difficult.

The word polymorphism means "many forms." Polymorphism allows a derived class to be passed to a method that expects a base class. It allows methods from a base class to be redefined in a derived class. It also allows methods to be declared with the same name but different arguments.

This chapter and Chapter 5 discuss many forms of polymorphism and how to use each form effectively. While inheritance and polymorphism are powerful tools for writing robust, reusable object hierarchies, they give the uninitiated an unprecedented opportunity to write some really bad code. Thus, rather than just discuss the syntax, a few fundamental concepts will be covered as well. Covering these concepts will ensure that these technologies be used in a way that is ultimately beneficial.

## Overloading

Look at `Payment.Bill` (in Example 4-1) for minute. In its current state, it does not take any parameters. Whatever amount was authorized is the amount that will be billed. But the online shopping world is strange. It is possible that when this payment is billed, not all of the items that were originally purchased will be in stock. Should the order be canceled? Of course not. You should notify the customer, bill for what you have, and ship the order. The problem is that the customer can't be billed for anything that hasn't shipped. And as it stands now, there is no way to bill a partially available order by using the `Payment` class.

You need an additional billing method that allows an amount to be specified. It is possible to define two or more methods that have the same name, but a different number of parameters. Then the functionality can be implemented for each case. Example 4-5 shows two versions of `Bill`: one that accepts an amount and one that does not. This process is called overloading.

*Example 4-5. Overloading a method*

```
Imports System

Public MustInherit Class Payment

  'Other class methods are here

  Public Function Bill() As Boolean
    'Bill authorized amount
  End Function

  Public Function Bill(ByVal amount As Double) As Boolean
    If amount > Me.amount Then
      amount = Me.amount
    End If
    'Bill specified amount here
  End Function

End Class
```

If a method is overloaded in a derived class, then it needs to be explicitly expressed by using the `Overloads` keyword:

```
Public Class CreditCard : Inherits Payment

  'Other methods here

  'Overloading method defined in Payment requires keyword
  Public Overloads Function Bill(ByVal amount As Double) As Boolean
    'Bill for amount specified
  End Function

End Class
```

The compiler knows which call is made based on the parameters that are passed, as the following code fragment shows:

```
Dim visa As New CreditCard("4111111111111111")
visa.Bill()      'Calls Payment.Bill
visa.Bill(3.33)  'Calls CreditCard.Bill
```

Overloading is based on the name of the method and the arguments it takes. A method cannot be overloaded by return type, so overloading properties is out of the question.

## Overloaded Constructors

It is not uncommon for a class designer to overload the constructor of a class and provide several different ways to initialize an object. In the .NET class library, for instance, the String class provides several different constructors.

A string can be initialized with a literal:

```
Dim someString As String = "Literal"
```

or an array of characters:

```
Dim otherString As New String(New Char() {"a"c, "r"c, "r"c, "a"c, "y"c})
```

The c following the individual elements of the array distinguishes each element as a type of Char versus a 1-character String.

The string can be initialized with a character and an integer that represents how many times the character should be repeated:

```
'A string that contains 10 question marks
Dim thatString As String = New String("?"c, 10)
```

These constructors are just a few that are defined for a string. This was accomplished by overloading the New method to handle the various types of arguments. Notice that no two constructors have the same signature. You can similarly define constructors with different signatures for your own classes to provide more than one way to initialize your object. However, you should know how overloading a constructor differs from overloading an ordinary method.

### The default constructor

Constructors are not inherited, so, technically, they cannot be overloaded from one class to the next. The compiler does, however, add a call to the default constructor (a constructor that has no arguments) in the parent class from the derived class, effectively chaining the classes together. This move is sensible because the derived class might rely on the parent class being in a known state. If a default constructor isn't explicitly defined, the compiler puts an empty one into the class during compilation. Example 4-6 demonstrates the process.

*Example 4-6. Constructor behavior*

```
Imports System

Public MustInherit Class Payment

  Public Sub New()
    Console.WriteLine("Payment.New")
  End Sub
```

*Example 4-6. Constructor behavior (continued)*

```
  Public Sub New(ByVal account As String)
    Console.WriteLine("Payment.New: {0}", acctNumber)
  End Sub

End Class

Public Class CreditCard : Inherits Payment

  Public Sub New()
    Console.WriteLine("CreditCard.New")
  End Sub

  Public Sub New(ByVal account As String)
    Console.WriteLine("CreditCard.New: {0}", account)
  End Sub

End Class

Friend Class Test
  Public Shared Sub Main()
    Dim visa As New CreditCard()
    Dim amex As New CreditCard("3111111111111")
  End Sub
End Class
```

Both the child class and the parent class define constructors with the same signatures. Regardless of which constructor is called in the subclass, though, the default constructor in the base class is always called first, even if the parameterized constructor is called:

```
Payment.New
CreditCard.New
Payment.New
CreditCard.New: 3111111111111
```

Remember that the default constructor is called first, *not* the New method with the matching signature. In this case, the base class constructor with the matching function signature should be called instead of the default constructor. You can call it by using the MyBase keyword to call the appropriate base class constructor directly from the derived constructor as follows:

```
Public Class CreditCard : Inherits Payment

    Public Sub New()
        Console.WriteLine("CreditCard.New")
    End Sub

    Public Sub New (ByVal acctNumber As String)
        MyBase.New(acctNumber)
        Console.WriteLine("CreditCard.New: {0}", acctNumber)
    End Sub

End Class
```

Now the following line of code:

```
Dim amex As New CreditCard("3111111111111")
```

Would produce this expected result:

```
Payment.New: 311111111111111
CreditCard.New: 311111111111111
```

The default constructor of the base class is not called at all.

When calling a constructor in the parent class using MyBase, make sure it is the first thing that happens in the derived class' constructor. For example:

```
Public Sub New(ByVal x As Integer)
    MyBase.New(x)
    'Do additional initialization here
End Sub
```

With other overloaded methods, the call to the base class method using MyBase can be at the beginning, the middle, or the end of a method call, depending on when the functionality provided by the parent implementation is needed. Or it may not be needed at all.

# Overriding

As an abstract base, Payment is pretty limited in its current state. You can only overload methods in the class; that is, you can add new methods that have the same name as existing methods. However, existing behavior cannot be redefined. Note that different payment types need to implement Authorize, Bill, and Credit in different ways. Credit cards and checks are authorized through outside companies. However, while credit-card billing is handled by one of those same outside companies, billing a check means that Racer Jim gets an email and the checks are taken down to the bank. Finally, gift certificates are handled in-house; the information is all stored in a database, so there is quite a bit of variation here.

## Overridable and Overrides

An existing behavior in a base class can be completely redefined by overriding it in the derived class, but only if the writer of the base class has made it permissible to do so. For a method to be overridden, it must be declared by using the Overridable modifier. Naturally, this suggests some foresight on the part of the class designer. If the method is not marked as overridable, one of two things is happening: the person who coded the class does not want the method to be overridden, or he or she was not thinking ahead of the game. In the latter case, there is a loophole of sorts (see "Shadowing" at the end of this chapter) in the language that allows circumvention of this grievous situation. But for now, assume that the person who wrote the base class had a thinking cap on and defined the Payment class as shown in Example 4-7.

*Example 4-7. Overridable methods*

```
Public MustInherit Class Payment

  'Other methods a data here

  Public Overridable Function Authorize(ByVal amount As Double) As Boolean
    'Base implementation
  End Function

  Public Overridable Function Bill() As Boolean
    'Base implementation
  End Function

  Public Overridable Function Credit() As Boolean
    'Base implementation
  End Function

End Class
```

The person deriving a new class can specify that the method is overridden using the Overrides modifier, as shown here:

```
Public Class CreditCard : Inherits Payment

  'Other methods and data here

  Public Overrides Function Authorize(ByVal amount As Decimal) _
    As Boolean
    'Authorize credit card
  End Function

  Public Overrides Function Bill() As Boolean
    'Bill credit card
  End Function

  Public Overrides Function Credit() As Boolean
    'Refund credit card
  End Function

End Class
```

When a method is overridden, the original definition in the base class is completely hidden. To extend the behavior, rather than merely override it, MyBase can be used to call the base class implementation, as shown in the following code:

```
Public Overrides Function Bill() As Boolean
  'Do credit card-specific things here
  'then call base class method
  '(which updates database)
  MyBase.Bill()
End Function
```

## MustOverride

Alternatively, the person writing the base class may say, "Hey, there really is no generic behavior for any of this!" It is not uncommon for an abstract base class to require that a behavior be present in a derived class but provide no implementation. As far as flexible design goes, defining an abstract base class with no implementation for its members is the way to go.

Think about the `Payment` class. No implementation could be provided for `Authorize`, `Bill`, or `Credit`. You have just deluded yourself all along. Yes, you've been in a fantasy world. These operations are handled so differently between one payment type and the next, what would a generic implementation do?

A more realistic way to deal with this issue is to *force* a derived class to implement a behavior. Derived classes like `CreditCard` or `GiftCertificate` can be made to expose a key set of operations by using the `MustOverride` modifier with the base class' public members, as shown in Example 4-8.

*Example 4-8. Creating a contract with MustOverride*

```
Public MustInherit Class Payment

  'No End Function required (Definition only, no implementation)

  Public MustOverride Function Authorize(ByVal amount As Double) _
      As Boolean

  Public MustOverride Function Bill() As Boolean

  Public MustOverride Function Credit() As Boolean

End Class
```

C++ programmers might recognize this example as a *pure virtual function*. This type of function is used when a default behavior cannot be adequately described. However, you also create a guarantee or a contract, which is enforced by the compiler. By creating this guarantee or contract, it is assured that every class deriving from `Payment` will support these three operations. `MustOverride` methods actually play an important role in polymorphism.

## NotOverridable

When a method is marked `Overridable`, it is considered that way all the way down the inheritance tree. Suppose the `Payment` class contains a method that is used internally to verify the validity of an account number. Knowing that every payment type needs a different way to validate this number, the creator of the class has made it overridable:

```
Public MustInherit Class Payment

    Protected Overridable Function IsValidNumber() As Boolean
        Return False
    End Function

End Class
```

Although `IsValidNumber` was initially defined as overridable, at some point, it might be practical to prevent this override by using the `NotOverridable` modifier:

```
Public Class CreditCard : Inherits Payment
  Protected NotOverridable Function IsValidNumber() As Boolean
    'Use LUHN Mod 10 algorith to validate
    'card number
  End Function
End Class
```

`NotOverridable` prohibits further overriding once it has begun. In this case, the base class `Payment` provides minimal functionality for the `IsValidNumber` method. It merely returns `False`. Realizing the simplicity of the provided functionality, the method is marked as `Overridable`.

The `CreditCard` class then overrides this behavior to use the Luhn Mod 10 algorithm to validate card numbers. At this point, it is decided that all credit cards that might be derived in the future should use this algorithm. Therefore, `NotOverridable` is used to prevent further overriding. This way, new credit card classes cannot be derived, which could potentially sidestep this part of the validation process. (If you are interested in seeing how this algorithm works, see the "Luhn Mod 10 Algorithm" sidebar.)

Don't confuse overriding with overloading. Overriding is the process of defining a method that *replaces* a method definition with the same signature somewhere up the inheritance tree. Overloading is the process of adding new methods with the same name, but with different arguments.

## Substitution

One of polymorphism's best features is that it allows you to use a derived class where a base class is expected. It sounds crazy, but it's true. And because of that, it also allows you to write some amazingly adaptable code. Look at the following fragment:

```
Dim pmt As Payment
pmt = New CreditCard()
pmt.Authorize(3.33)
```

Guess what method is called as a result of running this code? If you guessed `CreditCard.Authorize`, you are right.

To use a real-world context as an example, some larger online retailers allow the use of multiple payments when placing an order. Theoretically, each payment could be

## Luhn Mod 10 Algorithm

The Luhn Mod 10 algorithm validates the numbers of most major credit card companies. Given the credit card number 4111111112127777, here's how it works:

1. Start from *right to left* and double the even-numbered digits. If the result is 10 or greater, store the result as two digits (i.e., 1 + 0 for 10, 1 + 1 for 11, 1 + 2 for 12, etc.). Add the results together.
2. Add the odd-numbered digits to the final result of step 1.
3. If the total from step 2 is divisible by 10, then the card is valid.

```
(Right)
7            = +7
7 * 2 = 14 = +1+4
7            = +7
7 * 2 = 14 = +1+4
2            = +2
1 * 2 =  2 = +2
2            = +2
1 * 2 =  2 = +2
1            = +1
1 * 2 =  2 = +2
1            = +1
1 * 2 =  2 = +2
1            = +1
1 * 2 =  2 = +2
1            = +1
4 * 2 =  8 = +8
----------------
(Left)       50 Mod 10 = 0 (Number is valid)
```

The source code for the Luhn function is:

```
Private Function Luhn(ByVal cc As String) As Boolean

  Dim i As Integer
  Dim total As Integer
  Dim even As String
  Dim len As Integer = cc.Length
  Dim digits(len - 1) As Integer

  For i = 0 To len - 1
      digits(i) = CInt(cc.Substring(i, 1))
  Next i

  For i = len - 1 To 1 Step -2
      total += digits(i)
      even = (digits(i - 1) * 2).ToString("00")
      total += Convert.ToInt32(even.Substring(0, 1))
      total += Convert.ToInt32(even.Substring(1, 1))
  Next i
```

—*continued*—

```
    If len Mod 2 <> 0 Then
        total += digits(0)
    End If

    If total Mod 10 = 0 Then
        Return True
    End If

    Return False

End Function
```

different: a credit card, a gift certificate, and maybe some kind of Internet-based cash. In a situation like this, you could create a very adaptable solution by writing the following code:

```
'Pseudo-code
Dim p As Payment
Dim payments() As Payment

payments(0) = New GiftCertificate(30.00)
payments(1) = New NuttyCash(15.00)
payments(2) = New CreditCard("1234")

For Each p In payments
    p.Bill()
Next p
```

An array of the base type, `Payment`, was declared. The array serves as a container that can hold any object derived from the base `Payment` type. When the `Bill` method is called for each element, the appropriate version of the method is called. If the payment is a credit card, then `CreditCard.Bill` is called. If it is a gift certificate, then `GiftCertificate.Bill` is called, and so on.

You can also declare methods that expect a base class like this:

```
Private Function ProcessPayment(ByVal p As Payment, _
                                ByVal amount As Double)
  If p.Authorize(amount) Then
    p.Bill()
  Else
    'Notify customer service
  End If
End Function
```

Each major function—`Authorize`, `Bill`, and `Credit`—is overridable. Overridable functions are often called *virtual methods*, indicating that the most derived implementation is called. It doesn't matter that each object is accessed through its base type. What matters is the actual type of aliased object.

If you made your base classes abstract, you should write methods that expect the base class and not a specific derivative. Writing your methods in this way will allow you to grow your applications over time without creating dependencies. Consider the following code fragment:

```
Select Case ClassName

  Case "CreditCard"
  'Do cc billing

  Case "GiftCertificate"
  'Do gift cert. billing

  Case "WireTransfer"
  'Do wire transfer billing

  Case "Check"
  'Do check billing

End Select
```

When you find yourself writing code in which you look at the actual type of an object like this, step back for a moment and reconsider your course of action. Polymorphism was designed as an alternative to this type of coding.

Why is this code fragment problematic? The function to which the code fragment belongs cannot be considered *closed*. This means that there is no way to add a new kind of payment to the system without revisiting the code shown in the fragment. When you add the new type, you have to add a new case to handle it. Adding this new case is a violation of a very important principle in object-oriented programming called the *open-closed principle*. This principle is responsible for many of the practices that programmers today consider "good." The fact that class members should always be private and global variables should be avoided comes from this principle. Honestly, people don't just make this stuff up.

## Open-Closed Principle

If you develop an application that will last through more than one version, you can be sure of one thing: change. And if a single change introduces more changes like a domino effect throughout your application, you probably have what is known in the industry as *bad code*. Designing software that is stable and impervious to change is pivotal to the open-closed principle. This principle comes from Bertrand Meyer, demigod of OOP and creator of the Eiffel programming language. It goes something like this:

> Software entities should be open for extension, but closed for modification.

Here, "entities" can mean a couple of things. A class is the obvious first choice, but it can also be applied to an entire module (a source file containing numerous related classes) or just a single method. When an entity is "open for extension," new behavior can be added as a result of changing requirements, but the entity itself cannot change. It is "closed for modification." Doesn't this concept seem like a contradiction?

Applications conforming to the open-closed principle are changed by adding new code, not by changing code that already works. Abstraction and polymorphism are key in implementing this principle. Abstract base classes allow you to define a specific set of behaviors that can be implemented in infinite ways through derived classes. As you have seen, methods can be written to expect these abstract base classes instead of concrete types. These methods and the modules they reside in can be considered *closed* because they rely on an abstraction that will not change.

Consider a class whose member variables are made public. If the member variables change, then every method that depends on those variables needs to be changed, too. Thus, no method that depends on those variables can be thought of as closed. Of course, you should expect that member functions of a class need to change (internally) in respect to its member data. But you should also expect a derived class to be closed to changes of those variables. This is encapsulation, after all.

Using abstraction and polymorphism is the way to successfully write code that adheres to the open-closed principle. These two mechanisms are enforced through inheritance. By using inheritance, you can derive classes that conform to the contract presented by the base class. Specifically, the abstract base class says that you must override certain functions to participate in this hierarchy or relationship.

Are there any rules or pitfalls to be aware of when using inheritance like this? Is it enough to say that Class B *is-a* Class A and be done with it? Or will you need to look at other considerations? Rest assured, devious traps lie in wait for those who use inheritance in a reckless and cavalier manner. However, what you need to watch out for is not always obvious.

## Liskov Substitution Principle

If you want a good grasp of proper inheritance, the Liskov Substitution Principle (LSP) is a good place to start. Basically, it says:

> Methods that use references to base classes must be able to use objects of derived classes without knowing it.

In other words, a derived class must behave like a base class; you should be able to swap the two classes in any given situation. Sounds easy, right? Well, let's see what happens when this principle is violated.

Because no book on OOP should omit an example involving a geometric shape of some kind, here is a token example of an application that uses rectangles. However, the charade ends here. This isn't a CAD program or a non-Windows GUI framework. This example is a rectangle application, pure and simple. The primary class used in this application is the `Rectangle`, shown in Example 4-9.

*Example 4-9. The amazing Rectangle class*

```
Public Class Rectangle

  Private myWidth As Double
  Private myHeight As Double

  Public Property Width() As Double
    Get
      Return myWidth
    End Get
    Set(ByVal Value As Double)
      myWidth = Value
    End Set
  End Property

  Public Property Height() As Double
    Get
      Return myHeight
    End Get
    Set(ByVal Value As Double)
      myHeight = Value
    End Set
  End Property

  Public ReadOnly Property Area() As Double
    Get
      Return myWidth * myHeight
    End Get
  End Property

  Public Overrides Function ToString() As String
    Dim s As String
    s = String.Format("Width: {0}, Height: {1}", _
        myWidth.ToString(), myHeight.ToString())
    Return s
  End Function

End Class
```

OK, so the rectangle application works well. It handles those rectangles like nobody's business, when suddenly, a highly intelligent person from marketing drops in and says that the application needs to work with squares. Incredible as it sounds, some people want squares, too.

Well, everyone knows that inheritance should represent an *is-a* relationship, and for the most part, a square is a rectangle. After all, it has four sides, right? You should be able to derive it from `Rectangle` like this:

```
Public Class Square : Inherits Rectangle

End Class
```

However, just using the *is-a* relationship as a yardstick for proper inheritance can lead to some subtle problems. First, a Square doesn't need to be described in terms of two sides. Thus, an extra member variable takes up 8 bytes of space. Remember that this isn't a CAD application in which there could be thousands of squares lying around. But even if you are not concerned with memory, there is another problem.

Square inherits the Width and Height properties from Rectangle. This inheritance is inappropriate because squares aren't usually described according to width and height. Again, a square is defined by the fact that both adjacent sides are the same. It is possible to override Width and Height so that when one is set, the other is set to the same value. In this way, the sides of the square would never be invariant.

The problem is that these properties are not Overridable. You might say that this problem is an oversight to be blamed on the writer of the base class, but is it really? After all, Width and Height are primitive operations in respect to a rectangle. Blaming this problem on an oversight is like saying, "We'd better give someone the ability to change the way multiplication works for integers!"

For the sake of argument, assume that the Width and Height properties are virtual. In that case, as the code in Example 4-10 shows, you can override them so that when one is set, the other is set to the same value. In this way, the sides of the Square are never discordant.

*Example 4-10. The Square class*

```
Public Class Square : Inherits Rectangle

  Public Overrides Property Width() As Double
    Get
      Return MyBase.Width
    End Get
    Set(ByVal Value As Double)
      MyBase.Width = Value
      MyBase.Height = Value
    End Set
  End Property

  Public Overrides Property Height() As Double
    Get
      Return MyBase.Height
    End Get
    Set(ByVal Value As Double)
      MyBase.Width = Value
      MyBase.Height = Value
    End Set
  End Property

End Class
```

When one side of the square is set, the other is set to match. Everything should work, right? Well, not exactly. In a fish tank, the assumptions made here seem to hold water, but what about the assumptions a user might make? Ahhhh, so many times, the user is forgotten! Look at the following code fragment to see the story unfold:

```
#Const Debug = True

Imports System
Imports System.Diagnostics

Public Class NotSomeCADProgram

  Public Sub Test(ByVal r As Rectangle)
    r.Width = 5
    r.Height = 10
    Debug.Assert(r.Area = 50)
  End Sub

End Class
```

What happens when a `Square` is passed to the `Test` method? It's going to blow up for sure. The area will end up being `100`. Is the person who wrote that method in error? It does seem reasonable to assume that changing the width of a rectangle would not alter its height. After all, a rectangle is described by two sides, and each is independent of the other.

A square might be a rectangle, but a `Square` is definitely not a `Rectangle`. Admittedly, the `Square` class did look valid until it was actually used. However, when viewed in terms of an actual user, the idea that a `Square` *is-a* `Rectangle` falls apart. Sure, they might share similar properties, but the behavior of a `Square` is different from that of a `Rectangle`; *is-a* is more about behavior than anything else.

## Shadowing

Overriding a method hides the method that has the same name and signature in the base class. However, another form of method-hiding hides by name alone. It is called *shadowing*.

Shadowing is very different from overriding. You are free to shadow any method in a base class that you choose; no permission is needed. Also, shadowed methods are not virtual. For example, look at this code fragment:

```
Imports System

Public Class A
  Public Sub Foo()
    Console.WriteLine("A.Foo")
  End Sub
End Class

Public Class B : Inherits A
  Public Shadows Sub Foo()
```

```
      Console.WriteLine("B.Foo")
    End Sub
  End Class

  Public Class Test
    Public Shared Sub Main()
      Dim myA As A = New B()
      myA.Foo()
    End Sub
  End Class
```

If you reference an instance of B through the base class A, A.Foo is still called as a result. With Overrides, you would expect B.Foo to be called. If you want to verify this process for yourself, add an Overridable modifier to A.Foo and replace Shadows with Overrides in B.Foo.

Shadowing hides every member in the base class. If your base class has 15 overloaded Foo methods and a derived class shadows it, all 15 methods will be hidden. The only usable version of Foo is the one in the derived class, unless you access the method through a base class reference (which is not very realistic in most situations).

Interestingly, shadowing solves the problem presented in Example 4-10. If the Width and Height properties were shadowed and an instance of Square were passed to the Test method, the assertion would have held because the base class version of the properties would have been called. However, the only reason this is mentioned is to remind those of you who may have noticed the fact that this is not a valid solution in this particular case.

# CHAPTER 5
# Interfacing .NET

The concept of separating the interface from the implementation has been around for some time. You have seen how code written against an abstract base class allows you to write applications that can grow over time and remain resistant to some of the more negative aspects of change. This is not a new idea. C++ programmers have been using the same technique for years. In fact, the open-closed principle (see Chapter 4) is based on this idea.

Visual Basic .NET provides a more formal declaration of this notion of separation called an *interface*. At the highest level, an interface contains a group of related methods to perform a task or describe a service. It is similar to an abstract base class that does not contain implementation, and it serves a similar purpose as well. It acts as a contract, describing a behavior that an object provides. Any object that implements an interface has to provide an implementation of everything included within the interface definition.

Although they have been with the language for some time now, interfaces are one of the most misunderstood features of VB.NET. Undoubtedly, interfaces will continue to be neglected in lieu of implementation inheritance. This is unfortunate because interface-based programming is as important now as it was in the past. And in terms of inheritance, it is not an either-or situation. Interfaces have their place alongside implementation inheritance. In fact, each principle and technique discussed in the last chapter is even more beneficial when used with interfaces.

Interfaces are declared in a manner similar to a class, but they contain only methods (such as `Function`, `Sub`, or `Property`) and events. Example 5-1 shows the definition of a simple interface.

*Example 5-1. Defining an interface*

```
Public Interface IPaintable

  Sub Paint(ByVal color As System.Drawing.Color)

  ReadOnly Property Color() As System.Drawing.Color
```

*Example 5-1. Defining an interface (continued)*

```
  Event Completed()

End Interface
```

While the interface itself can be declared with any visibility, the individual methods and events are inherently public, so no modifier is used. In fact, the compiler complains if you try to use one.

A class describing an object that can be painted can now implement the interface, as Example 5-2 demonstrates.

*Example 5-2. Implementing an interface*

```
Imports System
Imports System.Drawing

Public Class Car
  Implements IPaintable

  Private myColor As Color

  Public Event Painted() Implements IPaintable.Completed

  Public Sub Paint(ByVal aColor As Color) Implements IPaintable.Paint
    myColor = aColor
    RaiseEvent Painted()
  End Sub

  Public ReadOnly Property Color() As Color Implements IPaintable.Color
    Get
      Return myColor
    End Get
  End Property

End Class
```

While each interface method needs to be implemented, you don't need to name it the same thing in the implementing class. Look closely and you will see that `IPaintable.Completed` was renamed "`Painted`" in the implementation. This feature is nice because "`Completed`" is vague in regard to the interface it is part of and it is also a common name. When a class implements several interfaces, the name "`Completed`" could be used in several places.

## Private Implementation

The `IPaintable` interface was defined as `Public`. In Example 5-2, methods are implemented as `Public`, too. This implementation allows you to call interface members through an instance of an object:

```
Dim myCar As New Car()
myCar.Paint(Color.LemonChiffon)
```

One school of thought says that a client should not be aware of objects. It should only know about interfaces, and all interaction with an object should be made through an interface reference instead of an object reference. While this example is extreme, it has a point. By now, you can probably guess that using interface references rather than object references enhances encapsulation. In this case, there is less of a dependency between the client and the object.

Just because an interface is public doesn't mean you have to implement it publicly. Implementing the interface privately is actually better. If you make every method implemented in Example 5-2 private, you can no longer access the IPaintable methods directly. You have to use a reference to the interface, as the following code fragment illustrates:

```
Dim myCar as New Car()
.
.
Dim paintable As IPaintable = myCar
.
.
paintable.Paint(Color.PapayaWhip)
```

Yes, this fragment lives in an unnatural setting. However, imagine client code that is only interface-aware. Think about how easy it would be to swap out new implementations without breaking anything. The key is that you do not care about what type of object you use; rather, you care about what the object can do or what services it provides.

## Versioning

An interface is a contract, and contracts are not meant to be broken. It is not hard to fathom that if you change an interface, the waters will get rough. Code that depends on an interface that has been changed will no longer work. Once an interface is published, it is imperative that it does not change. This rule applies to the public and protected interfaces of a class, as well as any interfaces that were implemented by a class.

In the tradition of the open-closed principle, when you need to extend an interface, simply create a new one. Usually, a number is appended to the original interface name. For example, the second version of IPaintable would be IPaintable2.

Working with interfaces is much easier than it used to be. When creating a new version of an interface, you can inherit from the old version to maintain integrity and add the new functionality to the derived interface. Overloading is also allowed:

```
Imports System
Imports System.Drawing

Public Interface IPaintable2 : Inherits IPaintable
    TransparentFill(color As System.Drawing.Color)
```

```
    Overloads Paint(color1 As Color, color2 As Color)
End Interface
```

Old clients can still obtain an IPaintable reference from IPaintable2, while new clients can use the new interface directly.

The versioning story of interfaces is debatably better than a base class. It is definitely more explicit. When you need something new, you define a new interface. It's as straightforward as that. Old clients can use the old interface, while new clients can take advantage of more recent offerings. Simply adding methods to a base class and sorting things out at runtime is not very safe, nor is it forward thinking. It opens you up to all kinds of failures.

## Interfaces Versus Abstract Base Classes

Interfaces provide all the benefits of polymorphism. You can code against an interface much like you can code an abstract base class:

```
Dim superSport As New Car()
.
.
.
PaintSomeStuff(superSport)
.
.
.
Public Sub PaintSomeStuff(someThing As IPaintable)
    someThing.Paint()
End Sub
```

So what is the difference between an interface and an abstract base class? When should you use one over the other?

If you are describing an *is-a* relationship, you can use an abstract base class. An interface, on the other hand, usually describes a service or facility that can be used across a wide variety of objects. For instance, House, Car, and Fence are three very different classes, but each could implement IPaintable and handle the painting process in a manner specific to its needs.

This describes a typical scenario and is a pretty good guideline to follow, but it is by no means set in stone. Just because an *is-a* relationship is described doesn't mean you can't use an interface in place of an abstract base class. If there is no implementation in the base class, there is no reason not to use an interface instead. The Payment class you have already seen could easily be rewritten as an interface:

```
Public Interface IPayment
    Function Authorize(amount As Decimal) As Boolean
    Function Bill() As Boolean
    Function Credit() As Boolean
End Interface
```

One advantage of using interfaces is that the number a class can implement is unlimited (in theory). You can implement as many interfaces as your class requires, but you are only allowed to derive from one base class. You will often hear of interfaces described primarily as a means of circumventing this limitation. It's true, but this description minimizes the importance of interface-based programming. Interfaces do have a place beyond this role.

Programming against an interface gives you all the benefits of coding against an abstract base class, at least in a polymorphic sense. It also gives you more flexibility in your design, at least in terms of component-to-component dependency.

This book has discussed the use of abstract base classes and inheritance to minimize dependencies in a system. You have seen how polymorphism allows the construction of flexible systems. However, you should consider several issues relating to polymorphism and the tendency of an application to grow over time.

It is reasonable to expect the requirements of a base class or a derived class to change over time. Changing a base class, however, could wreak havoc with classes that are derived from it. This well-known problem is called the *fragile base class*.

As inheritance trees grow, modifying classes at the top can impact classes below significantly. This is especially true of classes that provide protected access to implementation details. Once a derived class calls a protected method, a dependency is created. You can no longer change the base class implementation without the possibility of breaking a derived class.

When overridable virtual functions are involved, you introduce the possibility that the client or base class will call functions overridden by a derived class. When these functions are called, it is no longer completely safe to change a base class implementation of an overridable method. You can't add functionality that is required by a derived class beyond this point or provide new functionality.

If you expect a class to be extended, it is just as important to encapsulate implementation details from a derived class as it is to encapsulate them from the client. You can minimize these dependencies by limiting or restricting protected access to a component altogether. You can also force derived classes to provide their own implementation through the use of the `MustOverride` modifier. Then you can use references to the abstract base class throughout your object model. However, even after considering this scenario, there are still a few issues at hand.

Although inheritance is good, it is best used in small doses, in situations that you control. Inheritance is considered *white box reuse*. This term implies that inheriting from a class requires knowledge or awareness of that class' internals.

If you use references to abstract base classes, you still create a layer of dependence, which may or may not be a problem for you. In fact, within a component, this issue is probably not very important. But step back for a moment.

Most systems are built using *object composition*. Components are built that contain various layers of the application, such as data access, business rules, and so forth. Then you use these components to build an application. In contrast to inheritance, object composition is known as *black box reuse*.

Now think about the "edges" of your system—the hinges, so to speak. If one component uses class-based references from another component, what does that mean? The two components are now dependent on each other. You are tied to an implementation, which is fine if you are satisfied with an implementation or you don't expect an implementation to change.

However, if the base class being referenced were to change, you might have some real problems on your hands. You've heard about the fragile base class problem. If you are solely responsible for an inheritance hierarchy, changes can be painful, but not detrimental. You can make your changes, recompile, and everything will be back in order. This solution is not ideal, but situations like this occur frequently outside of academia.

However, if you expose a class-based reference through a public interface, you could cause problems that would leak outside of your domain of influence. Another component that uses yours may no longer work. For this reason, many people believe that using an object as a parameter to a method should be outright illegal.

To reiterate, the use of interfaces and abstract base classes does not have to be mutually exclusive. You can use both. Example 5-3 shows a possible way to code the Payment class.

*Example 5-3. Using interfaces and ABCs*

```
Public Interface IPayment
  Function Authorize(ByVal amount As Decimal) As Boolean
  Function Bill() As Boolean
  Function Credit() As Boolean
End Interface

Public MustInherit Class Payment
  Implements IPayment

  Public MustOverride Function Authorize(ByVal amount As Double) _
    As Boolean Implements IPayment.Authorize

  Public MustOverride Function Bill() As Boolean _
      Implements IPayment.Bill

  Public MustOverride Function Credit() As Boolean _
      Implements IPayment.Credit

End Class
```

Rather than show two pages of database access code, you can assume that the Payment class contains base functionality that pulls payment information from a relational store. Classes that need this base functionality, like types of payments (e.g., credit cards or gift certificates), can inherit from the `Payment` class. Code that *uses* the hierarchy could refer to the interface instead of the class.

# Interfaces in .NET

The .NET Framework class library doesn't contain much in the way of interfaces, but every object designer should be familiar with a few of them. `IDisposable` is probably the most important because it plays an important role in garbage collection. Comparing and copying objects are also relatively common tasks; therefore, you should look at `IComparable` and `ICloneable`. `ISerializable` (discussed in Chapter 8) converts an object to a stream to persist it to disk or transport it across a network. Undoubtedly, though, constructing collections is one of the most essential programming tasks used in building object hierarchies. In .NET, collections are built by using `IEnumerable` and `IEnumerator`. These two interfaces allow your objects to be exposed through a `For...Each` loop, among other things.

## IDisposable

As you have seen, the lifespan of an object is nondeterministic; there is no way to know when an object will be freed. At some given point, the garbage collector (GC) decides that an object is no longer in use and reclaims its memory. If the object has a `Finalize` method, the GC calls it; it acts as a rough analog to a destructor.

This scenario creates two problems. First, calling `Finalize` is expensive. Garbage collection runs twice for these objects. On the first pass, the GC puts all objects that implement `Finalize` into the finalization queue and frees everything else. On the second pass, it must call `Finalize` for all objects in the queue, and only then is the memory released. Objects with finalizers take longer to be freed.

The second problem occurs in situations when a class wraps a limited resource, such as a file, a window, or, more commonly, a database connection. Best practice says that you should acquire a resource, use it, and free it as quickly as possible so you don't run out of resources. There are three varieties of *resource wrappers*:

- A class that holds both unmanaged and managed resources
- A class that holds only unmanaged resources
- A class that holds only managed resources

Managed resources are contained within .NET. They include such things as database connections and sockets and are defined in the .NET class library. Unmanaged resources exist outside of the framework. COM objects are one example. Another is a handle obtained from Win32, a device context (HDC) perhaps.

If at all possible, avoid using a `Finalize` method. If you can, write your classes so that the resource is used and then released. This is not always possible, however. If a held resource is used in several places in an object, the cost of obtaining the resource could far outweigh the overhead incurred from a call to Finalize. The solution is simple—provide your own cleanup method. Implementing this method, though, is not straightforward.

There is actually an established pattern in .NET for handling cleanup situations. A resource wrapper first needs to implement IDisposable, which is defined in the System namespace. As Example 5-4 shows, this interface contains one method, Dispose.

*Example 5-4. IDisposable*

```
Imports System

'Defined in System
'Public Interface IDisposable
'    Sub Dispose()
'End Interface


Public Class ResourceBase
  Implements IDisposable

End Class
```

The class shown in Example 5-5 holds two limited resources. The first is an instance of OleDbConnection, which is a database connection. The second is a file handle obtained from calling the Win32 API CreateFile function. Both are obtained from the constructor and are used in several places within the class. The interop code for making Win32 API calls was left out for brevity's sake.

*Example 5-5. Implementing IDisposable, Part I*

```
Public Class ResourceBase
  Implements IDisposable

  Private conn As OleDbConnection
  Private connString As String
  Private hFile As IntPtr

  Public Sub New(ByVal connString As String)
    Me.connString = connString
    InitResources()
  End Sub

  Private Sub InitResources()

    Me.conn = New OleDbConnection(Me.connString)
    Me.conn.Open()

    Me.hFile = CreateFile("data.txt", _
                          GENERIC_WRITE, _
                          0, _
```

*Example 5-5. Implementing IDisposable, Part I (continued)*

```
                              Nothing, _
                              OPEN_ALWAYS, _
                              FILE_ATTRIBUTE_NORMAL, _
                              Nothing)
  End Sub

  'IDisposable implementation here

End Class
```

Classes that implement IDisposable place the responsibility of cleanup in the hands of the user. Dispose must be called directly; it's not as elegant as a destructor, which is called automatically when an object goes out of scope, but that's the price you pay for managed memory. The good news is that all the classes in .NET do the same thing, so you should get used to it quickly.

If an object implements IDisposable, it should have a Finalize method, too. Finalize acts as a backup plan if Dispose is not called. Should this happen, any resources that might be lying around can be freed when the garbage collector fires up.

If Dispose is called, finalization should be canceled for the object. This cancelation prevents the cleanup code from being called twice and keeps well-behaved code from incurring the Finalize call's performance penalty.

Example 5-6 shows a common pattern for implementing Dispose. Notice how GC. SuppressFinalize is called to cancel finalization for the class when Dispose is called.

*Example 5-6. Implementing IDisposable, Part II*

```
Public Class ResourceBase
  Implements IDisposable

  'Other methods

  Private disposed As Boolean = False

  Public Sub Dispose() Implements IDisposable.Dispose
    Dispose(True)
    GC.SuppressFinalize(Me)
  End Sub

  Protected Overridable Sub Dispose(ByVal disposing As Boolean)
    If Not (Me.disposed) Then
      Me.disposed = True
      If (disposing) Then
        'Free managed resources here
        Me.conn.Close()
      End If
      'Free unmanaged resources here
      CloseHandle(Me.hFile)
    End If
```

*Example 5-6. Implementing IDisposable, Part II (continued)*

```
  End Sub

  Public Overrides Sub Finalize()
    Dispose(False)
  End Sub

End Class
```

For now, ignore the fact that Dispose is overloaded. Just understand that two things that can happen: a client can call Dispose like it should, or Finalize can do all the dirty work. In either case, the drudgery is delegated to the protected version of Dispose.

A private flag in the class determines whether the class is already disposed. If it isn't, the resources held by the class are released. Beyond this point, subtleties are all that matter. If disposing is True, which is the case when IDisposable.Dispose is called, the database connection is closed.

Finalize calls Dispose with a False argument. In this case, the database connection is *not* closed because conn is a managed object; it is an instance of OleDbConnection (defined in the System.Data.OleDb namespace). If a client fails to call ResourceBase.Dispose, two objects will end up in the finalization queue: ResourceBase *and* OleDbConnection.

When the garbage collector frees the memory associated with these objects, the order of their release is not guaranteed. If OleDbConnection is freed first, conn will no longer refer to a valid object when ResourceBase is finalized. Then when ResourceBase.Dispose is called, an exception will be thrown.

The disposing parameter determines whether Dispose is called or if the object is finalized. In the first case, you know the reference to conn is still valid, so you can call conn.Close (which essentially calls the OleDbConnection implementation of IDisposable) and free it. In the latter instance, it is best to let the GC deal with both objects on its own time.

All methods in a resource wrapper should be aware of the disposed flag and handle the situation accordingly. If the object was disposed, you should throw an exception, as shown in the following code:

```
Public Class ResourceBase

    Private disposed As Boolean = False

    Public Sub ResourceMethod()

        If Me.disposed Then
            Throw New ObjectDisposedException(...)
        End If

        'Continue
```

```
    End Sub

End Class
```

In addition to implementing IDisposable, you can expose a Close method. In the framework itself, many classes expose this method. When a class has a Close method, it implies that it can be reused. The OleDbConnection class from the example has a Close method. Once Close is called, the connection can be reopened by calling Open. While Close is standard across the framework, though, the implementer determines how an object is reused; a corresponding Open method is not required.

Writing a Close method can be as simple as routing the call to IDisposable.Dispose:

```
Public Sub Close()
    Dispose()
End Sub
```

However, consider the following when your object is reused in this type of situation. When Dispose is called, finalization is suppressed. What happens if you close an object, reopen it, and forget to call Dispose? The object will not be finalized. If you reuse an object, you need to make sure that finalization will occur. You can do this by calling GC.ReRegisterForFinalize.

Example 5-5 shows that the constructor calls a private function known as InitResources. Usually, a constructor needs to share code that is used to reopen an object:

```
Public Sub New(connString As String)
    Me.connString = connString
    InitResources()
End Sub

Public Sub Open(connString As String)
    Me.connString = connString
    InitResources()
    GC.ReRegisterForFinalize(Me)
End Sub
```

The protected version of Dispose exists for the benefit of derived classes, as shown in Example 5-7. In the derived class, Dispose is overridden and implemented in a manner similar to the base class. The only difference is that before the derived version exits, MyBase.Dispose is called. IDisposable is already implemented in the base class. Reimplementing the interface is unnecessary.

*Example 5-7. Deriving from classes that implement IDisposable*

```
Public Class ResourceDerived : Inherits ResourceBase

  Private disposed As Boolean = False

  Public Sub New(ByVal connString As String)
    MyBase.New(connString)
  End Sub
```

*Example 5-7. Deriving from classes that implement IDisposable (continued)*

```
  Protected Overloads Overrides Sub Dispose(ByVal disposing As Boolean)

    If Not (Me.disposed) Then
      Me.disposed = True
      If (disposing) Then
        'Free managed resources here
      End If

      'Release unmanaged resources here

      'Call Dispose in base class
      MyBase.Dispose(disposing)
    End If
  End Sub

End Class
```

You do not need to override `Finalize`. The base class implementation you inherited is suitable. `Dispose` is a virtual function. Even though `Finalize` is called from the base class, `ResourceDerived.Dispose` will be called. If `ResourceDerived` needs to encapsulate additional resources, it is free to do so, and the pattern maintains its integrity.

This pattern for implementing `Dispose` in this chapter is not thread-safe. A second object could call `IDisposable.Dispose` before the ***disposed*** flag was set to `True`. If you find that multiple threads call `Dispose`, you should consider a redesign.

By calling `Dispose`, you imply ownership of the object. If you don't own an object, you shouldn't call it. If you do have ownership, then you can call it, but make sure no one else does. There can be only one owner.

One of the drawbacks to the previous `Dispose` pattern is that the parameterized version of `Dispose` needs to be reimplemented for every derived class. The pattern works well and is recommended in the .NET documentation, but it is not the only available option. An alternative, lightweight pattern (one of many, no doubt) allows `Dispose` to be implemented once in the base class.

Start with the `BaseResource` class from the previous `Dispose` pattern and add the following two methods:

```
Overridable Protected Sub DoDispose()
    'Do nothing here - this will be overriden in the subclass
End Sub

Protected Sub CheckDispose()
    If (disposed) Then
        'Throw exception here
    End If
End Sub
```

Remove the Overrides modifier from the parameterized Dispose method; this method no longer needs to be virtual because it will be implemented only once in the base class—but it can still be called from derived classes because it remains protected.

Now, instead of freeing managed resources, call the new DoDispose method instead. Also, remove any code that frees unmanaged resources. The method should now look like this:

```
Protected Sub Dispose(ByVal disposing As Boolean)
    If Not disposed Then
        disposed = True
        'If this is a call to Dispose, dispose all managed resources
        If (disposing) Then
            DoDispose()    'Should be overridden in subclass
        End If
    End If
End Sub
```

The entire listing for the alternative ResourceBase class is shown in Example 5-8.

*Example 5-8. Alternative IDisposable pattern*

```
Imports System

Public Class ResourceBase
  Implements IDisposable

  Private disposed As Boolean = False

  Protected Overridable Sub DoDispose()
    'Do nothing here - this will be overriden in the subclass
  End Sub

  Public Sub Dispose() Implements IDisposable.Dispose
    Dispose(True)
    GC.SuppressFinalize(Me)
  End Sub

  Protected Sub Dispose(ByVal disposing As Boolean)
    If Not (Me.disposed) Then
      Me.disposed = True
      If (disposing) Then
        DoDispose()         'Should be overridden in subclass
      End If
    End If
  End Sub

  Protected Sub CheckDispose()
    If (disposed) Then
      'Throw exception here
    End If
  End Sub
```

*Example 5-8. Alternative IDisposable pattern (continued)*

```
  Protected Overrides Sub Finalize()
    Dispose(False)
  End Sub

End Class
```

As demonstrated in Example 5-9, the derived class no longer needs to implement a `Dispose` method. However, it overrides the `DoDispose` method that was added to the base class. This override frees resources allocated by the derived class, regardless of whether or not they are managed; no distinction is made.

*Example 5-9. Alternative ResourceDerived class*

```
Public Class ResourceDerived : Inherits BaseResource

  'Unmanaged resource
  Private handle As IntPtr

  'Managed resource
  Private Components As Component

  Public Sub New()
    'Constructor
  End Sub

  Protected Overrides Sub DoDispose()
    Components.Dispose()
    Release(handle)
    handle = IntPtr.Zero
  End Sub

  Public Sub DoSomething()

    CheckDispose()  'Make sure object is still alive

    'Do something important

  End Sub

End Class
```

Every public method in the class begins with a call to `CheckDispose` (which also is implemented once in the base class), which determines whether or not the object is still alive. If it was disposed, an exception is thrown from the base class.

## IComparable

Objects wishing to take advantage of `Array.Sort` or `Array.BinarySearch` (`System.Array` is the base class for all arrays in the runtime) can implement the `IComparable` interface. The interface defines a single method named `CompareTo` and looks like this:

```
Public Interface IComparable
    Function CompareTo(ByVal obj As Object) As Integer
End Interface
```

The return value of CompareTo indicates how obj relates to the object that actually implements the interface. Possible values are shown in Table 5-1.

*Table 5-1. CompareTo return values*

| Return value | Relationship |
|---|---|
| < 0 | x is less than y. |
| = 0 | x equals y. |
| > 0 | x is greater than y. |

How this method is implemented is arbitrary; it all depends on the object's needs. Example 5-10 contains an unembellished listing for the MuscleCar class. You could implement IComparable to base sorting on the car's horsepower.

*Example 5-10. The MuscleCar class*

```
Imports System

Public Class MuscleCar

  Public ReadOnly year, make, model As String
  Public ReadOnly horsePower As Short

  Public Sub New(ByVal year As String, _
                 ByVal make As String, _
                 ByVal model As String, _
                 ByVal horsePower As Short)
    Me.year = year
    Me.make = make
    Me.model = model
    Me.horsePower = horsePower
  End Sub

End Class
```

First, specify that the class will implement the IComparable interface:

```
Imports System

Public Class MuscleCar
    Implements IComparable
```

Next, the CompareTo method must be added to the class. This implementation is interesting because the horsepower of the MuscleCar is stored as a Short, and the Short data type also implements IComparable. This means that the call can be forwarded to the Short implementation, saving you a few lines of code:

```
Public Function CompareTo(ByVal obj As Object) As Integer _
    Implements IComparable.CompareTo
```

```
        'Cast obj to a MuscleCar
        Dim otherCar As MuscleCar = CType(obj, MuscleCar)
        Return Me.horsePower.CompareTo(otherCar.horsePower)

    End Function
```

Given two instances of a MuscleCar, you can now compare them:

```
Dim car1 As MuscleCar = New MuscleCar("1966", "Shelby", "Cobra", 425)
Dim car2 As MuscleCar = New MuscleCar("1969", "Pontiac", "GTO", 370)

Console.WriteLine(car1.CompareTo(car2))
```

The result is 55, the difference of 425 and 370, meaning car1 is "greater" than car2 (no flames, please).

You can also sort the class by calling Array.Sort. First, though, you must override the ToString method so that you can print the sort results to the console in a meaningful way. Simply add the following method to MuscleCar:

```
Overrides Public Function ToString() As String
    Return String.Format( _
        "MuscleCar - Year:{0} Make:{1} Model:{2} HP:{3}", _
        Me.year, Me.make, Me.model, Me.horsePower)
End Function
```

You can now test the sorting by declaring a few different instances of MuscleCar and calling Array.Sort, which is a shared method:

```
Friend Class Test
    Public Shared Sub Main()
        Dim car As MuscleCar
        Dim cars(3) As MuscleCar
        cars(0) = New MuscleCar("1970", "Plymouth", "Hemi-Cuda", 425)
        cars(1) = New MuscleCar("1966", "Shelby", "Cobra", 425)
        cars(2) = New MuscleCar("1969", "Pontiac", "GTO", 370)
        cars(3) = New MuscleCar("1969", "Chevy", "Chevelle SS", 375)

        Array.Sort(cars)

        For Each car In Cars
            Console.WriteLine(car.ToString())
        Next car
    End Sub
End Class
```

After the array is sorted, you can write each element to the console window (thanks to the ToString override). The last two cars have the same horsepower. In this case, the order is determined by the position of the cars in the array:

```
C:\>muscle
MuscleCar - Year:1969 Make:Pontiac Model:GTO HP:370
MuscleCar - Year:1969 Make:Chevy Model:Chevelle SS HP:375
MuscleCar - Year:1970 Make:Plymouth Model:Hemi-Cuda HP:425
MuscleCar - Year:1966 Make:Shelby Model:Cobra HP:425
```

## ICloneable

Implementing ICloneable does not give your object the ability to take advantage of amazing .NET features. The interface just exists to provide a standard mechanism for making a copy of an object. ICloneable contains a single method, Clone, that returns a copy of the object:

```
Public Interface ICloneable
    Function Clone() As Object
End Interface
```

Clone can provide a deep or shallow copy—the choice is yours. *Deep copies* are exact copies of the original object, including private member state. A *shallow copy* is just a reference to the original object; there is still only one instance after the call.

A deep copy is a little more difficult to implement if the object you copy is part of a containment relationship with other objects; all contained objects need to be copied, too. The section "ICloneable and MemoryStream" in Chapter 8 covers this topic in more depth.

Example 5-11 shows a simple deep-copy implementation for the MuscleCar class. The class contains no additional objects or state variables beyond what is passed in to the constructor, so you only need to create a new object and return it.

*Example 5-11. ICloneable implementation for MuscleCar*

```
Imports System

Public Class MuscleCar
  Implements ICloneable

  Public ReadOnly year, make, model As String
  Public ReadOnly horsePower As Short

  Public Sub New(ByVal year As String, _
                 ByVal make As String, _
                 ByVal model As String, _
                 ByVal horsePower As Short)
    Me.year = year
    Me.make = make
    Me.model = model
    Me.horsePower = horsePower
  End Sub

  Public Function Clone() As Object Implements ICloneable.Clone
    Return New MuscleCar(Me.year, Me.make, Me.model, Me.horsePower)
  End Function

End Class
```

You could implement Clone by using Return Me, but doing so is not in the spirit of the interface. Me simply returns a reference to the existing object. Instead, you should have two distinct objects when the call returns. In a shallow copy, though, the object and its clone can share object references for any contained items.

## IEnumerable and IEnumerator

The System.Collections namespace contains classes and interfaces that facilitate most of the common, collection-oriented tasks such as stacks, lists, queues, and dictionaries. At its heart lies the IEnumerable interface, which provides iteration support for all collections. This support makes it possible to use the For...Each language construct to access members of a collection. Even common arrays support collection-like access as a result of this interface (all arrays are derived from System.Array, which implements IEnumerable).

IEnumerable contains a single method:

```
Public Interface IEnumerable
    Function GetEnumerator() As IEnumerator
End Interface
```

GetEnumerator has one job: to return an object that provides access to the items in the collection. This object, usually called an enumerator, must implement the IEnumerator interface:

```
Public Interface IEnumerator
    Function MoveNext() As Boolean
    ReadOnly Property Current() As Object
    Sub Reset()
End Interface
```

Every call to GetEnumerator should return a new object that enumerates the collection in its current state. Calling GetEnumerator, adding items to the collection, and calling GetEnumerator a second time should result in two enumerators—each with a different idea about what the collection contains. The first enumerator does not know about the additional items added to the collection.

The framework's collection classes contain a private member named _version (disassemble System.Collections.Stack to see it) that is incremented every time the collection is modified. The enumerator is returned from GetEnumerator and is passed this version number and a reference to (rather than a copy of) the items in the collection. Whenever the collection is accessed, the enumerator's version is compared to the current version of the collection. If they are different, then an InvalidOperationException is thrown.

For example, consider a primitive, three-dimensional object that contains a collection of points describing it, as shown in Example 5-12.

*Example 5-12. Implementing IEnumerable*

```
Imports System
Imports System.Collections
```

*Example 5-12. Implementing IEnumerable (continued)*

```
Public Structure ThreeDPoint
  Public x, y, z As Single
  Public Overrides Function ToString() As String
    Return String.Format( _
    "x={0},y={1},z={2}", x.ToString(), y.ToString(), z.ToString())
  End Function
End Structure

Public MustInherit Class ThreeDObject
  Implements IEnumerable

  Private myPoints() As ThreeDPoint

  Public Function GetEnumerator() As IEnumerator _
      Implements IEnumerable.GetEnumerator
    Return New ThreeDEnumerator(myPoints)
  End Function

  Protected WriteOnly Property Points() As ThreeDPoint()
    Set(ByVal p() As ThreeDPoint)
      myPoints = p
    End Set
  End Property

End Class
```

Internally, the points that comprise the object are maintained in an array. These points will be initialized in a derived class because 3-D objects like cubes, spheres, and pyramids can contain any number of points. The protected `Points` property passes the initialized point from the subclass back to `ThreeDObject`. There is no need to reimplement an interface that was implemented in a base class:

```
Public Class Pyramid : Inherits ThreeDObject

  '5-sided pyramid - 3 walls and a bottom

  Private myPoints(3) As ThreeDPoint

  Public Sub New()
    'Initialize points to pyramid shape then pass to
    'protected property in base class
    Points = myPoints
  End Sub

End Class
```

Implementing `GetEnumerator` is straightforward. It merely creates a new instance of `ThreeDEnumerator` (shown in Example 5-13), passing a reference to the `ThreeDPoint` array. It is possible to initialize a new enumerator with a copy of the elements in the array instead of passing the array by reference, but there would be a performance hit: one from the copy and another for all duplicated items in memory. Making a copy of all the items in a collection for an enumerator is preferable only when the collection contains a small number of items that need to reflect the exact state of the collection at any given time.

*Example 5-13. Implementing IEnumerator*

```
Public Class ThreeDEnumerator
  Implements IEnumerator

  Private myPoints() As ThreeDPoint
  Private index As Integer

  Public Sub New(ByVal p() As ThreeDPoint)
    myPoints = p
    index = -1
  End Sub

  Public ReadOnly Property Current() As Object _
      Implements IEnumerator.Current
    Get
      If (index < 0) OrElse (index = myPoints.Length) Then
        Throw New InvalidOperationException( _
            "Collection index is out of bounds!")
      End If
      Return myPoints(index)
    End Get
  End Property

  Public Function MoveNext() As Boolean _
      Implements IEnumerator.MoveNext
    If (index < myPoints.Length) Then
      index += 1
    End If
    Return Not (index = myPoints.Length)
  End Function

  Public Sub Reset() Implements IEnumerator.Reset
    index = -1
  End Sub

End Class
```

When the constructor for `ThreeDEnumerator` is called, a reference to the `myPoints` array is stored as private data and the current index of the array is set to `-1`. This step is important. The initial position of the collection cursor should be before the first element, which is element `0` (arrays are `0`-based). This position allows the collection to be accessed easily from a `While` loop without having to first check to see if the collection contains any items:

```
'First call to MoveNext moves cursor to
'the first item (if it exists)
```

```
While (myEnumerator.MoveNext())
    'Get item from collection here
End While
```

After minimal validation, `Current` returns element `index` from the `myPoints` array. `MoveNext` checks to see if `index` is less than the number of points in the array and increments it if it is still within the bounds of the array. `Reset` sets the index back to `-1`.

You can access the collection in several ways. The first is a strictly generic technique that uses only interfaces:

```
Friend Class Test

    Public Shared Sub Iterate(ByVal enumerable As IEnumerable)
        Dim enumerator As IEnumerator = enumerable.GetEnumerator()
        While (enumerator.MoveNext())
            Dim p As Object
            p = enumerator.Current
            Console.WriteLine(p.ToString())
        End While
    End Sub

    Public Shared Sub Main()
        Dim myPyramid As New Pyramid()
        Iterate(myPyramid)
    End Sub

End Class
```

This technique is a great example of polymorphism at work. As you can see, the `Iterate` function can enumerate any collection, whether it is a `ThreeDObject`, an array, stack, or queue. The only requirement is that the object implement `IEnumerable`.

You can also declare a specific type that implements `IEnumerable`:

```
Friend Class Test
    Public Shared Sub Main()
        Dim pmid As New Pyramid()
        Dim myEnumerator As IEnumerator = pmid.GetEnumerator()

        While (myEnumerator.MoveNext)
            Dim p As Object
            p = myEnumerator.Current
            Console.WriteLine(p.ToString())
        End While
    End Sub
End Class
```

Of course, doing so is definitely more abrasive than just using `For...Each`:

```
Friend Class Test
    Public Shared Sub Main()
        Dim pmid As New Pyramid()
        Dim p As ThreeDPoint
```

```
        For Each p In pmid
            Console.WriteLine(p.ToString())
        Next p
    End Sub
End Class
```

### Performance issues

This implementation has two major performance problems. The collection contains value types (ThreeDPoint structures), but enumerators are designed to work with reference types. For instance, before Current can return a ThreeDPoint, it must box it. This means that an object is allocated from the managed heap and the value of the ThreeDPoint is copied into this object. Not only will this object need to be garbage collected, but when the collection is iterated, the object will be unboxed—the values from the object will be copied back to a ThreeDPoint structure. Thus, for every element in the array, you end up copying memory twice and are left with an object on the managed heap waiting to be garbage collected.

There are a few things that can be done to make this collection (and others) work with value types without incurring performance penalties. Start with the ThreeDObject class and add the following method:

```
'This is not apart of IEnumerator
Public Function GetEnumerator() As ThreeDEnumerator
    Return New ThreeDEnumerator(myPoints)
End Function
```

This example is a new version of GetEnumerator. Don't be confused by it. This method is not an implementation of IEnumerator.GetEnumerator; it's just a method with the same name. The only difference between this method and IEnumerator.GetEnumerator is the fact that it returns an instance of ThreeDEnumerator instead of a reference to IEnumerator. Adding this method causes a naming conflict with IEnumerator.GetEnumerator (methods can't be overloaded on return type alone), so the interface implementation needs to be renamed. Any name will do:

```
Public Function OldGetEnumerator() As IEnumerator _
    Implements IEnumerable.GetEnumerator
    Return GetEnumerator()
End Function
```

Don't worry about the method name being different from the interface name. The method still implements IEnumerable.GetEnumerator, so the following code still works:

```
Dim enumerable As IEnumerable = New Pyramid()

'This will call OldGetEnumerator
Dim enumerator As IEnumerator = enumerable.GetEnumerator()
```

If you call the method directly, you will have to refer to it by its new name. Example 5-14 contains the new listing for ThreeDObject.

*Example 5-14. Implementing collections for value types*

```
Public MustInherit Class ThreeDObject
  Implements IEnumerable

  Private myPoints() As ThreeDPoint

  Public Function OldGetEnumerator() As IEnumerator _
      Implements IEnumerable.GetEnumerator
    Return GetEnumerator()
  End Function

  Public Function GetEnumerator() As ThreeDEnumerator
    Return New ThreeDEnumerator(myPoints)
  End Function

  Protected WriteOnly Property Points() As ThreeDPoint()
    Set(ByVal p() As ThreeDPoint)
      myPoints = p
    End Set
  End Property

End Class
```

You need to make a couple of modifications to the ThreeDEnumerator class to finish off the optimization. First, change Current to return a ThreeDPoint instead of an Object, and then remove the Implements statement:

```
Public ReadOnly Property Current() As ThreeDPoint
    Get
        If (index < 0) OrElse (index = myPoints.Length) Then
            Throw New InvalidOperationException(_
            "Collection index is out of bounds!")
        End If
        Return myPoints(index)
    End Get
End Property
```

Add a new implementation of IEnumerator.Current that calls the type-specific version. As in ThreeDObject, this method must be renamed to avoid a conflict at compile time. Again, any name will be fine:

```
Public ReadOnly Property OldCurrent() As Object _
    Implements IEnumerator.Current
    Get
       Return Me.Current  'Call non-interface version
    End Get
End Property
```

If the collection is accessed with a For...Each loop, the GetEnumerator method for the class is called before the IEnumerable implementation. If you do not need to access your collection in a generic manner, all you need is a GetEnumerator method. You don't need to implement IEnumerable at all, but you are advised to do so. The same holds true for the enumerator object. As long as the enumerator has a Current method and a MoveNext method, the For...Each loop will compile successfully. However, these interfaces should be implemented regardless. Remember that the noninterface versions of GetEnumerator, Current, and MoveNext are called first in a For... Each construct. Example 5-15 contains the new listing for ThreeDEnumerator.

*Example 5-15. Implementing an enumerator to handle value types*

```
Public Class ThreeDEnumerator
  Implements IEnumerator

  Private myPoints() As ThreeDPoint
  Private index As Integer

  Public Sub New(ByVal p() As ThreeDPoint)
    myPoints = p
    index = -1
  End Sub

  Public ReadOnly Property ICurrent() As Object _
      Implements IEnumerator.Current
    Get
      Return Me.Current
    End Get
  End Property

  Public ReadOnly Property Current() As ThreeDPoint
    Get
      If (index < 0) OrElse (index = myPoints.Length) Then
        Throw New InvalidOperationException( _
        "Collection index is out of bounds!")
      End If
      Return myPoints(index)
    End Get
  End Property

  Public Function MoveNext() As Boolean _
      Implements IEnumerator.MoveNext
    If (index < myPoints.Length) Then
      index += 1
    End If
    Return Not (index = myPoints.Length)
  End Function

  Public Sub Reset() Implements IEnumerator.Reset
    index = -1
  End Sub

End Class
```

If the collection is accessed generically through interfaces only, the actual implementations of the interfaces are called. However, since those implementations delegate to the noninterface versions (OldGetEnumerator and OldCurrent), no boxing will take place.

## Design Considerations

You shouldn't necessarily look to the .NET framework itself as a guide to using interfaces. You were meant to use the framework, not extend it. The sheer number of sealed classes in the library should convince you of that.

Simplicity and scalability are, unfortunately, mutually exclusive terms. The former was chosen over the latter in .NET; interfaces are used only when necessary.

If you inherit from a class, 99% of your work is done. However, when you implement an interface, your work has only begun. Developing a system around interfaces does require more work, but the rewards are great; you will end up with an application that scales very well.

Does your application need to scale? If so, then a system built around interfaces is best for that purpose. If not, you can still use interfaces in situations when you need to expose behavior that is not object-specific.

Unless you build a framework similar to .NET, you will not use inheritance as much as you think. You might not believe this statement, but keep it in mind and see if it holds true. You will use containment more than anything else.

Regardless of what you decide, here are some guidelines to take with you:

- Once an interface is published, don't change it. This is true for your class' protected and public interfaces, as well as any formally declared interface in use.
- Consider using class-based references internally and interfaces on the "edges" of your components.
- In places where you don't want to be tied to an implementation, use an interface.

# CHAPTER 6
# Exceptional Objects

Take a Zen-like approach to coding and accept the fact that bugs will always exist in your code—at least if you write anything significantly large. This statement doesn't imply that you shouldn't try to write bug-free code; it just means you accept the reality of bugs and plan for the worst scenerio. Having a solid framework in place for handling errors is *the* most important part of an application. Unfortunately, error handling is something that is added to many applications as an afterthought—tacked on at the end with duct tape and bailing wire or, worse yet, written inconsistently throughout the application. Approached like this, these applications force the people who support them to pay the price later. A piece of advice: write your error handling first. Then watch how smoothly things go the next time you develop an application.

## The Basics of Exception Handling

Visual Basic .NET supports two different systems for handling errors: structured and unstructured exception handling. This chapter focuses primarily on the structured approach. Unstructured error handling is a throwback to earlier versions of the language, while the structured approach is far more elegant. Structured exception handling was specifically designed to be a part of the language from the beginning, instead of tacked on as an addendum.

### Try Block

Example 6-1 shows the typical form of a structured exception handler. The `Try... End Try` block is somewhat misleading because it is not actually a single block; it is composed of several different blocks: a `Try` block, one or more `Catch` blocks, and a `Finally` block. A variable declared in a `Try` block is not available from a corresponding `Catch` or `Finally` block—each has its own scope. The term "structured" reflects the block-like nature of the exception handler; it's structured much like the rest of VB.NET, hence the term.

*Example 6-1. Try...Catch...Finally*

```
Try

    'Code where error can occur

Catch SpecificException [When condition]

    'Code to execute when exception is caught

Catch NotSoSpecificException [When condition]

    'Code to execute when exception is caught

Catch GeneralException [When condition]

    'Code to execute when exception is caught

Finally

    'Code to execute before leaving Try block

End Try
```

The `Try` block contains code in which a possible error can occur. If the unthinkable happens, VB.NET looks for a `Catch` block that is capable of dealing with the exception, and control is transferred there. If an appropriate handler is not found, the call stack is searched until a suitable `Catch` block is found. Therefore, it is important that `Catch` blocks be ordered from the most specific to the least specific exception. For example, a structured error handler for file open operation places the `FileNotFoundException` first, followed by the `FileLoadException`, and then the general `Exception` handler. Additionally, each `Catch` block can specify a filter expression that determines whether the exception should be handled. This is done by placing a `When` clause after the exception and defining a Boolean condition, such as:

```
Catch Exception When (x > 4 And y < 10)
```

Regardless of whether or not an exception occurs, the code in the `Finally` block executes.

Note that the `Finally` clause always executes before the exception handler goes out of scope. If an exception occurs and a `Catch` block is not found in the local scope, the `Finally` block is executed before the call stack is traversed. Example 6-2 demonstrates this idea and shows how an exception is thrown by using the `Throw` statement.

*Example 6-2. Throwing an exception*

```
Imports System

Public Class Jump
  Public Sub Go()
    Try
```

*Example 6-2. Throwing an exception (continued)*

```
      Console.WriteLine("Jump: Try")
      Throw New InvalidOperationException("Simulated Error")
    Catch e As ArgumentException
      Console.WriteLine("Jump: Catch")
    Finally
      Console.WriteLine("Jump: Finally")
    End Try
  End Sub
End Class

Friend Class Test
  Public Shared Sub Main()
    Try
      Console.WriteLine("Main: Try")
      Dim j As New Jump()
      j.Go()
    Catch e As InvalidOperationException
      Console.WriteLine("Main: Catch")
    Finally
      Console.WriteLine("Main: Finally")
    End Try
  End Sub
End Class
```

When `Jump.Go` is called, a deliberate `InvalidOperationException` is thrown. The `Try` block in `Go` does not contain a `Catch` block that is capable of handling the exception (it only handles exceptions of type `ArgumentException`), but the `Try` block in `Main` does. If you examine the output of this program, you will see the following code:

```
C:\>try
Main: Try
Jump: Try
Jump: Finally
Main: Catch
Main: Finally
```

After the `InvalidOperationException` is thrown, control is transferred to the `Finally` clause in `Jump` before the exception is caught in `Main`.

If a `Catch` block handler is not found, the exception is considered unhandled and the runtime shuts the application down. This is the only situation in which a `Finally` block will not execute.

Using a `Try` block is fundamentally similar to the following unstructured error handling technique:

```
Public Sub Foo()
    On Error Goto errHandler
        'Do work here
    Exit Sub
errHandler:
    'Handle error and recover here
End Sub
```

Although you can use structured and unstructured error handling in the same program, you can't mix and match them in the same method.

## Creating Your Own Exceptions

As shown in Figure 6-1, all exceptions are ultimately derived from `System.Exception`. When you create your own exceptions, though, you should never derive directly from this class. Runtime exceptions used by the CLR are derived from `System.SystemException`, and user-defined exceptions are derived from `System.ApplicationException`.

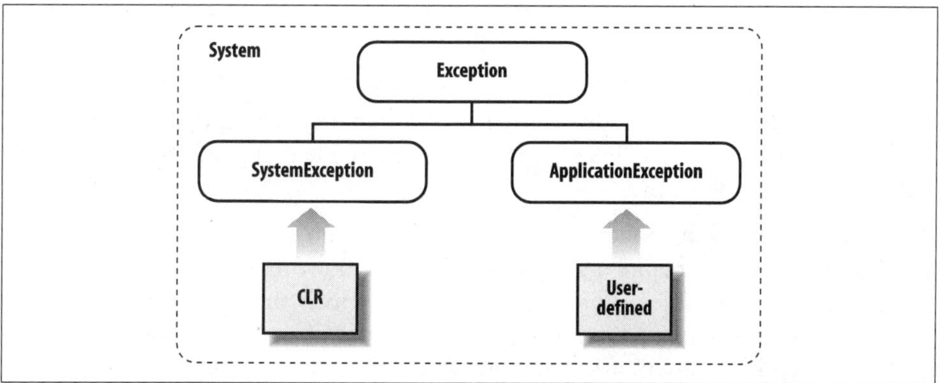


*Figure 6-1. Only the CLR should derive from SystemException. Everything else should derive from ApplicationException.*

Whenever possible, you should try to use an exception that is already defined in the .NET Framework. If invalid parameters are passed to a method, throw an `ArgumentException`. If an object is not in a valid state when a method is called, throw an `InvalidOperationException`.

Scanning namespace documentation for classes ending with "Exception" is a good way to learn about the various exceptions provided by the framework. If a method in the .NET Framework can throw an exception, the exception's type is usually listed in a table after the parameters and return values in the documentation. Eventually, you will become familiar with the available exceptions.

You should create a new exception class only when there is a programmatic benefit to doing so. Usually, derived classes contain new members or extend the base class in some way; with exceptions, this is not always the case. Many exception classes in .NET are member-for-member, exact copies of the classes they are derived from. The only difference is the name of the exception class itself. The kind of information provided is generally the same from one exception class to another. It is the type itself that allows the programmer to write granular exception handling code. Remember, deriving new exceptions does not necessarily involve extensibility at the source code level.

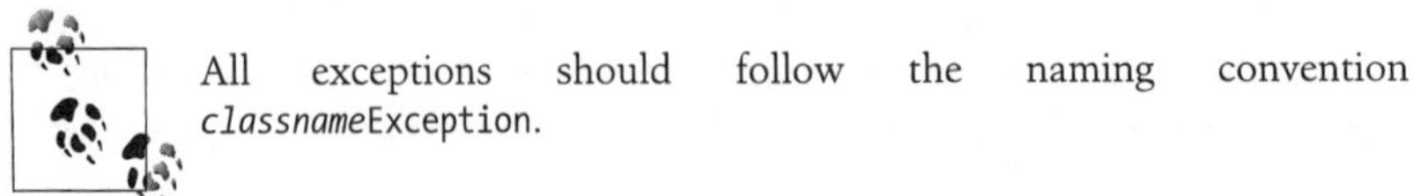

All exceptions should follow the naming convention *classname*`Exception`.

## Return Codes Versus Exceptions

Like inheritance, exceptions are easy to overuse. A neophyte programmer tends to use them everywhere because they are convenient and easy to use, even if the code is harder to read or a client has to code around a method that throws 15 different "exceptions."

When you consider the use of exceptions, keep the following statement in mind: exceptions are used to handle exceptional conditions. They are exceptions, not the rule.

You can think of exceptional conditions as things that can't ever happen, but do anyway (every once in a while). On a properly configured system, a table in an average database application exists 99.99% of the time. The code that goes against that table "always" executes perfectly.

But what happens if the system is not properly configured? Configuration problems are usually sorted out before a system is deployed. However, what if someone accidentally deletes the table? What if the server on which the database resides goes down? These external situations can happen outside of an application's control—they are exceptional situations. The normal use of a class should not result in any exceptions being thrown.

Let's examine a specific case in the .NET Framework in which an exception would have been inappropriate because the condition it would have indicated is not exceptional. `String.IndexOf` returns the location of one or more characters within the current instance of a `String` object. If the character or substring cannot be found, the method returns `-1`. This behavior is not exceptional—it's expected. It would not be appropriate for this method to throw an exception when a substring could not be found.

On the other hand, the following code fragment does indicate exceptional behavior. Here, an oversight results in a substring search on an uninitialized string:

```
Dim address As String
address.IndexOf("Don't Mess with Texas")
```

This code will compile because `address` is an actual `String` reference. When it is run, though, a `System.NullReferenceException` is thrown because the reference doesn't refer to anything.

However, don't underuse exception handling by writing methods that return error codes. The problem with using a return code to report an error is that you don't have to examine it. The discipline of handling errors in this situation rests on your shoulders alone. Exceptions *force* you to deal with an error or at least acknowledge that it occurred (an empty Catch block is one way to ignore an exception, as is a When clause that ignores errors under certain conditions). You can't just pretend that a thrown exception does not exist. If left unhandled, it eventually bubbles to the top of your application, forcing it to shut down. Consider Example 6-3, which does just that.

*Example 6-3. Unhandled exception*

```
Imports System

Public Class BadClass
  Public Sub BadMethod()
    Throw New ArgumentException("Bad things happened")
  End Sub
End Class

Friend Class Test
  Public Shared Sub Main()
    Dim b As New BadClass()
    b.BadMethod()
  End Sub
End Class
```

Ignoring a return code can cause your program to fail unpredictably. In the worst case, it could cause your application to crash. Not so with exceptions. If left alone, an exception bubbles up the call stack and eventually reaches the top, where it causes your program to shut down. When the program does shut down, you get a stack trace showing exactly what type of exception was thrown, what file it occurred in, the class and method, and the line number where it occurred:

```
Unhandled Exception: System.ArgumentException: SimulatedError
   at BadClass.BadMethod() in C:\bad.vb:line 5
   at Test.Main() in C:\bad.vb:line 12
```

## Unhandled Exception Handler

The stack trace that results from an unhandled exception is a default handler. It's a nice feature, but it is not very robust. It might work well for grandma's little recipe program, but in a bulletproof, industrial-strength application, it just won't do. Errors need to be logged to the event log or a database, emails need to be sent to technical support, and programmers need to be paged in the wee hours o' the morning. More than likely, you will probably need to use the stack trace information in conjunction with other forms of error reporting.

Fortunately, the .NET Framework is very giving in this area. You are free to substitute your own handler for unhandled exceptions, as demonstrated in Example 6-4.

Note the call to the AppDomain.CurrentDomain method in the Main procedure in Example 6-4. Calling AppDomain.CurrentDomain returns an object that represents the current application domain. Recall from the "Application Domains" section of Chapter 2 that an application domain is the execution environment for a .NET assembly. The instance of `AppDomain` that is returned as a result of this call provides a number of interesting properties and methods. Here are a few:

`BaseDirectory` *property*
: Returns the path of the application. It is similar to `App.Path` in earlier versions of VB.

`FriendlyName` *property*
: Returns the name of the executable. It is similar to `App.EXEName` in earlier versions of VB.

`ExecuteAssembly` *method*
: Executes the specified assembly. It is similar to `Shell` in earlier versions of VB.

`AppDomain` also provides an event that is called when an unhandled exception occurs. You only need to provide an event handler for it by using `AddHandler`. Then you can write the error to the event log, fire off an email, or do whatever needs to be done, as Example 6-4 illustrates.

*Example 6-4. Unhandled exception handler*

```
'vbc /t:exe /r:system.dll /r:system.web.dll

Imports System
Imports System.Diagnostics
Imports System.Web.Mail

Friend Class ReallyBadClass
  Public Sub ReallyBadMethod()
      'Throw an exception
      Throw New ArgumentException("Simulated Error")
  End Sub
End Class

Friend Class BadClass
  Public Sub BadMethod()
      Dim rb As New ReallyBadClass()
      rb.ReallyBadMethod()
  End Sub
End Class

Public Class App

  'Unhandled exception handler
  Public Shared Sub MyExceptionHandler( _
              ByVal sender As Object, _
              ByVal e As UnhandledExceptionEventArgs)

      Dim break As New String("-"c, 70)
      Console.WriteLine()
      Console.WriteLine("Unhandled Exception")
      Console.WriteLine(break)
      Console.WriteLine("{0}", e.ExceptionObject)
```

*Example 6-4. Unhandled exception handler (continued)*

```
        Console.WriteLine(break)
        Console.WriteLine("Writing to event log...")
        Console.WriteLine("Sending email to tech support...")

        'Write to event log
        Dim myLog As EventLog = New EventLog()
        myLog.Source = "Application Log"
        myLog.WriteEntry("My Bad Application", _
            e.ExceptionObject.ToString(), EventLogEntryType.Error)

        'Can sending an email be easier?
        Dim mailMsg As New MailMessage()
        mailMsg.To = "techsupport@somedomainhere.com"
        mailMsg.Subject = "My Bad Application - Exception"
        mailMsg.Body = e.ExceptionObject.ToString()

        'Your outgoing SMTP server goes here
        Try
          SmtpMail.SmtpServer = "mail.someserver.com"
          SmtpMail.Send(mailMsg)
        Catch x As Exception
          Debug.Write("Use a real SMTP server")
        End Try

        'Keep the example code up and running
        Console.WriteLine()
        Console.WriteLine("Press ENTER to continue...")
        Console.ReadLine()

    End Sub

    Public Shared Sub Main()
      'This replaces the default unhandled exception
      'handler with ours
      Dim domain As AppDomain = AppDomain.CurrentDomain()
      AddHandler domain.UnhandledException, _
          AddressOf MyExceptionHandler

      'Cause exception on purpose
      Dim b As New BadClass()
      b.BadMethod()
      Console.ReadLine()
    End Sub

End Class
```

The output from this program contains the call stack that the default handler provides via `e.ExceptionObject`:

```
Unhandled Exception
--------------------------------------------------------------------
System.ArgumentException: Simulated Error
```

```
        at ConsoleApplication3.ReallyBadClass.ReallyBadMethod()
            in C:bad.vb:line 12
        at ConsoleApplication3.BadClass.BadMethod()
            in C:\bad.vb:line 19
        at ConsoleApplication3.App.Main()
            in C:\bad.vb:line 67
    --------------------------------------------------------------------
    Writing to event log...
    Sending email to tech support...
```

It also shows how code could be added to handle exceptions in a variety of different ways. You can easily add an entry to the event log, and sending email has never been easier. Just a few lines of code are all it takes.

# The StackTrace Object

Whenever a method call is made, the Common Language Runtime creates information about that call. This information includes the location of the call within your program, the arguments that have been passed, and the local variables of the target method. The information is saved in a block of data called a *stack frame*. These stack frames are allocated in a region of memory called the *call stack*. The call stack contains all the methods that were called but have not returned to their callers. You saw this output to the console in Example 6-4.

This information can be very helpful when you track down bugs in your code. Even more helpful is the fact that you can inspect the call stack programmatically whenever you want. Example 6-5 demonstrates the process of iterating the call stack to obtain the method names that are currently active.

*Example 6-5. Iterating the call stack*

```
Imports System
Imports System.Diagnostics
Imports System.Reflection

Public Class StackTest

  Public Sub MethodA()
    MethodB()
  End Sub

  Public Sub MethodB()
    MethodC()
  End Sub

  Public Sub MethodC()

    Dim i As Integer = 0
    Dim st As New StackTrace()
    For i = 0 To st.FrameCount - 1
```

*Example 6-5. Iterating the call stack (continued)*

```
      Dim sf As StackFrame = st.GetFrame(i)
      Console.WriteLine(sf.GetMethod.Name)
    Next i
  End Sub

End Class

Public Class Application

  Public Shared Sub Main()
    Dim test As New StackTest()
    test.MethodA()
    Console.ReadLine()
  End Sub

End Class
```

The output from this program looks like this:

```
MethodC
MethodB
MethodA
Main
```

This is not quite useful, but it's getting there. The `System.Diagnostics.StackTrace` class used in Example 6-5 is really just a collection of `StackFrame` objects. Alone, it doesn't do much. The `StackFrame` object is where your interest should lie. With it, you can obtain the filename (the `GetFileName` method) and line number (the `GetFileLineNumber` method) of the method call, as well as explicit information about the method itself, including its namespace, class, name, and the data types of the parameters passed to it. Information about the method is available from the `GetMethod` method, which returns an instance of the `MethodBase` class. This class can be used to obtain information about a method, such as whether it is public or private, its return type, or its parameters. Chapter 7 discusses this class in more detail.

As shown in Example 6-6, it is also possible to create an instance of `StrackTrace` that takes an exception constructor argument. This is useful for viewing the call stack at the time an exception was thrown. In this example, several methods are called in succession, and then an exception is thrown deliberately. In the `Catch` block of the exception handler, the caught exception is passed to a new instance of `ExceptionInfo`, an application-defined class designed to provide information about an exception along with the call stack.

The filename and line numbers supplied by `StackFrame` are removed from the executable in release builds. If you compile from the command line, use the `/D+` compiler switch to include debugging information.

*Example 6-6. Accessing the call stack*

```
Imports System
Imports System.Diagnostics
Imports System.Reflection

Public Class StackTest

  Public Sub Start()
    Try
      MethodA()
    Catch e As Exception
      Dim exInfo As New ExceptionInfo(e)
      Console.WriteLine(exInfo.ToString())
    End Try
  End Sub

  Public Sub MethodA()
    MethodB()
  End Sub

  Public Sub MethodB()
    MethodC()
  End Sub

  Public Sub MethodC()
    Throw New ArgumentException("Simulated Error")
  End Sub

End Class

'Reusable class for getting exception information
Public Class ExceptionInfo

  Private exInfo As String

  Public Sub New(ByVal e As Exception)
    'Get exception message
    exInfo = e.Message & Environment.NewLine

    Dim i As Integer = 0
    Dim trace As New StackTrace(e, True)
    For i = 0 To trace.FrameCount() - 1
      Dim frame As StackFrame = trace.GetFrame(i)

      'Add line number, column number and file information
      Dim sFileInfo As String = _
        String.Format("Line {0}: Col {1}: File: {2}{3}", _
                      frame.GetFileLineNumber(), _
                      frame.GetFileColumnNumber(), _
                      frame.GetFileName(), _
                      Environment.NewLine)
      exInfo &= sFileInfo
```

*Example 6-6. Accessing the call stack (continued)*

```
      'Add method information
      Dim mi As MethodBase = frame.GetMethod( )
      Dim sMethodInfo As String
      exInfo &= mi.DeclaringType.Namespace & "." & _
                mi.DeclaringType.Name & "." & mi.Name & _
                Environment.NewLine
      exInfo &= Environment.NewLine
    Next i

  End Sub

  Public Overrides Function ToString( ) As String
    Return exInfo
  End Function

End Class

Public Class Application

  Public Shared Sub Main( )
    Dim test As New StackTest( )
    test.Start( )
    Console.ReadLine( )
  End Sub

End Class
```

`MethodInfo` is one of several classes that are part of a .NET technology called *reflection*. Using reflection, you can obtain runtime information about anything you might want to know about a given object, including its methods, properties, parameters, events, enumerations, and member variables—even the stuff that's declared private. If you are curious about it, play around with the `ExceptionInfo` class and examine `MethodInfo`. Chapter 7, which deals with reflection, should give you a good understanding of this powerful tool.

# Resuming Code

Sometimes you'll just want to keep on trucking after an error has occurred rather than handle it. Example 6-7 demonstrates an unstructured approach to ignoring errors. Normally this code would throw a `DivideByZeroException`, but here `On Error Resume Next` is used to prevent exceptions from propagating out of the method.

*Example 6-7. On Error Resume Next*

```
'Throws System.DivideByZeroException
Public Class App
  Public Shared Sub Main( )
    On Error Resume Next
    Dim x As Integer = 0
```

*Example 6-7. On Error Resume Next (continued)*

```
    Dim y As Integer = 10 \ x
    'Use x and y here
  End Sub
End Class
```

Many of you know that ignoring errors like this is considered bad practice. Even so (or so you say), sometimes it needs to be done. A safer approach would be to turn off error handling specifically where you need to, and then turn it back on when you are done:

```
Public Sub SomeMethod()
    On Error Goto errHandler

    On Error Resume Next
    'Code that might trigger errors goes here
    On Error Goto errHandler

    Exit Sub
errHandler:
    'Handle errors here
End Sub
```

There are several arguments against this approach. Handling (or not handling) errors in this way does not produce the most readable code. Program flow jumps all over the place. Also, if this technique is used in a method that contains even a small degree of complexity, debugging could turn into a nightmare.

`On Error Resume Next` results in inefficient code. It might be one line of code in VB, but you'd be amazed by the IL spaghetti that is generated by the compiler. Remember Example 6-7? It uses `On Error Resume Next`, declares two integers, and performs a division. Example 6-8 shows the IL produced by this example. We will not even attempt to discuss the listing for this "simple" example. The listing is provided only for its magnitude. Just scan it and remember it the next time you are tempted to turn off error handling in your code.

*Example 6-8. Disassembly of Resume Next*

```
//  Microsoft (R) .NET Framework IL Disassembler.  Version 1.0.3705.0
//  Copyright (C) Microsoft Corporation 1998-2001. All rights reserved.

.assembly extern mscorlib
{
  .publickeytoken = (B7 7A 5C 56 19 34 E0 89 )  // .z\V.4..
  .ver 1:0:3300:0
}
.assembly extern Microsoft.VisualBasic
{
  .publickeytoken = (B0 3F 5F 7F 11 D5 0A 3A )  // .?_....:
  .ver 7:0:3300:0
}
```

*Example 6-8. Disassembly of Resume Next (continued)*

```
.assembly extern System
{
  .publickeytoken = (B7 7A 5C 56 19 34 E0 89 )  // .z\V.4..
  .ver 1:0:3300:0
}
.assembly extern System.Data
{
  .publickeytoken = (B7 7A 5C 56 19 34 E0 89 )  // .z\V.4..
  .ver 1:0:3300:0
}
.assembly extern System.Xml
{
  .publickeytoken = (B7 7A 5C 56 19 34 E0 89 )  // .z\V.4..
  .ver 1:0:3300:0
}
.assembly extern System.Web
{
  .publickeytoken = (B0 3F 5F 7F 11 D5 0A 3A )  // .?_....:
  .ver 1:0:3300:0
}
.assembly temp3
{
  .custom instance void [mscorlib]System.Reflection.AssemblyTrademarkAttribute::
    .ctor(string) = ( 01 00 00 00 00 )
  // --- The following custom attribute is added automatically, do not uncomment -------
  //  .custom instance void [mscorlib]System.Diagnostics.DebuggableAttribute::.ctor(bool,
  //                                                                                 bool)
  //                                                          = ( 01 00 01 01 00 00 )
  .custom instance void [mscorlib]System.Runtime.InteropServices.GuidAttribute::
    .ctor(string) = ( 01 00 24 38 31 36 37 39 30 37 42 2D 30 35 35 38  // ..$8167907B-0558

2D 34 38 33 30 2D 41 36 34 30 2D 35 44 31 46 46    // -4830-A640-5D1FF

44 42 43 41 34 43 34 00 00 )                        // DBCA4C4..
  .custom instance void [mscorlib]System.CLSCompliantAttribute::.ctor(bool) = ( 01 00 01
                                                                             00 00 )
  .custom instance void [mscorlib]System.Reflection.AssemblyProductAttribute::
    .ctor(string) = ( 01 00 00 00 00 )
  .custom instance void [mscorlib]System.Reflection.AssemblyCopyrightAttribute::
    .ctor(string) = ( 01 00 00 00 00 )
  .custom instance void [mscorlib]System.Reflection.AssemblyCompanyAttribute::
    .ctor(string) = ( 01 00 00 00 00 )
  .custom instance void [mscorlib]System.Reflection.AssemblyDescriptionAttribute::
    .ctor(string) = ( 01 00 00 00 00 )
  .custom instance void [mscorlib]System.Reflection.AssemblyTitleAttribute::.ctor(string)
= ( 01 00 00 00 00 )
  .hash algorithm 0x00008004
  .ver 1:0:830:30783
}
.module temp3.exe
// MVID: {667EE811-3A5C-4236-8B2C-5703ED42C24C}
.imagebase 0x11000000
```

*Example 6-8. Disassembly of Resume Next (continued)*

```
.subsystem 0x00000003
.file alignment 512
.corflags 0x00000001
// Image base: 0x02df0000
//
// ============== CLASS STRUCTURE DECLARATION ==================
//
.namespace temp3
{
  .class public auto ansi App
         extends [mscorlib]System.Object
  {
  } // end of class App

} // end of namespace temp3


// =============================================================


// =============== GLOBAL FIELDS AND METHODS ===================


// =============================================================


// =============== CLASS MEMBERS DECLARATION ===================
//   note that class flags, 'extends' and 'implements' clauses
//          are provided here for information only

.namespace temp3
{
  .class public auto ansi App
         extends [mscorlib]System.Object
  {
    .method public specialname rtspecialname
            instance void  .ctor() cil managed
    {
      // Code size       9 (0x9)
      .maxstack  8
      IL_0000:  ldarg.0
      IL_0001:  call       instance void [mscorlib]System.Object::.ctor()
      IL_0006:  nop
      IL_0007:  nop
      IL_0008:  ret
    } // end of method App::.ctor

    .method public static void  Main() cil managed
    {
      .entrypoint
      .custom instance void [mscorlib]System.STAThreadAttribute::.ctor() =
                                                             ( 01 00 00 00 )
      // Code size       134 (0x86)
```

*Example 6-8. Disassembly of Resume Next (continued)*

```
.maxstack  2
.locals init ([0] int32 x,
         [1] int32 y,
         [2] int32 _Vb_t_CurrentStatement,
         [3] class [mscorlib]System.Exception _Vb_t_Exception,
         [4] int32 _Vb_t_Resume,
         [5] int32 _Vb_t_OnError)
IL_0000:  nop
IL_0001:  call       void [Microsoft.VisualBasic]Microsoft.VisualBasic.
                     CompilerServices.ProjectData::ClearProjectError()
IL_0006:  ldc.i4.1
IL_0007:  stloc.s    _Vb_t_OnError
IL_0009:  ldc.i4.1
IL_000a:  stloc.2
IL_000b:  ldc.i4.0
IL_000c:  stloc.0
IL_000d:  ldc.i4.2
IL_000e:  stloc.2
IL_000f:  ldc.i4.s   10
IL_0011:  ldloc.0
IL_0012:  div
IL_0013:  stloc.1
IL_0014:  leave.s    IL_007b

IL_0016:  ldloc.s    _Vb_t_Resume
IL_0018:  ldc.i4.1
IL_0019:  add
IL_001a:  ldc.i4.0
IL_001b:  stloc.s    _Vb_t_Resume
IL_001d:  switch     (
                      IL_0001,
                      IL_0009,
                      IL_000d,
                      IL_0014)
IL_0032:  leave.s    IL_0079

IL_0034:  isinst     [mscorlib]System.Exception
IL_0039:  brtrue.s   IL_003d

IL_003b:  br.s       IL_0048

IL_003d:  ldloc.s    _Vb_t_OnError
IL_003f:  brfalse.s  IL_0048

IL_0041:  ldloc.s    _Vb_t_Resume
IL_0043:  brtrue.s   IL_0048

IL_0045:  ldc.i4.1
IL_0046:  br.s       IL_004b

IL_0048:  ldc.i4.0
IL_0049:  br.s       IL_004b
```

*Example 6-8. Disassembly of Resume Next (continued)*

```
    IL_004b:  endfilter
    IL_004d:  castclass  [mscorlib]System.Exception
    IL_0052:  dup
    IL_0053:  call       void [Microsoft.VisualBasic]Microsoft.VisualBasic.
        CompilerServices.ProjectData::SetProjectError(class [mscorlib]System.Exception)
    IL_0058:  stloc.3
    IL_0059:  ldloc.s    _Vb_t_Resume
    IL_005b:  brfalse.s  IL_005f

    IL_005d:  leave.s    IL_0079

    IL_005f:  ldloc.2
    IL_0060:  stloc.s    _Vb_t_Resume
    IL_0062:  ldloc.s    _Vb_t_OnError
    IL_0064:  switch     (
                          IL_0073,
                          IL_0075)
    IL_0071:  leave.s    IL_0077

    IL_0073:  leave.s    IL_0077

    IL_0075:  leave.s    IL_0016

    IL_0077:  rethrow
    IL_0079:  ldloc.3
    .try IL_0001 to IL_0034 filter IL_0034 handler IL_004d to IL_0079
    IL_007a:  throw

    IL_007b:  nop
    IL_007c:  ldloc.s    _Vb_t_Resume
    IL_007e:  brfalse.s  IL_0085

    IL_0080:  call       void [Microsoft.VisualBasic]Microsoft.VisualBasic.
                         CompilerServices.ProjectData::ClearProjectError()
    IL_0085:  ret
  } // end of method App::Main

} // end of class App

// =============================================================

} // end of namespace temp3

//*********** DISASSEMBLY COMPLETE ***********************
// WARNING: Created Win32 resource file C:\Programming VB.NET Objects\book - version 2\5\
Example6-7.res
```

The best way to write code that needs to resume is to use structured error handling in place of outdated, unstructured approaches. Anywhere you need to resume from an error, use nested Try blocks instead. These blocks result in more code, but the code is more readable, easier to debug, and flows nicely from top to bottom:

```
    Try

        'Resume #1
        Try
            'Resume if this code fails
        Catch e As Exception
            'Handle error
        Finally
            'Clean up
        End Try

        'Resume #2
        Try
            'Resume if this code fails
        Catch e As Exception
            'Handle error
        Finally
            'Clean up
        End Try

    Catch e As Exception
       'Handle error
    Finally
       'Clean up
    End Try
```

## Retrying Code

Sometimes it is necessary to rerun code that has triggered an error. Unfortunately, there is no good way to rerun code by using structured exception handling. Example 6-9 shows one method that uses nested Try blocks, which is ideal if you need to retry code only a few times.

*Example 6-9. Retrying a method*

```
Public Shared Sub Main()

  Try
    RetryMethod()
  Catch e As Exception

    Try
      RetryMethod()
    Catch e As Exception
      'Fail
    End Try

  End Try

End Sub
```

Nested Try blocks are great unless you want to retry your code more than a few times. Beyond that, reading the code becomes more difficult. If someone has to scroll the code window out to column 420 to see what you have done—well, they will laugh at you and tell people about it on the elevator.

Try blocks are re-entrant, so you can use a Goto to jump back into a Try block that already executed. Example 6-10 demonstrates this technique.

*Example 6-10. Retrying code after a failure*

```
Imports System

Public Class App

  Public Shared Sub Main()

    Dim attempts As Integer = 0
    Dim maxRetries As Integer = 5

    Try
      'Code to be retried n times
retry:
      attempts += 1
      Console.WriteLine("Attempt {0}", attempts.ToString())

      'Simulate error - jumps to Catch block
      Throw New Exception()

    Catch e As Exception

      If attempts = maxRetries Then
        GoTo done
      End If

      GoTo retry
done:
    End Try

  End Sub

End Class
```

This code does not flow well, and it is difficult to read. It exists just in case someone out there decides to be clever. Stop trying to be clever when you code. There is a better way to retry a path of execution; you can use recursion from a Catch block and monitor how many attempts were made on the method with a private instance variable, which is shown in Example 6-11.

### The Goto Is Obsolete

Don't believe the hype. Before structured error handling, the Goto did have a place in structured code. When several resources, such as database connections and file handles, were allocated, the Goto allowed a single "cleanup" location. Consider the following pseudocode:

```
Public Sub PseudoCode()
    Dim conn As New OleDbConnection(...)
    Dim fStream As FileStream = File.Open(...)

    If error Then
        Goto cleanup
    End If

    If error Then
        Goto cleanup
    End If

    If error Then
        Goto cleanup
    End If

cleanup:
    conn.Close()
    fstream.Close()
End Sub
```

This pattern allows cleanup to be performed in a single place rather than being repeated whenever an error occurs. However, this pattern is no longer necessary because with structured exception handling, cleanup code can be placed in a Finally block.

*Example 6-11. A better way to retry code*

```
Imports System

Public Class Retry

  Private attempts As Integer = 0
  Private Const maxRetries As Byte = 5

  Public Sub Go()

    Try
      'Code to retry0
      Console.WriteLine("Attempt #{0}", _
          attempts.ToString())
      'Simulate error
      Throw New Exception()
    Catch e As Exception When attempts < maxRetries
```

*Example 6-11. A better way to retry code (continued)*

```
      attempts += 1
      Go() 'Call method again
    Catch e As Exception
      'Failed so handle here
    End Try

    'Reset attempt counter
    attempts = 0

  End Sub

End Class

Public Class App
  Public Shared Sub Main()
    Dim r As New Retry()
    r.Go()
    Console.ReadLine()
  End Sub
End Class
```

Retrying code multiple times is considerably easier with the conditional handling of exceptions. Remember, exceptions are caught in the order they are received. In Example 6-11, the first exception handler's `When` clause provides a simple alternative to rerunning a block of code:

```
Try
    Go() 'Code that you want to re-run on failure
Catch e As Exception When attempts < maxRetries
    attempts += 1
    Go() 'Call method again
Catch e As Exception
    'Failed so handle here
End Try
```

After the internal counter exceeds its limit, the condition on the first `Catch` block is no longer valid, and the second handler catches any exception. The example ignores the exception, but in this situation, you could probably log the error as discussed earlier in the chapter.

Use unstructured exception handling only when migrating from earlier versions of VB to the .NET environment. New projects should always use structured exception handling.

## Performance Counters

Tucked away in the Administrative Tools folder within the Control Panel is the infamous Windows Performance Monitor. For years, network administrators have used this tool (shown in Figure 6-2) to profile everything from network traffic, SQL Server performance, memory, threads, and the cache. It is a very useful tool made even better by several additional counters provided by .NET.

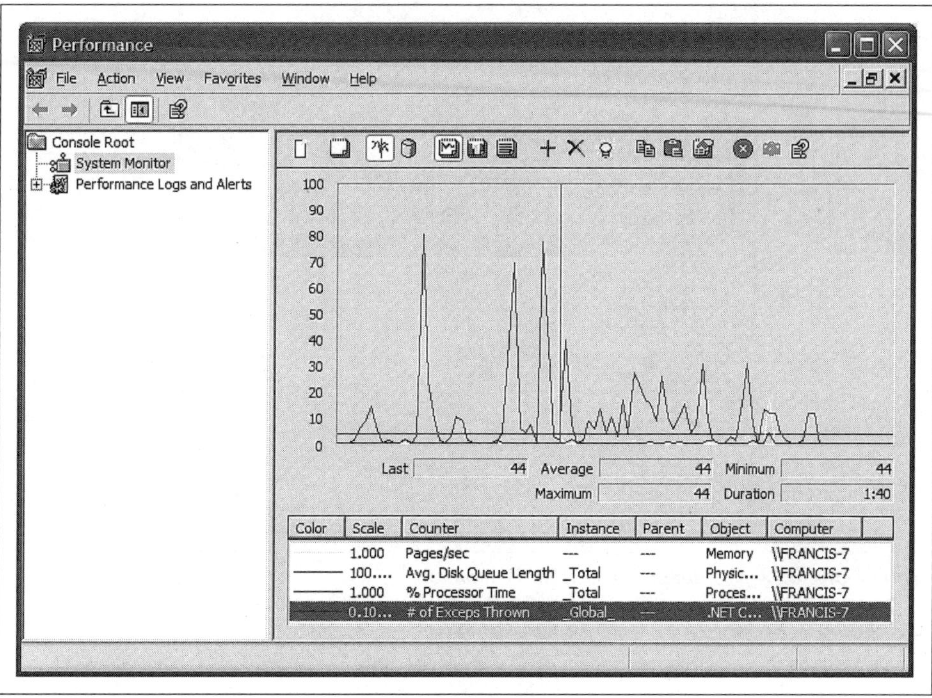


*Figure 6-2. The extremely useful Performance Monitor*

These supplementary counters allow you to profile low-level processes such as CLR memory allocation and the JIT compiler. In addition, ASP.NET provides several useful counters for keeping an eye on sessions, requests, and the cache.

## .NET CLR Exceptions

ASP.NET also provides a counter for monitoring exceptions thrown by the CLR. You can add it to the performance monitor by right-clicking on the performance graph and selecting "Add Counters" from the context menu. This step will bring you the dialog shown in Figure 6-3.

Then in the Performance object drop-down listbox, select ".NET CLR Exceptions." This category contains several counters, including "# of Exceps Thrown." There are several instances of this counter: `_Global_`, zero or more `devenv` counters, and `mmc`.

In the `System.Diagnostics` namespace, classes allow you to access any performance counter. Example 6-12 shows how to read values from a performance counter. Also shown is the "`# of Exceps Thrown`" counter, which tells you how many exceptions were thrown since the CLR was started.

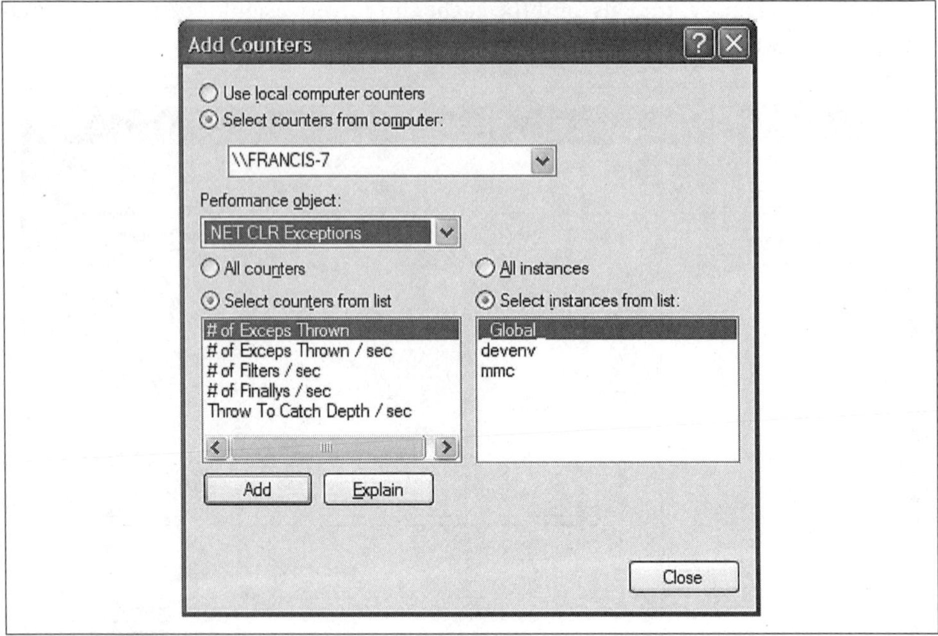


*Figure 6-3. Adding performance objects to the monitor*

*Example 6-12. Accessing known performance counters*

```
Imports System
Imports System.Diagnostics

Friend Class Test

  Public Shared Sub Main()
    If PerformanceCounterCategory.Exists(".NET CLR Exceptions") Then
      Dim pc As New PerformanceCounter(".NET CLR Exceptions", _
        "# of Exceps Thrown", "_Global_", True)
      Console.WriteLine(pc.RawValue().ToString())
    End If
  End Sub

End Class
```

The code first checks for the existence of the performance counter category by calling the shared method `PerformanceCounterCategory.Exists`. If it is found, an instance of `PerformanceCounter` is created by using the performance category, the counter name, and the instance name. These values can be readily obtained by looking in the Add Counters dialog from Figure 6-3. Finally the value is written to the console. It's not the greatest example, but the performance data is there, and you can access it.

## Custom Performance Counters

What does the number of exceptions thrown by the CLR tell you as a software developer? Well, not much. It would probably be more useful to monitor the number of exceptions thrown in your own application versus the entire runtime. Luckily, as Example 6-13 demonstrates, the .NET Framework provides ample support for creating custom profiling counters.

*Example 6-13. Creating a custom performance counter*

```
Imports System
Imports System.Diagnostics

Friend Class Test

  Public Shared Sub Main()

    If Not PerformanceCounterCategory.Exists("My Apps") Then

      'Create your performance counters
      Dim perfCounters As CounterCreationDataCollection _
          = New CounterCreationDataCollection()

      'Create exception performance counters
      Dim exceptionCounter As CounterCreationData = _
          New CounterCreationData( _
              "Exceptions Thrown", _
              "This counter tracks the " & _
              "total number of exceptions thrown " & _
              "by all of my applications.", _
              PerformanceCounterType.NumberOfItems32)

      'Add counter
      perfCounters.Add(exceptionCounter)

      'Create another counter to show executions
      Dim runCounter As CounterCreationData = _
          New CounterCreationData( _
              "Run Count", _
              "This counter profiles the " & _
              "total number of times " & _
              "my applications have run on this machine.", _
              PerformanceCounterType.NumberOfItems32)

      'Add second counter
      perfCounters.Add(runCounter)

      'Add counters to Performance Monitor
      PerformanceCounterCategory.Create("My Apps", _
                                        "My Counters Help", _
                                        perfCounters)
    End If
```

*Example 6-13. Creating a custom performance counter (continued)*

```
    End Sub

End Class
```

As in Example 6-12, the existence of the performance category is checked. In this example, the category is called "`My Apps`." If the category does not exist, it is created. Each performance category can contain any number of counters. In the example, one counter is created to track exceptions and another is created to track the number of times an application is run. Each counter is an instance of `System.Diagnostics.CounterCreationData`.

When creating the counter, the name of the counter, its help text, and its data type are provided. The help text is included for the benefit of the Add Counters dialog. A message box displays this text when the Explain button is pressed, as shown in Figure 6-4.

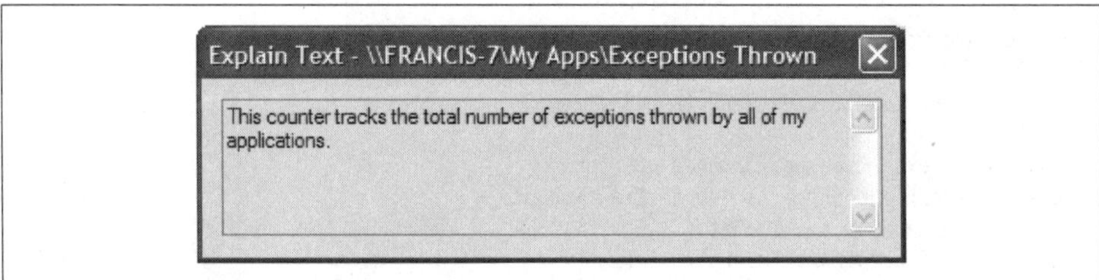


*Figure 6-4. Custom performance counter help text*

The important thing to remember is that counters cannot be added once the performance category is created, so think before jumping in head first.

After the counter is created, it is added to a collection of type `CounterCreationDataCollection`, which ends up as the third parameter to the `PerformanceCounterCategory.Create` method. The first two parameters are the name of and the help text for the category. This method makes the category and counters available to the `Performance` utility. If you want to track exceptions, you could place code similar to Example 6-13 into the startup routines of your application. If the category does not exist and you try to access it, an exception will be thrown. The irony!

To delete a custom performance counter, use the following code:

```
PerformanceCounterCategory.Delete("My Apps")
```

## Providing Performance Data

Now that a performance category exists, you need a way to write to the counter. If you were looking for an excuse to create your own exception object, here it is. Example 6-14 contains a derived exception class that writes to the exception counter that was just discussed.

*Example 6-14. Exception class that writes to performance counter*

```
Public Class MyBaseException : Inherits ApplicationException
  Public Sub New()
    If PerformanceCounterCategory.Exists("My Apps") Then
      Dim pc As New PerformanceCounter("My Apps", _
          "Exceptions Thrown", False)
      'Increment the counter
      pc.Increment()
    End If
  End Sub
End Class
```

In this instance, the constructor of the `PerformanceCounter` class takes the category name, the counter name, and whether or not the counter is read-only. Of course, to access the counter for a write operation, this last parameter must be `False`. Here, the Increment method adds one to the current counter value. To test the entire process, use code like this:

```
Try
    Throw New MyBaseException()
Catch e As MyBaseException
    If PerformanceCounterCategory.Exists("My Apps") Then
        Dim pc As New PerformanceCounter("My Apps", _
                                  "Exceptions Thrown")
        'Increment the counter
        Console.WriteLine(pc.RawValue().ToString())
    End If
End Try
```

As an exercise, you might consider adding the `ExceptionInfo` class or the functionality it provides to your performance tracking exception class.

CHAPTER 7

# Object Inspection

At this point, you should be familiar with the fundamentals of object-oriented programming and design within the .NET Framework. You've learned about classes, methods, and properties. You've seen inheritance, containment, and polymorphism. You have also tackled structured exception handling.

Hopefully, you have learned not only how to use these constructs but when to use them and why. Whether you know it or not, much of what you have gained is portable to other languages within the .NET Framework and beyond.

Now is the time to take what you learned and push forward. This chapter will discuss a few .NET-centric technologies that will be paramount when you consider architectures for your next big project. They include reflection (which you saw briefly in the last chapter), attributes, streams, and serialization. If you understand these technologies, you will have a solid foundation in programming applications for .NET.

## Reflection

Assemblies (either an *.exe* or a *.dll*) can contain one or more modules, though they usually contain just one. In turn, these modules contain one or more types; types in .NET include classes, interfaces, arrays, structures, delegates, and enumerations. Types contain members: fields, methods, properties, events, and parameters. The .NET class library supplies objects that encapsulate all these entities, letting you load an assembly at runtime (over the network, if you need to) and inspect all types in that assembly. Using the introspective properties of these objects, you can determine if a class is abstract, a method is public, or how many class constructors are available. In fact, anything you can describe with VB.NET code can be discovered at runtime. This process is called *reflection*.

Reflection is one of the .NET Framework's core technologies. In addition to runtime type discovery, you can use it to create assemblies, modules, and types at runtime and persist them to disk as *.exe* or *.dll* files. JScript .NET uses reflection to build symbol tables. The .NET Framework SDK, in fact, contains C# source code for two compilers that are written using reflection: a LISP compiler and a compiler for a subset of C called MyC. Serialization and remoting, both major players in .NET, also rely heavily on reflection.

# Runtime Type Discovery

Example 7-1 contains a listing for a class called ServerInfo. Consider it the humble beginnings of a load balancer. It can provide the machine name, an IP address, the processor usage, and the available memory of the machine on which it runs. However, in this chapter, it serves more form than function, so for now, forget about what it does and look at what it contains: an event, an enumeration, three methods (a sub, a function, and a shared function), and two read-only properties. While pondering these contents deeply, save it to a file named *ServerInfo.vb* and compile it to a class library. You will need this assembly as the basis of the rest of the chapter.

*Example 7-1. Reflection test class*

```
'vbc /t:library serverinfo.vb /r:system.dll

Imports System
Imports System.Diagnostics
Imports System.Net
Imports System.Threading

Public Class ServerInfo

    Private machine As String
    Private ip As IPAddress

    Public Enum Tasks
        EnterInfiniteLoop = 1
        WasteMemory = 2
        Allocate2GigForTheBrowser = 3
        RandomlyDestroyProcess = 4
    End Enum

    Public Event TaskCompleted As EventHandler

    Public Sub New()
        'Get machine info when object is created
        machine = Dns.GetHostName()
        Dim ipHost As IPHostEntry = Dns.GetHostByName(machine)
        ip = ipHost.AddressList(0)
    End Sub

    'This routine only fires an event right now
    Public Sub DoTask(ByVal task As Tasks)
        RaiseEvent TaskCompleted(Me, EventArgs.Empty)
    End Sub
```

*Example 7-1. Reflection test class (continued)*

```
    'Shared method
    Public Shared Function GetMachineTime() As DateTime
        Return DateTime.Now
    End Function

    'Get % of process currently in use
    Public Function GetProcessorUsed() As Single
        If PerformanceCounterCategory.Exists("Processor") Then
            Dim pc As New PerformanceCounter("Processor", _
                "% Processor Time", "_Total", True)
            Dim sampleA As CounterSample
            Dim sampleB As CounterSample

            sampleA = pc.NextSample()
            Thread.Sleep(1000)
            sampleB = pc.NextSample()
            Return CounterSample.Calculate(sampleA, sampleB)
        End If
    End Function

    'Get MBytes of free memory
    Public Function GetAvailableMemory() As Long
        If PerformanceCounterCategory.Exists("Memory") Then
            Dim pc As New PerformanceCounter("Memory", "Available MBytes")
            Return pc.RawValue()
        End If
    End Function

    Public ReadOnly Property MachineName() As String
        Get
            Return machine
        End Get
    End Property

    Public ReadOnly Property IPAddress() As IPAddress
        Get
            Return ip
        End Get
    End Property

End Class
```

The listing for *ServerInfo.dll* is in plain sight, so seeing its contents is easy. However, pretend that the source code doesn't exist. Can the assembly be queried programmatically for its type information? Sure it can. That's what reflection is all about.

The `System.Reflection` namespace and the `System.Type` class together will meet most reflection needs. This chapter will not discuss everything that can be accomplished with these classes. By the end of the chapter, though, your handle on reflection should be tighter than a G.I. Joe with Kung-Fu Action Grip.

The first step in type discovery is loading the assembly (the executable or library) in question; Example 7-2 shows the code that does this. Note that "`Assembly`" is a reserved word, so it is enclosed in square brackets in Example 7-2. If this were not done, `System.Reflection.Assembly` would have to be used instead. Who wants to type all that? The example also assumes that *ServerInfo.dll* is located in the same directory where the compiled executable will reside. If it is not, you will have to provide a full path to the `Assembly.LoadFrom` method.

*Example 7-2. Runtime type inspection*

```
Imports System
Imports System.Reflection

Public Class ObjectInfo

    Public Sub New (ByVal assemblyName As String)
        Dim a As [Assembly] = [Assembly].LoadFrom(assemblyName)
    End Sub

End Class

Public Class Application
    Public Shared Sub Main()
        Dim oi As New ObjectInfo("ServerInfo.dll")
        Console.ReadLine()
    End Sub
End Class
```

Save this example to a file called *reflect.vb*. Or, as an alternative, add the `Application` class and the `ObjectInfo` class to the *ServerInfo.dll* assembly and recompile it as an executable. In that case, the constructor to `ObjectInfo` needs modification so it obtains a reference to the current assembly instead of *ServerInfo.dll*. Modify it by replacing the call to `Assembly.LoadFrom` with `Assembly.GetExecutingAssembly`:

```
'Get the currently executing assembly
Dim a As [Assembly] = [Assembly].GetExecutingAssembly()
```

At this point, the `ObjectInfo` class does not do much more than load an assembly. Before compiling, remedy the situation by grabbing all the types in *ServerInfo.dll* and writing them out to the console. Doing so will get the ball rolling. The code is as follows:

```
Public Class ObjectInfo

    Public Sub New (ByVal assemblyName As String)
        Dim a As [Assembly] = [Assembly].LoadFrom(assemblyName)

        Dim t As Type
        Dim types As Type() = a.GetTypes()

        For Each t In  types
            Console.WriteLine(t.FullName)
        Next t

    End Sub
```

```
End Class

Public Class Application
    Public Shared Sub Main()
        Dim oi As New ObjectInfo("ServerInfo.dll")
        Console.ReadLine()
    End Sub
End Class
```

`Assembly.GetTypes` returns an array of `System.Type`. This array represents every type in the assembly. The types contained in *ServerInfo.dll* will come back as follows:

```
ServerInfo.ServerInfo
ServerInfo.ServerInfo+Tasks
```

There are two types in the assembly: the `ServerInfo` class and an enumeration named `Tasks`. To avoid confusion, properties, methods, and constructors are not categorized as types. They are considered elements of types.

Theoretically, the *ServerInfo.dll* assembly could contain more classes. As the types contained in the assembly are iterated in the `ObjectInfo` class, it might be beneficial to know what is what. `System.Type` contains several Boolean properties, shown in Table 7-1, that can help determine what a `Type` object represents.

*Table 7-1. Type classification properties in System.Type*

| Method | Description |
| --- | --- |
| `IsArray` | Type is an array. |
| `IsClass` | Type is a class. |
| `IsCOMObject` | Type is a COM object. |
| `IsEnum` | Type is an enum. |
| `IsInterface` | Type is an interface. |
| `IsPointer` | Type is a pointer. |
| `IsPrimitive` | Type is a primitive data type. |
| `IsValueType` | Type is a structure. |

It's a good idea to modify the constructor in `ObjectInfo` to look for class types only, since for the sake of simplicity, this chapter will discuss only classes. If a class is found, we'll pass the type along to a private method named `DumpClassInfo` (the source code for which is presented later in this chapter):

```
For Each t In  types
    If t.IsClass() Then
        DumpClassInfo(t)
    End If
Next t
```

Try to follow the discussion for now. Don't worry about coding along. After everything is discussed, a final code listing will contain everything.

The private method, DumpClassInfo, relies on several methods provided by the System.Type class that return Info objects. This is a general name given to the .NET class library classes of the following types: ConstructorInfo, EventInfo, FieldInfo, MethodInfo, ParameterInfo, and PropertyInfo. Each class represents the attributes of a class entity, and each is derived from a common parent, MemberInfo.

You can obtain references for these objects by calling a corresponding Get method on System.Type. For instance, Type.GetConstructors returns an array of ConstructorInfo objects, and Type.GetMethods returns an array of MethodInfo objects. These classes provide information about the constructors and methods of a class, respectively. Each Get method also has a single form: Type.GetConstructor, Type.GetProperty, and so forth. Table 7-2 summarizes these methods.

*Table 7-2. Info methods from System.Type*

| Method | Returns |
|---|---|
| GetConstructor/GetConstructors | ConstructorInfo |
| GetEvent/GetEvents | EventInfo |
| GetField/GetFields | FieldInfo |
| GetMethod/GetMethods | MethodInfo |
| GetParameter/GetParameters | ParameterInfo |
| GetProperty/GetProperties | PropertyInfo |

Using the specific classes in Table 7-2 is not necessary, but they do make life easier. Type.GetMembers returns an array of MemberInfo objects. From here, you can determine the specific type of each member by examining the MemberInfo object that corresponds to it. Here's a quick example. Given that t is an instance of Type (that represents a class), the following code is possible:

```
Dim member As MemberInfo
Dim members() As MemberInfo = t.GetMembers()

For Each member In members

    Select Case member.MemberType
        Case MemberTypes.Constructor

        Case MemberTypes.Event

        Case MemberTypes.Field

        Case MemberTypes.Method

        Case MemberTypes.Property
    End Select

Next member
```

However, using the specific Info methods provided through Type is easier.

The time to write ObjectInfo.DumpClassInfo draws nigh. This method, once written, can be used to examine any class. The final listing will be fairly long, so this chapter will examine the code one step at a time. All pretenses aside, the primary motivation of this example is to cover as much of reflection as possible without turning the chapter into a reference manual.

Regardless, the example needs some semblance of credibility. To give it a purpose, let's approach it as if it will be used to generate class documentation. This is a practical for reflection.

DumpClassInfo should first output the name of the class by calling Type.FullName. This step returns the fully qualified name of the type (meaning it includes the namespace):

```
Private Sub DumpClassInfo(ByVal t As Type)
    Console.WriteLine(New String("-"c, 80))
    Console.WriteLine("Class: {0}", t.FullName)
```

## Constructor Information

It's easy to get the constructors by calling Type.GetConstructors. This method returns an array of ConstructorInfo. One of the overrides of GetConstructors accepts a bitmask containing values from the BindingFlags enumeration as a parameter. This enumeration provides a means to restrict what is searched during reflection. Here, the Public and Instance members of the BindingFlags enumeration are used, so only the public instance constructors are asked for. Any nonpublic constructors will not be returned:

```
    'Get constructors
    Dim c As ConstructorInfo
    Dim ci() As ConstructorInfo = _
        t.GetConstructors(BindingFlags.Public Or BindingFlags.Instance)

    Console.WriteLine("Constructors:")

    For Each c In ci
        Console.WriteLine("    {0}", c)
    Next c
```

If BindingFlags.Instance (or BindingFlags.Static) is not used in conjunction with BindingFlags.Public (or BindingFlags.NonPublic), no members will be returned.

Examining the output of the previous block of code, note that the enumeration is no longer listed. It is not listed because the call to Type.IsClass wraps the call to DumpClassInfo. The output, thus far, should look similar to this:

```
--------------------------------------------------------------------------------
Class: ServerInfo.ServerInfo
Constructors:
    Void .ctor()
```

Now, this example is definitely not Visual Basic. In C, C++, C#, and Java, void denotes a function that does not return a value. In VB.NET, a function that does not return a value is a Sub. To make this code readable to VB.NET programmers, you only need to replace Void with Public Sub. The .ctor is short for "constructor," or in VB.NET-speak, New.

Translating the output into VB.NET is a fairly straightforward string replacement. Instead of writing the raw constructor signature to the console, use this code:

```
For Each c In ci
    Dim s As String = String.Format("{0}{1}", vbTab, c.ToString())
    Console.WriteLine(s.Replace("Void .ctor", "Public Sub New"))
Next c
```

Even if the BindingFlags enumeration were not used as a filter in this example, the ConstructorInfo class (like all the Info classes) contains all the members needed to determine everything about a class' attributes: Is it public? Is it private? Is it abstract? Is inheritance allowed? And so on.

This chapter does not cover the minutiae of it all. Just understand that all the classes that derive from MemberInfo are very similar in form and function.

## Property Information

The code for obtaining public instance properties is similar to that for constructors. Additionally, a call to PropertyInfo.CanRead and PropertyInfo.CanWrite can determine the property's accessibility. The following code, when added to the DumpClassInfo method, displays property information:

```
Dim p As PropertyInfo
Dim pi() As PropertyInfo = _
    t.GetProperties(BindingFlags.Public Or BindingFlags.Instance)

Console.WriteLine()
Console.WriteLine("Properties:")

For Each p In pi
    Console.Write("Public ")
    If p.CanRead And p.CanWrite Then
    ElseIf p.CanRead Then
        Console.Write("ReadOnly ")
    ElseIf p.CanWrite Then
        Console.Write("WriteOnly ")
    End If
    Console.WriteLine("Property {0}() As {1}", p.Name, _
        p.PropertyType.ToString())
Next p
```

This code returns the properties as VB.NET declarations:

```
-----------------------------------------------------------------------
Class: ServerInfo.ServerInfo
Constructors:
```

```
        Public Sub New()

    Properties:
    Public ReadOnly Property MachineName() As System.String
    Public ReadOnly Property IPAddress() As System.Net.IPAddress
```

Apparently, the PropertyInfo class does not return as much information about a property as some of the other Info classes do for their counterparts. For instance, if you look at the class definition, there does not appear to be a way to do much beyond determining whether a property is read-only, write-only, or both (using the CanWrite and CanRead properties).

However, this impression is not completely accurate. Behind the scenes, VB.NET properties are implemented with corresponding Get and Set methods (see the "Properties" section in Chapter 3). To get additional information about the property (such as whether it is private, inheritable, or shared), you must work with these methods rather than with the PropertyInfo class. The next section details the type of information you can obtain by examining a method. First, though, you need to get to the accessor methods.

You can access the accessor methods in one of two ways: by calling either PropertyInfo.GetGetMethod or PropertyInfo.GetSetMethod. Each returns a MethodInfo class that represents the appropriate accessor. Also, it is possible to call PropertyInfo.GetAccessors, which returns an array of MethodInfo objects. This class is very similar to ConstructorInfo and contains all the functionality necessary to describe the method in question.

## Method Information

To get the methods of a class, call Type.GetMethods, which returns an array of MethodInfo objects. This time, however, in the name of pure, unadulterated entertainment, the BindingFlags bitmask will not be used. Our goal is to demonstrate how the information provided by BindingFlags can be determined without using the bitmask.

While iterating through each method, you can see if the method is declared in the current class by calling MethodInfo.DeclaringType. Calling it filters out all methods that are inherited from System.Object or from another base class, had we used inheritance explicitly when creating the ServerInfo class. This way, the listing reflects the only current type, the ServerInfo class, and its unique methods and events. The following code accomplishes this:

```
'Get public shared methods
Dim i As Integer
Dim returnType As Type
Dim returnString As String
Dim m As MethodInfo
Dim mi() As MethodInfo = t.GetMethods()
```

```
Console.WriteLine("Methods:")

For Each m In mi

    If m.DeclaringType.Equals(t) Then
```

You can filter out inherited members in the call to GetMethods by supplying the BindingFlags.DeclaredOnly constant using a method call like the following:

```
mi = t.GetMethods(BindingFlags.Public Or _
                  BindingFlags.Instance Or _
                  BindingFlags.DeclaredOnly)
```

To determine the accessibility of a method, various properties are available from MethodInfo. See how these property names map IL to VB.NET:

```
If m.IsPublic Then
    Console.Write("Public ")
ElseIf m.IsPrivate Then
    Console.WriteLine("Private ")
ElseIf m.IsFamily Then
    Console.WriteLine("Protected ")
ElseIf m.IsAssembly Then
    Console.WriteLine("Friend ")
ElseIf m.IsFamilyAndAssembly Then
    Console.WriteLine("Protected Friend ")
End If

If m.IsStatic Then
    Console.Write("Shared ")
End If
```

These properties, such as IsPublic, IsFamily, and IsStatic, are defined in a class named MethodBase, which is the parent class of both MethodInfo and ConstructorInfo. ConstructorInfo functions the same way as MethodInfo, except it is focused on constructors.

To cut the example's size, polymorphic attributes like MustOverride, Overridable, and Overrides were left out. However, MethodInfo allows you to ascertain this information.

The return type for the reflected method can be snagged by calling, oddly enough, the property named ReturnType. Who could have guessed? If the return type is equal to System.Void, the method is a Sub; otherwise, it's a Function. After determining which is which, our code calls MethodInfo.Name to retrieve the name of the method.

```
returnType = m.ReturnType

If String.Compare(returnType.ToString(), "System.Void") <> 0 Then
    Console.Write("Function {0}(", m.Name)
    returnString = String.Format(" As {0}", returnType.ToString())
Else
    Console.Write("Sub {0}(", m.Name)
End If
```

Divining the parameters for the method is as simple as calling `MethodInfo.GetParameters`, which returns an array of `ParameterInfo` objects. This class can query the parameter's name and type, as shown in the next code fragment for `DumpClassInfo`:

```
            Dim parms() As ParameterInfo = m.GetParameters()

            For i = 0 To parms.Length - 1
                Console.Write(parms(i).Name)
                Console.Write(" As ")
                Console.Write(parms(i).ParameterType())
                If (i < parms.Length - 1) Then
                    Console.Write(", ")
                End If
            Next i

            Console.Write(")")
            Console.WriteLine(returnString)

        End If

    Next m
```

Up to this point, the output of `ServerInfo` looks like this (if you reformatted it to fit in a book):

```
Methods:
Public Sub remove_TaskCompleted(obj As
    ServerInfo.ServerInfo+TaskCompletedEventHandler)
Public Sub add_TaskCompleted(obj As
    ServerInfo.ServerInfo+TaskCompletedEventHandler)
Public Sub DoTask(task As ServerInfo.ServerInfo+Tasks)
Public Shared Function GetMachineTime() As System.DateTime
Public Function GetProcessorUsed() As System.Single
Public Function GetAvailableMemory() As System.Int64
Public Function get_MachineName() As System.String
Public Function get_IPAddress() As System.Net.IPAddress
```

`get_MachineName` and `get_IPAddress` are the read-only accessor methods of the `MachineName` and `IPAddress` properties, so they should probably not be listed here because they were already handled in the properties section. An additional property of the `MethodInfo` class called IsSpecialName can prevent the display of accessor methods. To use it, modify the `If` statement that tests to eliminate inherited members as follows:

```
If m.DeclaringType.Equals(t) AndAlso m.IsSpecialName = False Then
```

If you disassemble *ServerInfo.dll*, you will see that both accessor methods have the `specialname` IL attribute associated with them. This flag is provided for compiler writers and tool vendors and allows a member to be treated specially. For instance, IntelliSense uses it to prevent the display of accessor methods. However, it doesn't do anything that affects the way code is run.

Once we eliminate methods with special names, the output appears as follows:

```
Methods:
Public Sub DoTask(task As ServerInfo.ServerInfo+Tasks)
Public Shared Function GetMachineTime() As System.DateTime
Public Function GetProcessorUsed() As System.Single
Public Function GetAvailableMemory() As System.Int64
```

## The Complete ObjectInfo Source Code

Example 7-3 contains a revised listing of the ObjectInfo class. It was rewritten slightly, but all the functionality is there (including events). Your assignment, should you choose to accept it, is to add support for other types, such as enumerations and value types. Also, nested types (that is, classes contained within classes) are not handled at all. To handle them, look at Type.GetNestedTypes, if possible. There is really nothing to it. Everything in reflection is aptly named. You can learn a lot just by hacking the example.

Example 7-3 is long, but don't run away. The wonderful world of reflection is far from fully explored. More needs to be covered before the topic can be put to rest. But check out the example and spend some quality time with it.

*Example 7-3. ObjectInfo reflection class*

```
Public Class ObjectInfo

    Private Sub DumpConstructors(ByVal t As Type)

        Dim c As ConstructorInfo
        Dim ci() As ConstructorInfo = _
            t.GetConstructors(BindingFlags.Public Or BindingFlags.Instance)

        Console.WriteLine()
        Console.WriteLine("Constructors:")

        For Each c In ci
            Dim s As String = c.ToString()
            Console.WriteLine(s.Replace("Void .ctor", "Public Sub New"))
        Next c

    End Sub

    Private Sub DumpEvents(ByVal t As Type)
        Dim e As EventInfo
        Dim ei As EventInfo() = _
                    t.GetEvents(BindingFlags.Public Or _
                                BindingFlags.Instance)

        Console.WriteLine()
        Console.WriteLine("Events:")

        For Each e In ei
```

*Example 7-3. ObjectInfo reflection class (continued)*

```
            Console.WriteLine(e.Name)
        Next e

    End Sub

    Private Sub DumpProperties(ByVal t As Type)

        Dim p As PropertyInfo
        Dim pi() As PropertyInfo = _
            t.GetProperties(BindingFlags.Public Or BindingFlags.Instance)

        Console.WriteLine()
        Console.WriteLine("Properties:")

        For Each p In pi
            Console.Write("Public ")
            If p.CanRead And p.CanWrite Then
            ElseIf p.CanRead Then
                Console.Write("ReadOnly ")
            ElseIf p.CanWrite Then
                Console.Write("WriteOnly ")
            End If
            Console.WriteLine("Property {0}() As {1}", _
                p.Name, p.PropertyType.ToString())
        Next p

    End Sub

    Private Sub DumpMethod(ByVal m As MethodInfo)

        Dim i As Integer
        Dim returnType As Type
        Dim returnString As String

        If m.IsPublic Then
            Console.Write("Public ")
        ElseIf m.IsPrivate Then
            Console.WriteLine("Private ")
        ElseIf m.IsFamily Then
            Console.WriteLine("Protected ")
        ElseIf m.IsAssembly Then
            Console.WriteLine("Friend ")
        ElseIf m.IsFamilyAndAssembly Then
            Console.WriteLine("Protected Friend ")
        End If

        If m.IsStatic Then
            Console.Write("Shared ")
        End If

        returnType = m.ReturnType

        If String.Compare(returnType.ToString(), "System.Void") <> 0 Then
```

*Example 7-3. ObjectInfo reflection class (continued)*

```
            Console.Write("Function {0}(", m.Name)
            returnString = String.Format(" As {0}", returnType.ToString())
        Else
            Console.Write("Sub {0}(", m.Name)
        End If

        Dim parms() As ParameterInfo = m.GetParameters()
        For i = 0 To parms.Length - 1
            Console.Write(parms(i).Name)
            Console.Write(" As ")
            Console.Write(parms(i).ParameterType())

            If (i < parms.Length - 1) Then
                Console.Write(", ")
            End If
        Next i

        Console.WriteLine(")")

    End Sub

    Private Sub DumpMethods(ByVal t As Type)

        Dim m As MethodInfo
        Dim mi() As MethodInfo = t.GetMethods()

        Console.WriteLine()
        Console.WriteLine("Methods:")

        For Each m In mi
            If m.DeclaringType.Equals(t) AndAlso _
               m.IsSpecialName = False Then
                DumpMethod(m)
            End If
        Next m

    End Sub

    Private Sub DumpClassInfo(ByVal t As Type)

        Console.WriteLine(New String("-"c, 80))
        Console.WriteLine("Class: {0}", t.FullName)

        DumpConstructors(t)
        DumpEvents(t)
        DumpProperties(t)
        DumpMethods(t)

        Console.WriteLine()

    End Sub

    Public Sub New(ByVal assemblyName As String)
```

*Example 7-3. ObjectInfo reflection class (continued)*

```
        Dim a As [Assembly]
        If (assemblyName = Nothing) Then
            a = [Assembly].GetExecutingAssembly()
        Else
            a = [Assembly].LoadFrom(assemblyName)
        End If

        Dim t As Type
        Dim types As Type() = a.GetTypes()

        For Each t In types
            If t.IsClass Then
                DumpClassInfo(t)
            End If
        Next t

    End Sub

End Class
```

# Dynamic Type Loading

The process of locating a type declaration and verifying that its methods are used correctly is called *binding*. Binding that occurs at compile time is called *early binding*. When it happens at runtime, it is known as *late binding*.

Visual Basic .NET uses reflection to implement late binding. Consider the following code:

```
Dim fourOneOne As Object
fourOneOne = New ServerInfo()
fourOneOne.DoTask(Allocate2GigForTheBrowser)
```

Here, `fourOneOne` is declared as an `Object` but instantiated as `ServerInfo` (from Example 7-1). The `DoTask` method call is a late-bound call. In situations like this, the method is called at runtime through the `Type.InvokeMember` method. Try to avoid writing code like this, if possible. You will incur a performance penalty for late binding.

In more exotic architectures, especially distributed systems, late binding is a must. Think about a system centered around SOAP, for instance. A SOAP envelope that describes an object and a method call is sent to a server located halfway around the world. The remote server spawns an instance of the object, calls the appropriate method, and sends the results back to the caller. This is late binding at the extreme!

## Using Dynamically Loaded Types

Reflection not only allows you to inspect the types contained within an assembly, it makes it possible for you to create instances of those types at runtime. You can then call methods on those objects and use them just like any other objects.

Loading a type at runtime and calling its methods is easy, but more details need to be discussed, so let's piece together the example one fragment at a time. Start with loading the assembly. As in Example 7-2, the assembly containing the type must first be loaded into an application domain. Then a call to `Assembly.GetType` can be used to get a *reference* (not an instance) to the needed type:

```
Imports System
Imports System.Reflection

'This examples assumes ServerInfo.dll is in the current directory
Dim a As [Assembly] = [Assembly].LoadFrom("ServerInfo.dll")
Dim siType As Type = a.GetType("ServerInfo")
```

You have already seen how the info classes can provide information about the specifics of a class. The exciting thing is that the same classes can be used to make runtime calls on an object. The starting point is to retrieve a `MethodInfo` or `PropertyInfo` object representing the method or the property to be called. To get a reference to a method, call `Type.GetMethod`; to get a reference to a property, call `Type.GetProperty`. Instead of calling the `GetProperty` method, you can also call `Type.GetMethod` to access the `MethodInfo` object representing either a property's get accessor or its set accessor. For example, the following code retrieves the `MethodInfo` object representing the `DoTask` method and also retrieves a `MethodInfo` object representing the `MachineTime` property's get accessor:

```
'Get DoTask method
Dim doTask As MethodInfo
doTask = siType.GetMethod("DoTask")

'This was done as a function instead of a property in order
'to demonstrate shared methods
Dim machineTime As MethodInfo
machineTime = siType.GetMethod("GetMachineTime")
```

### System.Activator

So far, although the code retrieved a `Type` object representing the `ServerInfo` class, an instance of `ServerInfo` doesn't actually exist. To create it, use the `System.Activator` class. This class contains all methods necessary to create objects locally or remotely, or to obtain references to existing objects.

To create an object of a given type, call `Activator.CreateInstance`, which simply takes the type to be created:

```
Dim si As Object
si = Activator.CreateInstance(siType)
```

If `ServerInfo`'s constructor had arguments, each would have to be packed into an object array and passed along with the type:

```
Dim d As Double = 10
Dim s As String = "Test"
Dim args() As Object = {d, s}
Dim si As Object = Activator.CreateInstance(siType, args)
```

### Dynamic event handling

Before invoking methods at runtime, it's probably a good idea to wire up the handler to deal with the event that is raised when ServerInfo.DoTask is invoked. Doing this dynamically is not difficult, but it does have to be done precisely in order to work. The first step is to create a method that matches the event's signature:

```
'The event handler for ServerInfo.TaskCompleted
Public Sub OnTaskCompleted(ByVal obj As Object, ByVal e As EventArgs)
    Console.WriteLine("The task has been completed")
End Sub
```

After having seen ConstructorInfo, MethodInfo, and PropertyInfo, what class could you use to obtain event information? It's called EventInfo, and to get it, call Type.GetEvent and ask for the event by name. Then finishing the job only requires calling EventInfo.AddEventHandler. This method takes the event source as the first parameter (the ServerInfo object) and a delegate of type EventHandler as the second:

```
'Dynamically hook up to event source
Dim evtInfo As EventInfo = siType.GetEvent("TaskCompleted")
Dim evtHandler As EventHandler = AddressOf OnTaskCompleted
evtInfo.AddEventHandler(si, evtHandler)
```

### Calling methods and properties dynamically

MethodInfo.Invoke calls methods at runtime. It takes two parameters: an object instance on which to call the method and an object array containing the parameters to the method.

ServerInfo.DoTask has one parameter: the task that is to be performed. The tricky part of making this call, however, is the fact that the parameter that must be passed is a member of the Tasks enumeration, which is also declared in the *ServerInfo.dll* assembly.

You must call Assembly.GetType to return a Type representing the Tasks enumeration. Then GetMember is called from the returned type. GetMember brings back the individual member of the enumeration—in this case, WasteMemory. Now the parameter array can be packaged. When the "task" is passed to Activator.CreateInstance, the declaring type is used:

```
'Package DoTask parameters and call
Dim taskType As Type = a.GetType("ServerInfo+Tasks")
Dim taskInfo() As MemberInfo = taskType.GetMember("WasteMemory")
Dim taskParam As Object = Activator.CreateInstance(taskInfo(0).DeclaringType)
Dim taskParams() As Object = {taskParam}
doTask.Invoke(si, taskParams)
```

This code should cause the OnTaskCompleted event to be called indirectly through the event handler that is assigned dynamically.

GetMachineName is a different story. It's a shared method, so an object instance is not required to call it. Furthermore, it takes no parameters, so Nothing can be passed for both arguments of the Invoke method:

```
'Call GetMachineTime
Dim result As Object = machineTime.Invoke(Nothing, Nothing)
Dim dt As DateTime = Convert.ToDateTime(result)
Console.WriteLine(dt.ToString())
```

Properties are handled differently. To get and set the value of a property, call PropertyInfo.GetValue and PropertyInfo.SetValue. The property can be referred to by name:

```
'Get machine name
Dim pi As PropertyInfo = siType.GetProperty("MachineName")
Console.WriteLine(pi.GetValue(si, Nothing))
```

Example 7-4 contains a complete listing of everything up to this point. Compile and try it. The output should look like this:

```
The task has been completed
4/18/2002 9:41:22 PM
LOGAN-5
192.168.1.101
288 MB Free
Processor: 1.5625% used
```

*Example 7-4. Dynamic type loading and method invocation*

```
'latebind.vb
'References ServerInfo.dll
'Assumes ServerInfo.dll is in same directory as executable

Imports System
Imports System.Net
Imports System.Reflection
Imports ServerInfo.ServerInfo

Public Class LateBind

    'Event Handler
    Public Sub OnTaskCompleted(ByVal obj As Object, ByVal e As EventArgs)
        Console.WriteLine("The task has been completed")
    End Sub

    Public Sub New()
        Dim a As [Assembly]
        a = [Assembly].LoadFrom("ServerInfo.dll")
        Dim siType As Type = a.GetType("ServerInfo.ServerInfo")

        'Get DoTask method
        Dim doTask As MethodInfo
        doTask = siType.GetMethod("DoTask")
```

*Example 7-4. Dynamic type loading and method invocation (continued)*

```
        'GetAvailableMemory
        Dim getMem As MethodInfo
        getMem = siType.GetMethod("GetAvailableMemory")

        'GetProcessorUsed
        Dim getProc As MethodInfo
        getProc = siType.GetMethod("GetProcessorUsed")

        'This was done as a function instead of a property in order
        'to demonstrate shared methods
        Dim machineTime As MethodInfo
        machineTime = siType.GetMethod("GetMachineTime")

        'Create instance of object
        Dim si As Object
        si = Activator.CreateInstance(siType)

        'Dynamically hook up to event source
        Dim evtInfo As EventInfo = siType.GetEvent("TaskCompleted")
        Dim evtHandler As EventHandler = AddressOf OnTaskCompleted
        evtInfo.AddEventHandler(si, evtHandler)

        'Package DoTask parameters and call
        Dim taskParams() As Object = {Tasks.WasteMemory}
        doTask.Invoke(si, taskParams)

        'Output results
        Dim result As Object = machineTime.Invoke(Nothing, Nothing)
        Dim dt As DateTime = Convert.ToDateTime(result)
        Console.WriteLine(dt.ToString())

        'Get machine name
        Dim pi As PropertyInfo = siType.GetProperty("MachineName")
        Console.WriteLine(pi.GetValue(si, Nothing))

        'Get IP
        pi = siType.GetProperty("IPAddress")
        result = pi.GetValue(si, Nothing)
        Dim ip As IPAddress = CType(result, IPAddress)
        Console.WriteLine(ip.ToString())

        'Get free memory
        result = getMem.Invoke(si, Nothing)
        Dim mbytesFree As Integer = Convert.ToInt32(result)
        Console.WriteLine(String.Format("{0} MB Free", mbytesFree))

        'Get processor
        result = getProc.Invoke(si, Nothing)
        Dim used As Single = Convert.ToSingle(result)
        Console.WriteLine(String.Format("Processor: {0}% used", used))

    End Sub
```

*Example 7-4. Dynamic type loading and method invocation (continued)*

```
End Class

Public Class Application

    Public Shared Sub Main()
        Dim test As New LateBind()
        Console.ReadLine()
    End Sub

End Class
```

# Attributes

Classes in .NET contain all kinds of declarative information that describes how the class works. Modifiers like `Public`, `Private`, and `Friend` describe the accessibility of a class, field, or method. Attributes like `MustInherit`, `NotInheritable`, and `Overrides` describe the inheritance- and polymorphic-related behaviors that a class exhibits. Also, data can be declared as a specific type.

Throughout this chapter, reflection has been used to query types, load them, and make method calls on them. Virtually any secret can be discovered by reflection. This ability by itself is pretty amazing when you think of the kinds of architectures that can be accommodated with it. However, there is another level beyond this: declarative attributes can be created programmatically and associated with any entity in .NET. These attributes are stored with the type's metadata and are available at all times: design time, compile time, and runtime. Reflection can examine this information and make decisions based on it.

Quite a few attributes are already defined in the framework. For instance, both the Visual Basic .NET and C# compilers recognize the `Obsolete` attribute. The attribute allows the programmer to associate a warning with a class.

In Visual Basic .NET, the `System.ObsoleteAttribute` attribute (like all attributes) is contained within angular brackets on the same line as the class definition. Unfortunately, this containment is unwieldy:

```
<Obsolete("Try NewClass instead.")> Public Class OldClass

End Class
```

Instead, use the line continuation character, which allows the attribute to be placed above the class:

```
<Obsolete("Try NewClass instead.")> _
Public Class OldClass

End Class
```

This attribute does not come into play until someone actually declares an instance of the class. Any code that uses this class compiles, but the compiler issues a warning announcing that the class is no longer in use. The attribute provides a string constructor that allows a resolution message to be specified. In this case, it tells the person compiling to try another class:

```
Microsoft (R) Visual Basic .NET Compiler version 7.00.9466
for Microsoft (R) .NET Framework version 1.00.3705.209
Copyright (C) Microsoft Corporation 1987-2001. All rights reserved.

C:\oc.vb(11) : warning BC40000: 'OldClass' is obsolete:
  'Try NewClass instead.'

    Dim oc As New OldClass()
```

The `Obsolete` attribute is a great way to inform other developers of newer classes that are available. Old classes can be left in place so that existing client code will not break and at the same time give users a push towards a newer implementation.

You can treat warnings as errors to prevent compilation by using the `/warnaserror+` compiler switch.

Even though the class is named `ObsoleteAttribute`, it can be referred to it as `Obsolete` when applied. This is true for any attribute, unless that attribute's short name is also a VB keyword.

The .NET class library contains numerous attribute definitions (the largest collection is contained in the `System` and `System.Reflection` namespaces), and each one is named using the *`attributename`*`Attribute` format. Thus, seeing which classes in the framework are attributes is fairly easy.

By now, you should recognize a pattern in the naming conventions for classes in the framework library. `Exception` classes end with "`Exception`"; `EventArgs` derivatives end with "`EventArgs`"; `EventHandler` classes end with "`EventHandler`"; and attribute classes are appended with "`Attribute`." When it comes to naming conventions, use the framework as your guide.

VB.NET uses other attributes to implement features of the language. For instance, when declaring a method with a variable argument list, the `ParamArray` keyword, as shown in Example 7-5, is used. This keyword actually resolves to an attribute.

*Example 7-5. Variable argument lists*

```
Imports System

Public Class Bag

    Public ReadOnly Objects() As Object
```

*Example 7-5. Variable argument lists (continued)*

```
    Public Sub New(ParamArray objects() As Object)
        Me.Objects = objects
    End Sub

    Public Sub ShowItems()
        Console.WriteLine("I have {0} items.", Objects.Length)
    End Sub

End Class

Friend Class Test
    Public Shared Sub Main()

        Dim o As New Object()

        Dim thisBag As Bag = New Bag(o,o,o,o,o)
        Dim thatBag As Bag = New Bag(o,o,o)

        thisBag.ShowItems()
        thatBag.ShowItems()

    End Sub
End Class
```

In Example 7-5, two instances of Bag are created—one with five objects, and the other with three. Any number of objects can be passed as individual arguments; the objects are used to initialize an array. Disassemble this listing and notice that the ParamArray keyword is implemented with a System.ParamArrayAttribute. Equivalently, it is possible to rewrite the constructor of the Bag class by using the attribute instead:

```
Public Sub New(<[ParamArray]()> objects() As Object)
    Me.Objects = objects
End Sub
```

The square brackets [...] are placed around ParamArray because the attribute name is a reserved word in VB. This behavior is possible with any VB reserved word.

Alternatively, remember that you can also apply attributes by using their full name. In the case of ParamArray (since it is a reserved word), it could be declared like this:

```
Public Sub New(<ParamArrayAttribute()> objects() As Object)
    Me.Objects = objects
End Sub
```

The ParamArray attribute is applied at the parameter level, but the Obsolete attribute is applied to the class (it can also be applied to a method). Attributes can be applied to any number of class elements, or even directly to the assembly; it all depends on how they were defined. Some, like ParamArray, can be applied to only one element.

The default property is another language feature that is built upon attributes—in this case, the DefaultMemberAttribute class, which is a class-level attribute defined in the

System.Reflection namespace. Recall that default properties allow objects to be indexed like an array. The properties themselves are prefixed with the Default keyword and are required to have at least one parameter. For example, the following code defines a default property named Item:

```
Imports System

Public Class WorthlessArray

    Default ReadOnly Public Property Item(ByVal index As Integer) _
        As Integer
        Get
            Return index
        End Get
    End Property

End Class
```

Considering the fragment above, an instance of WorthlessArray can be treated as if it were an array:

```
Dim wa As New WorthlessArray ()
Dim answer As Integer = wa(5) 'Returns 5
```

This same behavior can be accomplished by adding the DefaultMember attribute to WorthlessArray:

```
Imports System
Imports System.Reflection

<DefaultMember("Item")> _
Public Class NewClass

    ReadOnly Public Property Item(ByVal index As Integer) _
        As Integer
        Get
            Return 42
        End Get
    End Property

End Class
```

The Default keyword is no longer necessary, so it is removed. To test this behavior, compile this class into a library and then reference the assembly from another executable.

Another interesting attribute is System.CLSCompliantAttribute, which can be applied to almost every element in an assembly. By decorating an assembly with this attribute, everything in the assembly is declared as CLS-compliant; by default, this is not the case. Even so, an assembly that declared compliance is permitted to contain noncompliant elements. However, these elements must be designated explicitly with the ClsCompliant attribute, as shown in the following code:

```
Imports System

<Assembly: CLSCompliant(True)>

Public Class NewClass

    <CLSCompliant(False)> _
    Public Sub NotCompliant(ByVal someNumber As SByte)
        'SByte is not CLS-compliant
    End Sub

End Class
```

The attribute is designed to trigger a compiler warning when compliance is suspect. In other words, removing the attribute from the `NotCompliant` method should trigger a warning in future versions of the VB compiler. The key phrase here is *future versions*. Currently, the compiler ignores this attribute, but this will not always be the case. You should start using this attribute now to prepare ahead.

The previous example is a good demonstration of assembly-level attribute application. Versioning is another object-related task that is handled with an attribute at the assembly level. In fact, there are quite a few assembly-specific attributes. These attributes allow miscellaneous information such as a company name, copyright, and trademark to be associated with an assembly, as the following code illustrates:

```
Imports System
Imports System.Reflection

<Assembly:AssemblyVersion("1.0.0.0")>
<Assembly:AssemblyCompany("Big Bad Software")>
<Assembly:AssemblyCopyright("(c) 2001 Big Bad Software.")>
<Assembly:AssemblyDescription("Chapter 7 Example.")>
<Assembly:AssemblyProduct("Object Attribute-thingy")>
<Assembly:AssemblyTrademark("Putting the YOU in Useless")>
```

All of these attributes are stored in the manifest. Fire up ILDASM and check it out. This information can be located and used by anyone interested in obtaining it. Visual Studio .NET, for instance, makes the description attribute available from its property window.

Several major attributes have not been covered so far in this chapter. One notable attribute is `System.SerializableAttribute`, which says that a class can be serialized. Serialization is the process by which an object is converted to a form that can be stored or transported across a network. The process usually involves writing the class' member variables to a database or some other form of persistent storage—a file perhaps—or encoding the object's state into binary or XML and transporting it across a network. Speaking of XML, several attributes are designed to map the member variables of a class to an XML document or SOAP header. These attributes play a major role in .NET remoting.

As for remoting, don't forget `WebMethodAttribute`, which is used to build a web service—undoubtedly, one of the most exciting features available in .NET. This attribute injects all plumbing necessary to call a class method over the Web by using standard XML and HTTP.

These attributes will have their day in the sun, but first things first. One final aspect of attributes, and possibly the coolest, is the ability to define your own. While the VB compiler will never know about these attributes, you could write code that can use these custom attributes meaningfully and productively.

## Custom Attributes

C# excels over VB as a .NET language in one particular area: XML documentation comments. C# allows you to embed XML comments into your code that can be compiled to documentation independently at a later time. Example 7-6 shows a simple class written in C# that contains XML comments.

*Example 7-6. C# class with XML comments*

```
using System;

/// <summary>
/// Summary for the BestLoveSong class.
/// </summary>
/// <remarks>
/// This is a longer description for the BestLoveSong class,
/// which is used as an example for Chapter 7.
/// </remarks>
public class BestLoveSong
{

    /// <summary>
    /// Name property </summary>
    /// <value>
    /// Returns the name of the best love song.</value>
    public string Name {
        get {
            return "Feelings";
        }
    }

    /// <summary>
    /// Plays the best love song.</summary>
    /// <param name="volume"> Volume to play the best love
    /// song.</param>
    public void Play(byte volume) {
        if (volume > 11)
            volume = 11;
    }
}
```

You can compile this example from the command line using the */doc* switch of the C# compiler as follows:

```
C:\>csc /target:library comments.cs /doc:comments.xml
```

Using this switch produces an XML file named *comments.xml*, as shown in Example 7-7.

*Example 7-7. XML documentation output*

```
<?xml version="1.0"?>
<doc>
    <assembly>
        <name>comments</name>
    </assembly>
    <members>
        <member name="T:BestLoveSong">
            <summary>
            Summary for the BestLoveSong class.
            </summary>
            <remarks>
            This is a longer description for the BestLoveSong
            class, which
            is used as an example for Chapter 7.
            </remarks>
        </member>
        <member name="M: BestLoveSong.Play(System.Byte)">
            <summary>
            Plays the best love song.</summary>
            <param name="volume">
            Volume to play the best love song.
            </param>
        </member>
        <member name="P: BestLoveSong.Name">
            <summary>
            Name property </summary>
            <value>
            Returns the name of the best love song.</value>
        </member>
    </members>
</doc>
```

This XML can now be processed in a variety of ways to create professional-looking documentation. In fact, this is how the class library documentation for the .NET Framework is created.

Example 7-6 demonstrates only a few of the most important XML comment tags: `<summary>`, `<remarks>`, `<param>`, and `<value>`. Pay close attention to the `<assembly>` and `<member>` tags. They were obtained using reflection and are not a direct part of the XML comments. There are actually quite a few more tags, but there is no time or space available to discuss them all.

Implementing XML comments in VB.NET by using custom attributes is possible. While similar results can be achieved, there is one major drawback to this approach. In C#, the XML tags are comments; they are not stored in the executable. The same cannot be said for attributes, which means that executable size could be significantly larger when using attributes in this manner. However, the degree to which executables expand can be offset greatly by using conditional compilation constants. The attributes might be added only in a debug build, for instance.

There is no doubt that XML comments will be available to VB.NET at some point in the future (if enough people scream for it), so consider this an interim solution. Or just consider it a fun lesson for custom attributes.

## Building a Custom Attribute

In addition to deriving from the `System.Attribute` class, custom attributes use an attribute: `AttributeUsage`.

`AttributeUsage` is actually `System.AttributeUsageAttribute`. From now on, though, attributes will be referred to by their shorthand names. Namespace prefixes and the "`Attribute`" suffix will not be used when discussing attributes.

`AttributeUsage` describes three things about the custom attribute that is being created:

- What class elements can the attribute be applied to?
- Will derived classes inherit the attributes once they are applied to the base class?
- Can the attribute be applied to the same class element more than once?

The first question is answered by the `AttributeTargets` enumeration, which contains all elements that can have attributes applied to them. The members of this enumeration, which are self-explanatory, are as follows: `All`, `Assembly`, `Class`, `Constructor`, `Delegate`, `Enum`, `Event`, `Field`, `Interface`, `Method`, `Module`, `Parameter`, `Property`, `ReturnValue`, and `Struct`.

Here is the basis of an attribute that can be applied to any element:

```
Imports System

<AttributeUsage(AttributeTargets.All)> _
Public Class SomeAttribute : Inherits Attribute

End Class
```

The target values can also be `ORed` together to provide a more granular selection. Here is a custom attribute that can be applied only to a class or a method:

```
Imports System

<AttributeUsage(AttributeTargets.Class Or AttributeTargets.Method)> _
Public Class SomeAttribute : Inherits Attribute

End Class
```

By default, attributes are inherited. However, this behavior can be changed using the `Attribute.Inherited` property:

```
Imports System

<AttributeUsage(AttributeTargets.All, Inherited:=False)> _
Public Class SomeAttribute : Inherits Attribute

End Class
```

Check out the := operator. When an attribute is applied, the constructor for the attribute class is actually called. For instance, the documentation for `AttributeUsage` looks like this:

```
Public Sub New(ByVal validOn As AttributeTargets)
```

The constructor has only one parameter, a member of the `AttributeTargets` enumeration. Inherited is a property of the `AttributeUsage` class. The := syntax is just a mechanism that allows an instance of an attribute to be created and a property to be set on that instance all in one go.

Attributes can be applied only once per element unless the `AllowMultiple` property is set to `True`:

```
Imports System

<AttributeUsage(AttributeTargets.All, _
                Inherited:=False, _
                AllowMultiple:=True)> _
Public Class SomeAttribute : Inherits Attribute

End Class
```

## SummaryAttribute

At this point, the concept of creating a custom attribute might still be nebulous. It's time to remedy that and start building the `SummaryAttribute` class used to imitate the `<summary>` comment tag defined by C#.

The process is actually quite simple. First, create a class that is derived from attribute:

```
Public Class SummaryAttribute : Inherits Attribute

End Class
```

The summary document comment is just a string. The desired behavior is essentially the following:

```
<Summary("This class does something really vague")> _
Public Class ThisClass
```

The attribute's string argument is actually the single argument passed to the constructor of SummaryAttribute:

```
Public Class SummaryAttribute : Inherits Attribute
    Public ReadOnly Text As String
    Public Sub New(ByVal text As String)
        Me.Text = text
    End Sub
End Class
```

A read-only field named Text is added to hold the string. Since the field is read-only, we can make it publicly accessible without difficulty. Later, when using reflection to get the summary attribute, it will be obtained through this field.

Adding the AttributeUsage attribute to the class is the final task. This step is shown in Example 7-8. The attribute can be applied to any element, so the AttributeTargets.All is used.

However, the SummaryAttribute class should not be inherited because this would prevent derived classes from having their own summary. Therefore, Inherited is set to False. Finally, the attribute will be used only once per element, so AllowMultiple is set to False as well.

*Example 7-8. SummaryAttribute class*

```
<AttributeUsage(AttributeTargets.All, _
               Inherited:=False, _
               AllowMultiple:=False)> _
Public Class SummaryAttribute : Inherits Attribute
    Public ReadOnly Text As String
    Public Sub New(ByVal text As String)
        Me.Text = text
    End Sub
End Class
```

You might wonder why the AllowMultiple property is set to False—because of this setting, the attribute is allowed only one application per element. After all, if multiple attributes were allowed, something like this would be possible:

```
<Summary("This class is used to demonstate the SummaryAttribute"), _
 Summary("class that has been created for Chapter 7."), _
 Summary("Unfortunately we cannot use multiple attributes like this")"> _
```

The problem is that attributes are not stored in the assembly in any particular order. It would be nice if they were stored in the order in which they were applied, but that is not the case. Using the summary attribute multiple times would require that we write an alternative sorting method, and possibly that we add an additional parameter in the constructor that specifies the sort order.

This leads to another issue: the formatting of the text stored with the Summary attribute (and the other attributes that will be defined in this chapter). Because the summary is stored as one block of text, a method of formatting it is needed (if, in fact, formatting is necessary).

## Additional Documentation Attributes

The remaining documentation attributes are about the same as Summary. The differences lie in where the attributes can be applied. The Remarks attribute is the same as Summary; it can be applied everywhere. The Param attribute can be applied only to a parameter. The Value attribute can be used only to describe a property's value.

The Param attribute is somewhat different from the others, since it can be applied multiple times. It contains an additional constructor argument that allows a name to be associated with the parameter:

```
<Param("key", "This is the key description"), _
 Param("entry", "This is the entry description")> _
Public Sub(ByVal key As Integer, ByVal entry As String)
```

Example 7-9 shows the code for the remaining attributes. Each class is implemented in basically the same manner; as in the case of exceptions, it is the name of the class that is important.

By distinguishing among the various types of attributes (rather than using the Summary attribute for everything), you can position and format each attribute based on its type.

*Example 7-9. Additional documentation attributes*

```
<AttributeUsage(AttributeTargets.All, Inherited:=False, AllowMultiple:=False)> _
Public Class RemarksAttribute : Inherits Attribute
    Public ReadOnly Text As String
    Public Sub New(ByVal text As String)
        Me.Text = text
    End Sub
End Class

<AttributeUsage(AttributeTargets.Method Or _
                AttributeTargets.Constructor, _
                Inherited:=False, AllowMultiple:=True)> _
Public Class ParamAttribute : Inherits Attribute
    Public ReadOnly Name As String
    Public ReadOnly Text As String
    Public Sub New(ByVal name As String, ByVal text As String)
        Me.Name = name
        Me.Text = text
    End Sub
End Class

<AttributeUsage(AttributeTargets.Property, Inherited:=False, AllowMultiple:=False)> _
Public Class ValueAttribute : Inherits Attribute
```

*Example 7-9. Additional documentation attributes (continued)*

```
    Public ReadOnly Text As String
    Public Sub New(ByVal text As String)
        Me.Text = text
    End Sub
End Class
```

## HistoryAttribute

Before using these attributes, we can add one more attribute that is not based on some C# document tag. Since tracking changes to a class throughout the development cycle is useful, an attribute that will help with the process could be very helpful. This attribute can be implemented similarly to the other attributes; it will just contain more parameters in its constructor. It needs a name field to track who made the change, a date field to mark when the change was made, and a text field to hold the description of the change that was made.

Given the specifics of what the attribute needs to contain (and the previous examples), this attribute is trivial to implement. There is nothing to say that has not already been said, which is why the `HistoryAtribute` class is listed now, in its entirety, in Example 7-10.

*Example 7-10. Class history attribute*

```
<AttributeUsage(AttributeTargets.Class, _
                Inherited:=False, _
                AllowMultiple:=True)> _
Public Class HistoryAttribute : Inherits Attribute
    Implements IComparable

    Public Author As String
    Public [Date] As DateTime
    Public Change As String

    Public Sub New(ByVal Author As String, _
                   ByVal ChangeDate As String, _
                   ByVal Change As String)
        Me.Author = Author
        Me.[Date] = Convert.ToDateTime(ChangeDate)
        Me.Change = Change
    End Sub

    Public Function CompareTo(ByVal obj As Object) As Integer _
        Implements IComparable.CompareTo
        Dim ha As HistoryAttribute
        If TypeOf obj Is HistoryAttribute Then
            ha = CType(obj, HistoryAttribute)
            Return DateTime.Compare(Me.Date, ha.Date)
        End If
    End Function

End Class
```

This class also implements `IComparable` (see Chapter 5), which allows an array of `History` attributes to be sorted based on the entry date. The implementation checks to make sure the object being passed in is a `HistoryAttribute`. If it is, the call is delegated to `DateTime.Compare`, which determines how the dates should be sorted. This will be put to use in the next example.

## Custom Attributes at Work

Save all documentation attributes to a file named *myattributes.vb* and compile it to a class library. Then look at Example 7-11—it shows the `ServerInfo` class from the beginning of the chapter with several custom documentation attributes applied to it. Add the attributes and recompile.

*Example 7-11. Custom documentation attributes*

```
Imports System
Imports System.Diagnostics
Imports System.Net
Imports System.Threading

'Assumes attribute have been compiled to a library
'called myattributes.dll which is referened at compile time
'vbc /t:library /r:system.dll /r:myattributes.dll serverinfo.vb

<Summary("The Amazing ServerInfo Class(tm)"), _
 Remarks("This class provides simple machine info."), _
 History("JPH", "04/05/2002", _
         "Added ability to dump custom attributes"), _
 History("JPH", "04/06/2002", _
         "Broke all of the code suddenly"), _
 History("JPH", "04/07/2002", _
         "Fixed everything that I broke.")> _
Public Class ServerInfo

    Private machine As String
    Private ip As IPAddress

    Public Enum Tasks
        EnterInfiniteLoop = 1
        WasteMemory = 2
        Allocate2GigForTheBrowser = 3
        RandomlyDestroyProcess = 4
    End Enum

    Public Event TaskCompleted(ByVal obj As Object, ByVal e As EventArgs)

    Public Sub New()
        'Get machine info when object is created
        machine = Dns.GetHostName()
        Dim ipHost As IPHostEntry = Dns.GetHostByName(machine)
        ip = ipHost.AddressList(0)
```

*Example 7-11. Custom documentation attributes (continued)*

```
    End Sub

    'This routine only fires an event right now
    <Param("task", "The task you want to perform")> _
    Public Sub DoTask(ByVal task As Tasks)
        RaiseEvent TaskCompleted(Me, EventArgs.Empty)
    End Sub

    <Summary("Gets date and time on machine")> _
    Public Shared Function GetMachineTime() As DateTime
        Return DateTime.Now
    End Function

    <Summary("Returns percentage of processor being used")> _
    Public Function GetProcessorUsed() As Single
        If PerformanceCounterCategory.Exists("Processor") Then
            Dim pc As New PerformanceCounter("Processor", _
                "% Processor Time", "_Total", True)
            Dim sampleA As CounterSample
            Dim sampleB As CounterSample

            sampleA = pc.NextSample()
            Thread.Sleep(1000)
            sampleB = pc.NextSample()
            Return CounterSample.Calculate(sampleA, sampleB)
        End If
    End Function

    <Summary("Returns available memory is megabytes")> _
    Public Function GetAvailableMemory() As Long
        If PerformanceCounterCategory.Exists("Memory") Then
            Dim pc As New PerformanceCounter("Memory", "Available MBytes")
            Return pc.RawValue()
        End If
        Return 0
    End Function

    <Value("Return the name of the machine")> _
    Public ReadOnly Property MachineName() As String
        Get
            Return machine
        End Get
    End Property

    <Value("Returns the IP address of the machine")> _
    Public ReadOnly Property IPAddress() As IPAddress
        Get
            Return ip
        End Get
    End Property

End Class
```

In comparison to gathering type information using reflection, retrieving information on custom attributes using reflection is quite easy. Only two methods are needed for retrieving custom attributes:

- `GetCustomAttribute`
- `GetCustomAttributes`

These methods are members of `System.Type` and of each of the `Info` classes (like `ConstructorInfo`, `MethodInfo`, and `PropertyInfo`). In addition, they are shared methods of the `Attribute` class.

Much of the code from previous examples is already in place for navigating types in an assembly (it's somewhat lacking, but it will work here), so Example 7-3 can be modified to handle custom attributes. The real work will be ordering the attribute, which are not returned in any particular order. Unfortunately, ordering the attribute means that the arrays of returned custom attributes will have to be iterated several times to get the needed information. The custom attributes are extracted in the following order:

*For classes*

- Summary
- Remarks
- History

*For methods*

- Summary
- Remarks
- Param

*For properties*

- Summary
- Remarks
- Value

Using the `ObjectInfo` class from Example 7-3, a method can be added to handle each custom attribute. The first is `DumpSummary`, which is shown here:

```
Private Sub DumpSummary(ByVal o As Object)

    Dim summary As SummaryAttribute

    If TypeOf o Is Type Then
        summary = Attribute.GetCustomAttribute( _
            CType(o, Type), GetType(SummaryAttribute), False)
    ElseIf TypeOf o Is MemberInfo Then
        summary = Attribute.GetCustomAttribute( _
            CType(o, MemberInfo), GetType(SummaryAttribute), False)
    End If
```

```
        If Not summary Is Nothing Then
            Console.WriteLine("{0}{1}", vbTab, summary.Text)
        End If

    End Sub
```

DumpSummary takes an Object parameter because it must be able to handle retrieval of attributes from a Type (a class) or some derivative of MemberInfo: ConstructorInfo, MethodInfo, or PropertyInfo.

Several overloaded GetCustomAttribute methods are available, depending on the program element to which the attribute is applied. The one that works best here allows the attribute to be retrieved by name. The first parameter to the call is the Type where the custom attribute is located. The second is the Type of the attribute itself. And the third is a Boolean flag that indicates whether or not the inheritance chain should be searched for the attribute. If the summary attribute exists, the SummaryAttribute.Text property can be written out to the console.

The Remarks and Value attributes are implemented in just about the same manner as Summary because each attribute can be applied only once per entity. Value is slightly different because it can be applied only to a property, so the method responsible for it will accept only a PropertyInfo object as a parameter. The code used to extract custom Remarks and Value attributes is:

```
    Private Sub DumpRemarks(ByVal o As Object)

        Dim remarks As RemarksAttribute

        If TypeOf o Is Type Then
            remarks = Attribute.GetCustomAttribute( _
                CType(o, Type), GetType(RemarksAttribute), False)
        ElseIf TypeOf o Is MemberInfo Then
            remarks = Attribute.GetCustomAttribute( _
                CType(o, MemberInfo), GetType(RemarksAttribute), False)
        End If

        If Not remarks Is Nothing Then
            Console.WriteLine("{0}{1}", vbTab, remarks.Text)
        End If

    End Sub

    Private Sub DumpValue(ByVal p As PropertyInfo)

        Dim value() As ValueAttribute = _
            p.GetCustomAttributes(GetType(ValueAttribute), False)

        If value.Length Then
            Console.WriteLine("{0}{1}", vbTab, value(0).Text)
        End If

    End Sub
```

The method responsible for Param attributes requires a little more work because attributes are not ordered in the assembly. However, the Param attributes can be matched on the parameter name using reflection, so this is not really a big problem. The code for the DumpParameters method is:

```
Private Sub DumpParameters(ByVal m As MemberInfo, _
                           ByVal params() As ParameterInfo)

    Dim param As ParameterInfo
    Dim attribute As ParamAttribute
    Dim attributes() As ParamAttribute
    attributes = m.GetCustomAttributes( _
                GetType(ParamAttribute), False)

    If attributes.Length Then
        Console.WriteLine(String.Format("{0}Parameters:", vbTab))
    Else
        Return
    End If

    For Each param In params
        For Each attribute In attributes
            If String.Compare(attribute.Name, param.Name) = 0 Then
                Console.WriteLine("{0}{1}{2}", _
                    vbTab, vbTab, attribute.Name)
                Console.WriteLine("{0}{1}{2}", _
                    vbTab, vbTab, attribute.Text)
            End If
        Next attribute
    Next param

End Sub
```

DumpParameters needs to handle constructors and methods, which is why the first parameter to the method is a MemberInfo object (the parent to both ConstructorInfo and MethodInfo). The second parameter is an array of ParameterInfo objects that are retrieved before the method is called, by either DumpMethods or DumpConstructors.

This section concludes the discussion on reflection and attributes. Example 7-12 contains the final listing with all calls to the custom attribute retrieval methods in place. It is a monster of a listing! It also includes DumpHistory, which handles the history attribute from earlier in the chapter. When run, the output generated from the *ServerInfo.dll* assembly should look like this:

```
---------------------------------------------------------------------------
Class:  ServerInfo2.ServerInfo
        The Amazing ServerInfo Class(tm)
        This class provides simple machine info.

        History:
         4/5/2002 JPH Came up with this a mere two months before
                  publishing.
```

```
            4/6/2002 JPH Tried to load assembly remotely but failed
            4/7/2002 JPH No one seems to know anything about auto deploy.

    Constructors:
    Public Sub New()

    Events:
    TaskCompleted

    Properties:
    Public ReadOnly Property IPAddress() As System.Net.IPAddress
            Returns the IP address of the machine
    Public ReadOnly Property MachineName() As System.String
            Return the name of the machine

    Methods:
    Public Sub DoTask(task As ServerInfo2.ServerInfo+Tasks)
            Parameters:
                    task
                    The task you want to perform
    Public Shared Function GetMachineTime()
            Gets date and time on machine
    Public Function GetProcessorUsed()
            Calculates percentage of processor being used
            This routine uses a sampling performance counter
    Public Function GetAvailableMemory()
            Returns available memory is megabytes
```

This example is not a pretty formatting job, but that's life in the fast lane. If everything is done already, anyone could program a computer, right?

The `ObjectInfo` class is woefully incomplete, mainly due to lack of space. Look at all the code in this chapter for the partial implementation. The code doesn't do events or member data, so look at `EventInfo` and `FieldInfo` if curiosity takes hold. It also lacks support for reflecting inheritance or polymorphic attributes. Furthermore, it cannot determine what interfaces are implemented by a class.

All the classes involved in pursuing a full implementation were discussed. That's the good news. Here's some more good news: these classes, and especially `System.Type`, are incredibly full featured (and large).

*Example 7-12. Final listing of ObjectInfo.vb*

```
'assumes serverinfo.dll is in the same directory

Imports Microsoft.VisualBasic
Imports System
Imports System.Reflection

Public Class ObjectInfo

    Private Sub DumpConstructors(ByVal t As Type)

        Dim c As ConstructorInfo
```

*Example 7-12. Final listing of ObjectInfo.vb (continued)*

```
        Dim ci() As ConstructorInfo = _
            t.GetConstructors(BindingFlags.Public Or BindingFlags.Instance)

        Console.WriteLine()
        Console.WriteLine("Constructors:")

        For Each c In ci
            Dim s As String = c.ToString()
            Console.WriteLine(s.Replace("Void .ctor", "Public Sub New"))
            DumpSummary(c)
            DumpRemarks(c)
            DumpParameters(c, c.GetParameters())
        Next c

    End Sub

    Private Sub DumpEvents(ByVal t As Type)
        Dim e As EventInfo
        Dim ei As EventInfo() = _
                t.GetEvents(BindingFlags.Public Or _
                            BindingFlags.Instance)

        Console.WriteLine()
        Console.WriteLine("Events:")

        For Each e In ei
            Console.WriteLine(e.Name)
        Next e

    End Sub

    Private Sub DumpProperties(ByVal t As Type)

        Dim p As PropertyInfo
        Dim pi() As PropertyInfo = _
            t.GetProperties(BindingFlags.Public Or BindingFlags.Instance)

        Console.WriteLine()
        Console.WriteLine("Properties:")

        For Each p In pi
            Console.Write("Public ")
            If p.CanRead And p.CanWrite Then
            ElseIf p.CanRead Then
                Console.Write("ReadOnly ")
            ElseIf p.CanWrite Then
                Console.Write("WriteOnly ")
            End If
            Console.WriteLine("Property {0}() As {1}", _
                p.Name, p.PropertyType.ToString())
            DumpSummary(p)
            DumpRemarks(p)
            DumpValue(p)
```

*Example 7-12. Final listing of ObjectInfo.vb (continued)*

```
        Next p

    End Sub

    Private Sub DumpMethod(ByVal m As MethodInfo)

        Dim i As Integer
        Dim returnType As Type
        Dim returnString As String

        If m.IsPublic Then
            Console.Write("Public ")
        ElseIf m.IsPrivate Then
            Console.WriteLine("Private ")
        ElseIf m.IsFamily Then
            Console.WriteLine("Protected ")
        ElseIf m.IsAssembly Then
            Console.WriteLine("Friend ")
        ElseIf m.IsFamilyAndAssembly Then
            Console.WriteLine("Protected Friend ")
        End If

        If m.IsStatic Then
            Console.Write("Shared ")
        End If

        returnType = m.ReturnType

        If String.Compare(returnType.ToString(), "System.Void") <> 0 Then
            Console.Write("Function {0}(", m.Name)
            returnString = String.Format(" As {0}", returnType.ToString())
        Else
            Console.Write("Sub {0}(", m.Name)
        End If

        Dim parms() As ParameterInfo = m.GetParameters()
        For i = 0 To parms.Length - 1
            Console.Write(parms(i).Name)
            Console.Write(" As ")
            Console.Write(parms(i).ParameterType())

            If (i < parms.Length - 1) Then
                Console.Write(", ")
            End If
        Next i

        Console.WriteLine(")")

        DumpParameters(m, parms)

    End Sub

    Private Sub DumpMethods(ByVal t As Type)
```

*Example 7-12. Final listing of ObjectInfo.vb (continued)*

```
        Dim m As MethodInfo
        Dim mi() As MethodInfo = t.GetMethods()

        Console.WriteLine()
        Console.WriteLine("Methods:")

        For Each m In mi
            If m.DeclaringType.Equals(t) AndAlso _
               m.IsSpecialName = False Then
                DumpMethod(m)
                DumpSummary(m)
                DumpRemarks(m)
            End If
        Next m

    End Sub

    Private Sub DumpClassInfo(ByVal t As Type)

        Console.WriteLine(New String("-"c, 80))
        Console.WriteLine("Class: {0}{1}", vbTab, t.FullName)

        DumpSummary(t)
        DumpRemarks(t)
        DumpConstructors(t)
        DumpEvents(t)
        DumpProperties(t)
        DumpMethods(t)

        Console.WriteLine()

    End Sub

    Private Sub DumpSummary(ByVal o As Object)

        Dim summary As SummaryAttribute

        If TypeOf o Is Type Then
            summary = Attribute.GetCustomAttribute( _
                CType(o, Type), GetType(SummaryAttribute), False)
        ElseIf TypeOf o Is MemberInfo Then
            summary = Attribute.GetCustomAttribute( _
                CType(o, MemberInfo), GetType(SummaryAttribute), False)
        End If

        If Not summary Is Nothing Then
            Console.WriteLine("{0}{1}", vbTab, summary.Text)
        End If

    End Sub

    Private Sub DumpRemarks(ByVal o As Object)
```

*Example 7-12. Final listing of ObjectInfo.vb (continued)*

```
        Dim remarks As RemarksAttribute

        If TypeOf o Is Type Then
            remarks = Attribute.GetCustomAttribute( _
                CType(o, Type), GetType(RemarksAttribute), False)
        ElseIf TypeOf o Is MemberInfo Then
            remarks = Attribute.GetCustomAttribute( _
                CType(o, MemberInfo), GetType(RemarksAttribute), False)
        End If

        If Not remarks Is Nothing Then
            Console.WriteLine("{0}{1}", vbTab, remarks.Text)
        End If

    End Sub

    Private Sub DumpValue(ByVal p As PropertyInfo)

        Dim value() As ValueAttribute = _
            p.GetCustomAttributes(GetType(ValueAttribute), False)

        If value.Length Then
            Console.WriteLine("{0}{1}", vbTab, value(0).Text)
        End If

    End Sub

    Private Sub DumpParameters(ByVal m As MemberInfo, _
                               ByVal params() As ParameterInfo)

        Dim param As ParameterInfo
        Dim attribute As ParamAttribute
        Dim attributes() As ParamAttribute
        attributes = m.GetCustomAttributes( _
                        GetType(ParamAttribute), False)

        If attributes.Length Then
            Console.WriteLine(String.Format("{0}Parameters:", vbTab))
        Else
            Return
        End If

        For Each param In params
            For Each attribute In attributes
                If String.Compare(attribute.Name, param.Name) = 0 Then
                    Console.WriteLine("{0}{1}{2}", _
                        vbTab, vbTab, attribute.Name)
                    Console.WriteLine("{0}{1}{2}", _
                        vbTab, vbTab, attribute.Text)
                End If
            Next attribute
        Next param
```

*Example 7-12. Final listing of ObjectInfo.vb (continued)*

```
    End Sub

    Private Sub DumpHistory(ByVal t As Type)
        If Not t.IsClass Then
            Return
        End If
        Dim history As HistoryAttribute
        Dim histories() As HistoryAttribute = _
            Attribute.GetCustomAttributes _
            (t, GetType(HistoryAttribute), False)

        If histories.Length Then
            Array.Sort(histories)
            Console.WriteLine()
            Console.WriteLine("{0}History:", vbTab)
            For Each history In histories
                Console.WriteLine("{0} {1} {2} {3}", _
                    vbTab, _
                    history.Date.ToShortDateString(), _
                    history.Author, _
                    history.Change)
            Next
        End If
    End Sub

    Public Sub New(ByVal assemblyName As String)

        Dim a As [Assembly]
        If (assemblyName = Nothing) Then
            a = [Assembly].GetExecutingAssembly()
        Else
            a = [Assembly].LoadFrom(assemblyName)
        End If

        Dim t As Type
        Dim types As Type() = a.GetTypes()

        For Each t In types
            If t.IsClass Then
                DumpClassInfo(t)
            End If
        Next t

    End Sub

End Class

Public Class Application
    Public Shared Sub Main()
        Dim oi As New ObjectInfo("ServerInfo.dll")
        Console.ReadLine()
    End Sub
End Class
```

# CHAPTER 8

# Object In, Object Out

I/O in the .NET framework centers on the *stream*. Think of a stream as a flow of data. The process of using a stream can be likened to two people standing at opposite ends of a river. The person upstream puts a message in a bottle and drops it in. Downstream, the other person waits with a net to pull the bottle out and get the message. The only difference between a .NET stream and this allegorical river is that the stream flows both ways.

The stream is a useful abstraction that makes it possible to read and write data to and from a variety of sources generically. For the most part, the operations for reading bytes from a file, from memory, or from a network socket are identical.

## Streams

.NET has several types of streams, each of which is derived from `System.IO.Stream`:

`System.IO.FileStream`
: Provides a buffered stream used to read and write data from files.

`System.IO.MemoryStream`
: Provides a stream that is buffered in memory instead of physical storage. This stream can alleviate the need for temporary buffers and files.

`System.Net.Sockets.NetworkStream`
: Forward-only stream used to send and receive data through network sockets.

`System.Security.Cryptography.CryptoStream`
: Provides a stream that associates data to cryptographic transformations.

Generally, streams support the following actions:

- Reading using `Read` (synchronous) or `BeginRead` (asynchronous).
- Writing using `Write` (synchronous) or `BeginWrite` (asynchronous).
- Seeking to determine a position or change a location within the stream using `Seek`.

Not all streams support every action. NetworkStream, which is used to send and receive data through network sockets, does not support seeking, for example. However, it is easy to determine what capabilities a stream supports by calling CanRead, CanWrite, or CanSeek.

.NET also supports a buffered stream, which is encapsulated by the System.IO.BufferedStream class. A *buffered stream* contains a backing memory store that acts as a cache for read and write operations. It is most commonly used in conjunction with a NetworkStream, as data is usually read and written in chunks over a socket. The FileStream class already contains internal buffering, and memory streams are inherently buffered, so a buffered stream is not applicable with these types.

## FileStream

Consider the file *everything.txt*, which contains the quotation, "When you understand one thing through and through, you understand everything."

It is fairly easy to obtain a stream that allows data to be read from the file. Example 8-1 demonstrates the process. The constructor of the FileStream class takes a path to a file and a combination of members of the FileMode or FileAccess enumerations designating the needed access.

*Example 8-1. Reading from a file stream*

```
Imports System
Imports System.IO
Imports System.Text

Public Class StreamTest

    Public Sub New()

        Dim bytesRead As Integer
        Dim buffer(256) As Byte
        Dim fs As New FileStream("everything.txt", _
                                 FileMode.Open, _
                                 FileAccess.ReadWrite)
        bytesRead = fs.Read(buffer, 0, buffer.Length)
        While (bytesRead > 0)
            Dim i As Integer
            For i = 0 To bytesRead - 1
                Console.Write(buffer(i).ToString)
            Next i
            bytesRead = fs.Read(buffer, 0, buffer.Length)
        End While

    End Sub

End Class
```

*Example 8-1. Reading from a file stream (continued)*

```
Public Class Application
    Public Shared Sub Main()
        Dim test As New StreamTest()
        Console.ReadLine()
    End Sub
End Class
```

After the stream is acquired, the file's contents are read into an array of `Byte`. Just to be clear, a `Byte` is not the same thing as a `Char`. When the buffer is dumped to the console, the output is the following, very uninformative sequence:

```
8710410111032121111117321171101001011141151169711010032111110101321161041051101033211
6104114111117103104329711010032116104114111117103104321211111173211711010010111411511
6971101003210111810111412111610410511010346
```

A `Byte` is an 8-bit unsigned integer, while a `Char` is a 2-byte Unicode character. Fundamentally, streams just involve reading and writing bytes. No underlying notion of data type or representation of data is built into the stream. For that, other classes elsewhere in the framework can help.

### System.Text.Encoding

The `System.Text` namespace contains a class called `Encoding` whose derivates contain facilities for conversion between bytes, characters, and strings in several different encoding schemes: ASCII, Unicode, UTF7, and UTF8. Each format is encapsulated by a class, but shared methods of the `Encoding` base class return instances of each one.

Assuming that the `System.Text` namespace is imported, the `Encoding.ASCII` method can convert the buffer into something more readily understandable by human eyes. The code from Example 8-1 then changes as follows:

```
'From Example 8-1
'Dim i As Integer
'For i = 0 To bytesRead - 1
'    Console.Write(buffer(i).ToString)
'Next i

Dim s As String = Encoding.ASCII.GetString(buffer)
Console.WriteLine(s)
```

This code returns something a little more meaningful:

```
When you understand one thing through and through you understand everything.
```

### Writing to a stream

The stream in Example 8-1 was opened explicitly for reading and writing, so it is possible to write back to it. Normally, when opening a file for writing, the `Seek` method must be called to move to the end of the stream (unless the file contents will be overwritten). This method takes the offset of the stream to seek from and the destination, which is of type SeekOrigin:

```
fs.Seek(0, SeekOrigin.End)
```

We do not have to call Seek here. The pointer is already positioned at the end of the stream because the entire stream was just read into *buffer*.

Before a write operation to a stream can occur, whatever is to be written to the stream must first be converted to an array of bytes. This process of conversion is called *serialization* and will be discussed in depth later in the chapter. In the case of strings, the Encoding class again comes to the rescue. It provides a method called GetBytes that can handle the necessary details of the conversion. Here, the name of the author of the quotation in Example 8-1 is written back to file via the stream:

```
bytesRead = fs.Read(buffer, 0, buffer.Length)
While (bytesRead > 0)
    Dim s As String = Encoding.ASCII.GetString(buffer)
    Console.WriteLine(s)
    bytesRead = fs.Read(buffer, 0, buffer.Length)
End While

Dim author() As Byte = Encoding.ASCII.GetBytes("Shunryu Suzuki")
fs.Write(author, 0, author.Length)
fs.Close()
```

There is an important concept to understand about streams. When the Write method is called, nothing is actually written to the file. How is that for a misleading method name? Instead, the data was written to the internal buffer of the FileStream. To get it to the file, one of two things must occur. If reading and writing is to continue, the buffer can be written to the file by calling Stream.Flush:

```
fs.Flush()
```

This method call clears the internal buffer and copies the contents into the file, but leaves the stream open for further reading and writing. If the stream is no longer needed, call Stream.Close:

```
fs.Close()
```

Close performs the same functions as Flush, but it also calls Dispose and releases the lock on the file. Remember that this behavior is the same, regardless of the type of stream. When working with streams, remember that like any limited resources (such as file handles and network connections), it is good practice to free the stream as soon as possible. Example 8-2 contains the complete listing for the exercise of reading and writing to a file.

*Example 8-2. Reading and writing to a file stream*

```
Imports System
Imports System.IO
Imports System.Text
```

*Example 8-2. Reading and writing to a file stream (continued)*

```
Public Class StreamTest

    Public Sub New()

        Dim bytesRead As Integer
        Dim buffer(256) As Byte
        Dim fs As New FileStream("everything.txt", _
                                 FileMode.Open, _
                                 FileAccess.ReadWrite)

        'Read from stream and write to the console
        bytesRead = fs.Read(buffer, 0, buffer.Length)
        While (bytesRead > 0)
            Dim s As String = Encoding.ASCII.GetString(buffer)
            Console.WriteLine(s)
            bytesRead = fs.Read(buffer, 0, buffer.Length)
        End While

        'Append author's name to the end of the file
        Dim author() As Byte = Encoding.ASCII.GetBytes("Shunryu Suzuki")
        fs.Write(author, 0, author.Length)
        fs.Close()

    End Sub

End Class

Public Class Application
    Public Shared Sub Main()
        Dim test As New StreamTest()
        Console.ReadLine()
    End Sub
End Class
```

## Readers and Writers

Although reading and writing directly to a stream is possible, working with an array of bytes can be difficult if the data in question is composed of integers, longs, doubles, or other primitive data types—or objects, for that matter. Fortunately, there are classes available (in `System.IO`) whose sole purpose is to assist in reading and writing data to streams.

`BinaryReader` and `BinaryWriter` read and write primitive data types from a stream. There are also several readers and writers designed for character-based input and output, as opposed to "raw" bytes. These classes are derived from `TextReader` and `TextWriter`. Specifically, they are called `StringReader/Writer` and `StreamReader/Writer`.

## BinaryReader and BinaryWriter

In Example 8-3, a file stream creates a stream to a file called *data.bin*. The stream instance constructs a `BinaryWriter`, which allows primitive data types to be written to the store.

*Example 8-3. Using BinaryWriter*

```
Imports System
Imports System.IO

Public Class StreamTest2

    Public Sub New()

        Dim stream As New FileStream("data.bin", _
                                     FileMode.Create, _
                                     FileAccess.ReadWrite)

        Dim writer As New BinaryWriter(stream)

        Dim b As Byte = 1
        Dim i As Integer = 2
        Dim l As Long = 3
        Dim d As Double = 3.1459
        Dim s As String = "It's easy as ABC"

        writer.Write(b)
        writer.Write(i)
        writer.Write(l)
        writer.Write(d)
        writer.Write(s)

        writer.Close()

        Console.WriteLine("File written...")

    End Sub

End Class

Public Class Application
    Public Shared Sub Main()
        Dim test As New StreamTest2()
        Console.ReadLine()
    End Sub
End Class
```

After initializing a few variables with arbitrary values, the program writes them to the stream by using the `BinaryWriter.Write` method, which is overloaded for every type defined in the `System` namespace. The writer is then closed, and two things happen. The underlying stream is closed and the contents are written to the file.

The Read method isn't overloaded because there is no way to distinguish a byte with a value of 1 from an integer with a value of 1. Instead, several Read*datatype* methods are defined for all the primitive types (including the non–CLS-compliant types). The following code, which reads back the data that was written to *data.bin*, illustrates the use of these Read... methods:

```
Dim stream2 As New FileStream("data.bin", _
                    FileMode.Open, _
                    FileAccess.Read)

Dim reader As New BinaryReader(stream2)

b = reader.ReadByte()
i = reader.ReadInt32()
l = reader.ReadInt64()
d = reader.ReadDouble()
s = reader.ReadString()

Console.WriteLine("{0} {1}, {2}, {3}, {4}", s, b, i, l, d)

reader.Close()
```

One element of this code might not be straightforward. When the string is written to the file, the length of the string is encoded as an integer and placed before the string. This value is calculated 8-bits at a time, which is very efficient in terms of physical storage.

Example 8-4 contains the entire listing used to write to and read from *data.bin*.

*Example 8-4. Using BinaryReader and BinaryWriter*

```
Imports System
Imports System.IO

Public Class StreamTest2

    Public Sub New()

        Dim stream As New FileStream("data.bin", _
                            FileMode.Create, _
                            FileAccess.ReadWrite)

        Dim writer As New BinaryWriter(stream)

        Dim b As Byte = 1
        Dim i As Integer = 2
        Dim l As Long = 3
        Dim d As Double = 3.1459
        Dim s As String = "It's easy as ABC"

        writer.Write(b)
        writer.Write(i)
```

*Example 8-4. Using BinaryReader and BinaryWriter (continued)*

```
        writer.Write(l)
        writer.Write(d)
        writer.Write(s)

        writer.Close()

        Console.WriteLine("File written...")

        Console.WriteLine("Reading from file...")

        Dim stream2 As New FileStream("data.bin", _
                          FileMode.Open, _
                          FileAccess.Read)

        Dim reader As New BinaryReader(stream2)

        b = reader.ReadByte()
        i = reader.ReadInt32()
        l = reader.ReadInt64()
        d = reader.ReadDouble()
        s = reader.ReadString()

        Console.WriteLine("{0} {1}, {2}, {3}, {4}", s, b, i, l, d)

        reader.Close()

    End Sub

End Class

Public Class Application
    Public Shared Sub Main()
        Dim test As New StreamTest2()
        Console.ReadLine()
    End Sub
End Class
```

## StreamReader and StreamWriter

Earlier in this chapter, the `System.Text.Encoding` class was used to convert an array of bytes into a string. This example demonstrated how difficult it could be to work directly with a stream. While using `Encoding` like this works, a better alternative uses `StreamReader`. This class contains a `Read` method similar to that of `Stream`, but it returns characters instead of bytes.

What about `StringReader`? It is not used for reading strings from a stream, but to stream data from a string. `StringWriter`, conversely, writes to a string.

Other Read methods simplify reading text-based input. StreamReader.ReadLine, shown here, reads from the stream until it finds a linefeed, a carriage return followed by a linefeed, or until it reaches the end of the stream. For example, the following code uses the StreamReader object's ReadLine method to read the single line of text from *everything.txt*:

```
Dim stream As New FileStream("everything.txt", _
                    FileMode.Open, _
                    FileAccess.Read)
Dim reader As New StreamReader(stream, Encoding.ASCII)
Console.WriteLine(reader.ReadLine())
reader.Close()
```

A method called ReadToEnd can also be useful at times. It reads the stream from the current position all the way to the end and returns the result in a string.

The best performance, however, is realized by using the StreamReader class' Read method with an external buffer (shown in Example 8-5) that matches the size of the reader's internal buffer. By default, if a size is not specified, the internal buffer will be 4k. However, a 256-byte buffer works well with small amounts of data.

*Example 8-5. High-performance stream access*

```
Imports System
Imports System.IO
Imports System.Text

Public Class StreamTest3

    Public Sub New()

        Dim count As Integer
        Dim buffer(256) As Char
        Dim stream As New FileStream("everything.txt", _
                            FileMode.Open, _
                            FileAccess.Read)

        Dim reader As New StreamReader(stream, _
                            Encoding.ASCII, _
                            False, _
                            buffer.Length)

        count = reader.Read(buffer, 0, buffer.Length)
        While count > 0
            Console.WriteLine(buffer)
            count = reader.Read(buffer, 0, buffer.Length)
        End While

    End Sub

End Class

Public Class Application
```

*Example 8-5. High-performance stream access (continued)*

```
    Public Shared Sub Main()
        Dim test As New StreamTest3()
        Console.ReadLine()
    End Sub
End Class
```

`StreamWriter` is not discussed here because it is merely the inverse of `StreamReader`. It contains an overloaded `Write` method just like `BinaryWriter`, as well as a `WriteLine` method, which writes to the stream just like `Console.WriteLine` writes to the console window. And speaking of the console ...

## Console

The console uses a `TextReader` object to get input from the keyboard (known as the standard input stream), a `TextWriter` object to write to the screen (known as the standard output stream), and another `TextWriter` object to write to the standard error stream, which, by default, is the screen. Each object is available through the shared properties `In`, `Out`, and `Error`, respectively.

You can also redirect any of these streams by using `SetIn`, `SetOut`, and `SetError`. For instance, console input and output could be redirected to a file or a socket. Example 8-6 demonstrates redirection by sending standard output to a file. An exception is then intentionally generated and written to a file using `Console.WriteLine`. The original `TextWriter` used by the console is saved before output is redirected. After the exception is written to the file, it restores the console to its original state.

*Example 8-6. Redirecting console output*

```
Imports System
Imports System.IO

Public Class StreamTest4

    Public Sub New()
        Dim stream As New FileStream("error.txt", _
                          FileMode.OpenOrCreate, _
                          FileAccess.Write)

        Dim writer As New StreamWriter(stream)

        'Save text writer
        Dim oldWriter As TextWriter = Console.Out

        'Set console output to error.txt
        Console.SetOut(writer)

        Try
            'Divide by zero
```

*Example 8-6. Redirecting console output (continued)*

```
            Dim x As Long = 0
            Dim y As Long = 8 \ x
        Catch e As Exception
            'Write to the error.txt
            Console.WriteLine(e)
        End Try

        writer.Close()

        'Restore old text writer
        Console.SetOut(oldWriter)

    End Sub

End Class

Public Class Application
    Public Shared Sub Main()
        Dim test As New StreamTest4()
        Console.WriteLine("Complete")
        Console.ReadLine()
    End Sub
End Class
```

Multithreaded programming provides a real-world scenario for redirecting standard output. If several threads write to the console, the calls need to be synchronized; `Console.WriteLine` is not thread-safe. Output in these conditions will contain some garbage because multiple calls to `Console.Write` or `WriteLine` will step on each other.

To remedy this problem, `TextWriter.Synchronized` can place a thread-safe wrapper around the console `TextWriter`:

```
Console.SetOut(TextWriter.Synchronized(Console.Out))
```

# Serialization

Reading and writing primitive data types to and from a stream is one thing, but what about objects? Converting an object to a stream is called *serialization*, and it is used for two primary purposes. The first is to persist an object to storage (such as a file) with the intent of recreating it later. The second is to send an object by value (marshal by value) to another computer or application domain. Serialization is necessary because an object is valid only within the application domain in which it was created. If the architecture demands that objects be shared or used in a distributed environment, then serialization is necessary. Serialization plays a major role in .NET remoting and, fortunately, the framework does most of the work.

When an object is serialized, the name of the assembly (this is the type boundary, after all), the class, and the member data are added to the stream. During this process, any referenced objects are serialized, too (if they are eligible). This is often called an *object graph*. Circular references are not a problem in the case of object graphs because the CLR keeps track of each serialized object to ensure that the object is not serialized more than once.

This chapter discusses two types of serialization:

- Binary serialization
- XML and SOAP serialization

Binary serialization maintains type integrity, which means that every aspect of the object is preserved, including private member data. Maintaining type integrity is useful in situations when state must be maintained, such as in a tightly coupled distributed application.

XML serialization, on the other hand, is not concerned with preservation. Only the public properties and fields of the class are serialized. The assembly name is not included, so technically an object that was serialized to XML no longer represents a type; it's just data. This is perfect in situations when the data must be consumed and its source is irrelevant.

For instance, a shopping cart object(s) could be serialized to XML to represent an order and passed to an order processor. The order processor doesn't care that the data came from the shopping cart; it just wants XML that conforms to a particular XSD schema. Because there is no affinity between the shopping cart and the order processor, it is now possible to get orders from anywhere—from an affiliated web site, perhaps. In other words, receiving orders is not limited to using a shopping cart on the web site. Using binary serialization in this situation would bind the shopping cart and the order processor together because the order processor would need specific knowledge of the shopping cart type to deserialize it.

## Serializable and NonSerialized Attributes

Regardless of the serialization technique, the runtime has to know that an object can be serialized. As shown in Example 8-7, this is done by applying the `Serializable` attribute to the type. Anything that requires exclusion from the serialization process can opt out with the `NonSerialized` attribute.

*Example 8-7. Serialization attributes*

```
<Serializable()> _
Public Class Employee

    Public Sub New()
        Console.WriteLine("Constructor called")
    End Sub

    <NonSerialized()> _
    Public employeeID As Integer 'Primary key in database

    Public FirstName As String
    Public LastName As String
    Public Department As String
```

*Example 8-7. Serialization attributes (continued)*

```
End Class

Public Class Test

    Public Shared Sub Main()

        Dim empIn As New Employee()
        empIn.employeeID = 42
        empIn.FirstName = "Bruce"
        empIn.LastName = "Banner"
        empIn.Department = "Nuclear Engineering"

        'Serialization code will go here

    End Sub

End Class
```

Normally, data that is excluded has no meaning outside the context of its current domain. Using the shopping cart/order processor example, quite a bit of data might be used to maintain the shopping cart that does not relate to an order directly. For instance, the order processor just needs item identifiers and payment information to do its job. It doesn't need descriptive text for the items in the cart (this text is used for the benefit of the customer when the shopping cart is rendered to HTML).

Ignore the fact that the `Employee` class is horribly designed. Just to keep things simple, everything that will be serialized is contained in a public field and left wide open, with no encapsulation of data whatsoever. The exception is the `employeeID` field, which is the primary key for the employee record in the database (assuming there is a database somewhere). This field demonstrates the `NonSerialized` attribute and gives the sample a minute degree of credibility.

## Binary Serialization

To serialize the `Employee` object from Example 8-7 into binary form, the `System.Runtime.Serialization.Formatters` namespace must be imported to provide access to the `BinaryFormatter` class.

A formatter is simply a class designed to serialize an object to a specific format. In .NET, there are two formatters: `BinaryFormatter` and `SoapFormatter`. Another class, called `XMLSerializer`, can serialize an object to XML. This process will be discussed shortly.

Once the object is ready for serialization (i.e., it has state), the binary formatter can be used in conjunction with a `FileStream` to write the object to a file in only a few lines of code. Example 8-8 illustrates this; it is identical to Example 8-7 except for the code that handles binary serialization, which is shown in boldface.

*Example 8-8. Binary formatters, Part I*

```
Imports System
Imports System.IO
Imports System.Runtime.Serialization.Formatters.Binary

<Serializable()> _
Public Class Employee

    Public Sub New()
        Console.WriteLine("Constructor called")
    End Sub

    <NonSerialized()> _
    Public employeeID As Integer 'Primary key in database

    Public FirstName As String
    Public LastName As String
    Public Department As String

End Class

Public Class Test

    Public Shared Sub Main()

        Dim emp As New Employee()
        emp.employeeID = 42
        emp.FirstName = "Bruce"
        emp.LastName = "Banner"
        emp.Department = "Nuclear Engineering"

        Dim formatter As New BinaryFormatter()
        Dim streamIn As New FileStream("employee.bin", _
                            FileMode.Create, _
                            FileAccess.Write)
        formatter.Serialize(streamIn, emp)
        streamIn.Close()

        Console.Write("Serialized. Press ENTER to continue...")
        Console.ReadLine()

        'Deserialization code will go here

    End Sub

End Class
```

The formatter contains all of the functionality: a Serialize method and a Deserialize method. The Serialize method requires a stream and an object instance to fulfill its obligations. As shown in Example 8-9, Deserialize requires only a stream to an object store—in this case, *employee.bin*.

*Example 8-9. Binary formatters, Part II*

```
Imports System
Imports System.IO
Imports System.Runtime.Serialization.Formatters.Binary

<Serializable()> _
Public Class Employee

    Public Sub New()
        Console.WriteLine("Constructor called")
    End Sub

    <NonSerialized()> _
    Public employeeID As Integer 'Primary key in database

    Public FirstName As String
    Public LastName As String
    Public Department As String

End Class

Public Class Test

    Public Shared Sub Main()

        Dim empIn As New Employee()
        empIn.employeeID = 42
        empIn.FirstName = "Bruce"
        empIn.LastName = "Banner"
        empIn.Department = "Nuclear Engineering"

        Dim formatter As New BinaryFormatter()
        Dim streamIn As New FileStream("employee.bin", _
                             FileMode.Create, _
                             FileAccess.Write)
        formatter.Serialize(streamIn, empIn)
        streamIn.Close()

        Console.Write("Serialized. Press ENTER to continue...")
        Console.ReadLine()

        Console.WriteLine("Deserializing...")
        Dim streamOut As New FileStream("employee.bin", _
                             FileMode.Open, _
                             FileAccess.Read)
        Dim empOut As Employee = _
            CType(formatter.Deserialize(streamOut), Employee)

        Console.WriteLine(empOut.employeeID.ToString())
        Console.WriteLine(empOut.FirstName)
        Console.WriteLine(empOut.LastName)
        Console.WriteLine(empOut.Department)

        Console.Write("Complete. Press ENTER to continue...")
        Console.ReadLine()
```

*Example 8-9. Binary formatters, Part II (continued)*

```
    End Sub

End Class
```

After opening *employee.bin* for reading, `formatter.Deserialize` is called to deserialize the object from the stream. `CType` casts the returned `Object` to an `Employee` type, and the object's state is then written to the console. It should appear as follows:

```
0
Bruce
Banner
Nuclear Engineering
```

The first item of displayed information, the `employeeID`, is `0` because it was not serialized. Really, the whole process is reminiscent of cooking dehydrated mashed potatoes from a box.

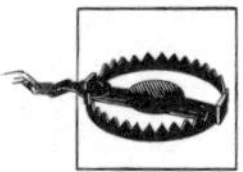

When designing objects that must be persisted or transported remotely, remember that constructors are not called when objects are deserialized.

### ICloneable and MemoryStream

Binary formatting is also used to clone objects. Chapter 5 discussed the `ICloneable` interface, but the details of how to implement it had to be left out until now; it requires a memory stream and a binary formatter.

The interface has one method called `Clone`, which is supposed to return a copy of an object. When the call is complete, there should be two identical object instances, as opposed to two references on one object.

Example 8-10 modifies the `Employee` class from the last example to implement the `ICloneable` interface. The implementation is actually contained in a private method called CloneImp. This is done because `ICloneable.Clone` returns an `Object`. By implementing the interface privately, the public method `Employee.Clone` can delegate to `CloneImp` and convert the returned `Object` into an `Employee` for the caller; definitely a more type-safe approach.

*Example 8-10. Object cloning*

```
Imports System
Imports System.IO
Imports System.Runtime.Serialization.Formatters.Binary

<Serializable()> _
Public Class Employee
    Implements ICloneable

    <NonSerialized()> _
    Public employeeID As Integer 'Primary key in database
```

*Example 8-10. Object cloning (continued)*

```
    Public FirstName As String
    Public LastName As String
    Public Department As String

    Public Function Clone() As Employee
        Return CType(CloneImp(), Employee)
    End Function

    Private Function CloneImp() As Object Implements ICloneable.Clone
        Dim stream As New MemoryStream()
        Dim formatter As New BinaryFormatter()
        formatter.Serialize(stream, Me)
        stream.Seek(0, SeekOrigin.Begin)
        Return formatter.Deserialize(stream)
    End Function

End Class

Public Class Test

    Public Shared Sub Main()
        Dim empIn As New Employee()
        empIn.employeeID = 42
        empIn.FirstName = "Bruce"
        empIn.LastName = "Banner"
        empIn.Department = "Nuclear Engineering"

        Dim empOut As Employee = empIn.Clone()

        Console.WriteLine(empOut.employeeID.ToString())
        Console.WriteLine(empOut.FirstName)
        Console.WriteLine(empOut.LastName)
        Console.WriteLine(empOut.Department)

        Console.ReadLine()

    End Sub

End Class
```

Nothing in this example is new. A memory stream works just like any other stream, and the binary formatter doesn't care about what type of stream it has. Once the object is serialized into the stream, a binary copy of the object is in memory. The only thing left to do is turn right around and deserialize it (don't forget to move the stream position back to the beginning first).

The `ICloneable` implementation is overkill for this class, but think about an extremely large object. Making a copy of an object that has a hundred members in only five lines of code is definitely worth this minimal amount of effort.

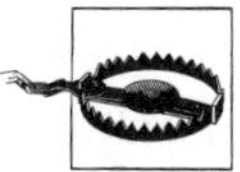

When writing Exception classes, make sure they are decorated with the `Serializable` attribute so that the exceptions can be thrown across application domains and machine boundaries.

## SOAP Serialization

Check the contents of *employee.bin* to verify that it contains binary data; with a few simple changes to Examples 8-7 through 8-9, it can be serialized to SOAP-compliant XML.

Only two things need to be done to this example to accomplish this goal. First, run a global find and replace on the source file and change every instance of "Binary" to "Soap." The second change occurs at compile time. An additional DLL must be referenced. It probably has the longest name in the modern programming world:

```
vbc /t:exe /r:System.Runtime.Serialization.Formatters.Soap.dll
    employee.vb
```

Change the name of the storage file to *employee.xml*. Then, as shown in Figure 8-1, the results can be viewed in Internet Explorer, which formats XML in a hierarchical display.

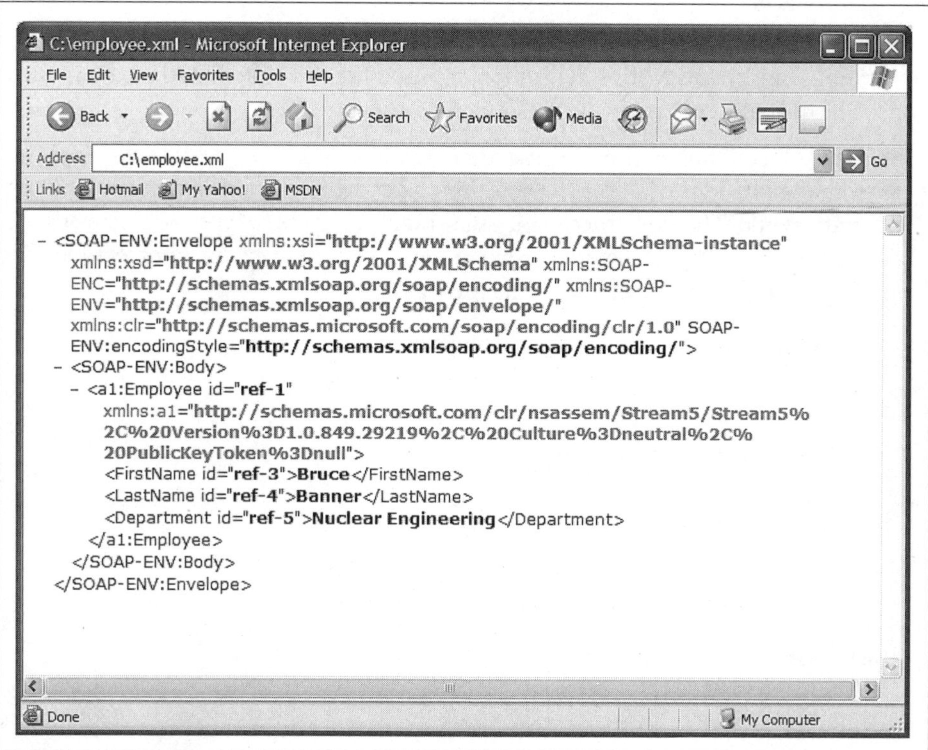


*Figure 8-1. Employee object as SOAP-compliant XML*

## XML Serialization

If absolute control over serialization is needed to ensure conformation to a specific XML schema definition (XSD), look no further than the `XmlSerializer` class found in the `System.Xml.Serialization` namespace. It does it all: defining namespaces, encoding fields as attributes or elements, and renaming elements and attributes to accommodate any need.

XML serialization has some limitations. For one, only public properties and fields are serialized. Also, properties and fields must be read/write; read-only properties and fields are not serialized. This limitation could lead to some very bad class design; in order for XML serialization to work, all data for a given class must be exposed.

Think about what it means to serialize an object as XML versus binary data, and then make the decisions regarding design. Binary serialization involves maintaining the complete state of an object between uses. The complete type is preserved (assembly, class name, and private variables) so that when deserialization occurs, *exactly the same object* is recreated. XML serialization, on the other hand, describes an object; after all, that is what the public properties of a class represent. This description is useful when parts of an application need to consume data and do not care about objects, let alone maintaining their state.

The tendency exists to expose more in order to serialize an object to XML. Resist the temptation. Binary and XML serialization are used for two different kinds of applications. The old rules still apply; hide as much data as possible.

Example 8-11 contains a short listing that demonstrates how to use the `Employee` class from the previous examples. It's nothing new, which is part of the beauty of the .NET framework. The constructor for `XmlSerializer` takes a `Type` parameter that is obtained by calling `Object.GetType`. Remember, a class represents an object of some kind. A `Type`, in this instance, represents the class itself.

*Example 8-11. XML serialization*

```
Imports System
Imports System.IO
Imports System.Xml.Serialization

<Serializable()> _
Public Class Employee

    <NonSerialized()> _
    Public employeeID As Integer 'Primary key in database

    Public FirstName As String
    Public LastName As String
    Public Department As String

End Class

Public Class Test
```

*Example 8-11. XML serialization (continued)*

```
    Public Shared Sub Main()
        Dim emp As New Employee()
        emp.employeeID = 9112001
        emp.FirstName = "Peter"
        emp.LastName = "Parker"
        emp.Department = "Photography"

        Dim employeeType As Type = emp.GetType()
        Dim serializer As New XmlSerializer(employeeType)
        Dim writer As New StreamWriter("employee.xml")
        serializer.Serialize(writer, emp)
        writer.Close()
    End Sub

End Class
```

The output to the *employee.bin* file (shown below) that results from this code is interesting because the XML serializer does not seem to care that the `employeeID` field is marked `NonSerialized`. To let the cat out of the bag, only the binary and the SOAP formatters are aware of `Serializable` and `NonSerialized`. The XML serializer does not care about the presence of these attributes, and it works off a whole different set of attributes and classes.

```
<?xml version="1.0" encoding="utf-8"?>
<Employee xmlns:xsd=http://www.w3.org/2001/XMLSchema
          xmlns:xsi=http://www.w3.org/2001/XMLSchema-instance>
  <employeeID>9112001</employeeID>
  <FirstName>Peter</FirstName>
  <LastName>Parker</LastName>
  <Department>Photography</Department>
</Employee>
```

By default, fields are serialized as XML elements, meaning they are wrapped in XML tags like this:

```
<FirstName>Peter Parker</FirstName>
```

If attributes are preferred, the `XMLAttribute` attribute can affect this change. It generates XML that looks like this:

```
<Employee FirstName="Peter Parker" .../>
```

Example 8-12 shows the `Employee` class again (it can replace the `Employee` class, shown in Example 8-11, with the rest of the code in Example 8-11 remaining unchanged). This time it is configured so that the fields are rendered as attributes. The `XMLIgnore` (as opposed to `NonSerialized`) attribute prevents the `employeeID` field from being serialized.

*Example 8-12. XML serialization as attributes*

```
Public Class Employee

    <XmlIgnore()> _
```

*Example 8-12. XML serialization as attributes (continued)*

```
    Public employeeID As Integer 'Primary key in database

    <XmlAttribute()> _
    Public FirstName As String
    <XmlAttribute()> _
    Public LastName As String
    <XmlAttribute()> _
    Public Department As String

End Class
```

Serializing this to XML now produces the output shown below. Notice that no elements are under Employee because all the fields were rendered as attributes:

```
<?xml version="1.0" encoding="utf-8"?>
<Employee xmlns:xsd=http://www.w3.org/2001/XMLSchema
          xmlns:xsi=http://www.w3.org/2001/XMLSchema-instance  FirstName="Peter"
LastName="Parker" Department="Photography" />
```

The System.Xml.Serialization namespace contains everything necessary to ensure that an object that conforms to any given schema can be serialized to XML. The XML output shown earlier declares two namespaces, and each has a qualifying prefix (*xsi* and *xsd*, respectively). This is the default behavior of the serializer, but it can be changed by using the XmlType attribute, as shown here (the local IP is used to protect the innocent):

```
<XmlType(Namespace:="http://192.168.1.1/", _
 TypeName:="NotoriousEmployee")> _
Public Class Employee

    <XmlIgnore()> _
    Public employeeID As Integer 'Primary key in database

    Public FirstName As String
    Public LastName As String
    Public Department As String

End Class
```

Running the code from Example 8-11 with this class produces the following output:

```
<?xml version="1.0" encoding="utf-8"?>
<NotoriousEmployee xmlns:xsd="http://www.w3.org/2001/XMLSchema" xmlns:xsi="http://
www.w3.org/2001/XMLSchema-instance">
  <FirstName xmlns="http://192.168.1.1/">Peter</FirstName>
  <LastName xmlns="http://192.168.1.1/">Parker</LastName>
  <Department xmlns="http://192.168.1.1/">Photography</Department>
</NotoriousEmployee>
```

Every field now has a namespace associated with it. However, this association might not be optimal. Namespace qualifiers are sometimes needed, but to get them, the serialization code needs to be modified. It's not done with an attribute—but it's done using the XmlSerializerNamespaces class.

XmlSerializerNamespaces has a method named Add that takes a key-value pair. As demonstrated in Example 8-13, the key is the prefix associated with the namespace, while the value is the XML namespace itself. After the qualifiers are defined, the object can be passed to XMLSerializer, which has an overloaded Serialize method that accepts an instance of XmlSerializerNamespaces.

*Example 8-13. Using XmlSerializerNamespaces*

```
<XmlType(Namespace:="http://192.168.1.1", _
 TypeName:="NotoriousEmployee")> _
Public Class Employee

    <XmlIgnore()> _
    Public employeeID As Integer 'Primary key in database

    Public FirstName As String
    Public LastName As String
    Public Department As String

End Class

Public Class Test

    Public Shared Sub Main()

        Dim emp As New Employee()
        emp.employeeID = 9112001
        emp.FirstName = "Peter"
        emp.LastName = "Parker"
        emp.Department = "Photography"

        Dim xmlNamespace As New XmlSerializerNamespaces()
        xmlNamespace.Add("eye", "http://192.168.1.1")

        Dim employeeType As Type = emp.GetType()
        Dim serializer As New XmlSerializer(employeeType)
        Dim writer As New StreamWriter("employee.xml")
        serializer.Serialize(writer, emp, xmlNamespace)
        writer.Close()

    End Sub

End Class
```

Now the output contains your own namespace, and all elements will be qualified with a prefix instead of an xmlns attribute—which is exactly what you want. The output appears as follows:

```
<?xml version="1.0" encoding="utf-8"?>
<NotoriousEmployee xmlns:eye="http://192.168.1.1">
  <eye:FirstName>Peter</eye:FirstName>
  <eye:LastName>Parker</eye:LastName>
  <eye:Department>Photography</eye:Department>
</NotoriousEmployee>
```

The namespace prefix that is passed to `XMLSerializerNamespaces` can be anything. However, the XML namespace *must* match the namespace used by the `XMLType` attribute.

XML in .NET is one of those topics that is so large that a whole book (and then some) could be written about it. If the chance arises, visit the `System.Xml.Serialization` documentation because what is covered here is only a small part of the picture. Just because this book doesn't discuss a topic doesn't mean it can't be done. XML in .NET is very robust; it has to be. After all, .NET uses XML serialization—it's a core part of the XML web services architecture.

## Schema Definition Tool

Help is available for applications in which XML is used extensively. The XML Schema Definition Tool makes it is possible to convert classes to an XSD document or convert an XSD document into a class. The tool is located in the *bin* directory of the .NET Framework SDK and is called *xsd.exe*. Given the schema:

```
<?xml version="1.0" encoding="utf-8"?>
<xs:schema elementFormDefault="qualified" xmlns:xs="http://www.w3.org/2001/XMLSchema"
>
  <xs:element name="Employee" type="Employee" />
  <xs:complexType name="Employee">
    <xs:sequence>
      <xs:element minOccurs="1" maxOccurs="1" name="employeeID"
                  type="xs:int" />
      <xs:element minOccurs="1" maxOccurs="1" name="FirstName"
                  type="xs:string" />
      <xs:element minOccurs="1" maxOccurs="1" name="LastName"
                  type="xs:string" />
      <xs:element minOccurs="1" maxOccurs="1" name="Department"
                  type="xs:string" />
    </xs:sequence>
  </xs:complexType>
</xs:schema>
```

The employee class can be generated like this:

```
C:\>xsd /classes /language:VB /namespace:MyApplication employee.xsd
```

This code generates a VB.NET class (versus an ADO.NET dataset) with the namespace `MyApplication`. The restriction is that the tool will only process schemas that contain the namespace `http://www.w3.org/2001/XMLSchema`, although additional namespaces can be part of the document. The output file, by default, has the same name as the schema definition, and in this case looks like this:

```
'------------------------------------------------------------------------------
' <autogenerated>
'     This code was generated by a tool.
'     Runtime Version: 1.0.3705.209
```

```
'
'     Changes to this file may cause incorrect behavior and will be lost if
'     the code is regenerated.
' </autogenerated>
'------------------------------------------------------------------------------

Option Strict Off
Option Explicit On

Imports System.Xml.Serialization

'
'This source code was auto-generated by xsd, Version=1.0.3705.209.
'
Namespace MyApplication

    '<remarks/>
    <System.Xml.Serialization.XmlRootAttribute([Namespace]:="", IsNullable:=false)>
_
    Public Class Employee

        '<remarks/>
        Public employeeID As Integer

        '<remarks/>
        Public FirstName As String

        '<remarks/>
        Public LastName As String

        '<remarks/>
        Public Department As String
    End Class
End Namespace
```

Going the other way, a schema can be generated for an existing assembly merely by providing the name to *xsd*:

```
C:\>xsd employee.dll
```

In this case, all classes in the assembly are added to the schema.

## Custom Serialization

Only public, read/write fields are serialized to XML, while binary serialization puts everything but the kitchen sink into the stream. Does this seem a little extreme? If more control is needed or if the default behavior doesn't do what needs to be done, the `ISerializable` interface provides an object with the means to control its own serialization. Implementing the interface is surprisingly simple. The interface contains a single method, called `GetObjectData`, with the following signature:

```
Sub GetObjectData(ByVal info As SerializationInfo, _
                  ByVal context As StreamingContext)
```

## SerializationInfo

As shown in Example 8-14, the first parameter to the GetObjectData method is a class called SerializationInfo that contains a method named AddValue. AddValue is overloaded to take all the native types from the System namespace, including Object and Type. Just pass it the data that needs to be serialized. Data is passed as a key-value pair so that values can be retrieved in any order (by name) during deserialization. Anything can be added to the stream, and additional business logic is easily incorporated.

*Example 8-14. Implementing ISerializable, Part I*

```
Imports System
Imports System.IO
Imports System.Runtime.Serialization
Imports System.Runtime.Serialization.Formatters.Binary

<Serializable()> _
Public Class Employee
    Implements ISerializable

    Private Sub GetObjectData(ByVal info As SerializationInfo, _
                              ByVal context As StreamingContext) _
                              Implements ISerializable.GetObjectData
        info.AddValue("First", FirstName)
        info.AddValue("Last", LastName)
        info.AddValue("Dept", Department)

        LastAccessed = DateTime.Now
        info.AddValue("AccessDate", LastAccessed)
    End Sub

    Public employeeID As Integer 'Primary key in database
    Public FirstName As String
    Public LastName As String
    Public Department As String
    Public LastAccessed As Date

End Class

Public Class Test

    Public Shared Sub Main()
        Dim empIn As New Employee()
        empIn.employeeID = 19283
        empIn.FirstName = "Lex"
        empIn.LastName = "Luthor"
        empIn.Department = "Operations"

        Dim formatter As New BinaryFormatter()
        Dim stream As New FileStream("employee.bin", _
                            FileMode.Create, _
                            FileAccess.ReadWrite)
```

*Example 8-14. Implementing ISerializable, Part I (continued)*

```
        formatter.Serialize(stream, empIn)

        'Leave stream open for now

    End Sub

End Class
```

ISerializable is somewhat special. For the process to work, a constructor with the same signature as GetObjectData must exist; this is where deserialization occurs. The use of this constructor is illustrated in Example 8-15, which both serializes and deserializes the Employee object. A side effect of adding this constructor is that a default constructor must now be declared explicitly. Values are retrieved in a manner similar to the way binary readers retrieve values. The incoming SerializationInfo instance contains several methods named with the following format: Get*datatype*, where *datatype* is a type defined in the System namespace. Each method takes the name of the parameter that is needed (which must match the key parameter in the AddValue call).

*Example 8-15. Implementing ISerializable, Part II*

```
Imports System
Imports System.IO
Imports System.Runtime.Serialization
Imports System.Runtime.Serialization.Formatters.Binary

<Serializable()> _
Public Class Employee
    Implements ISerializable

    Public Sub New()
        'Empty
    End Sub

    'Assure this constructor is not available in the public interface of
    'the class by making it a friend
    Friend Sub New(ByVal info As SerializationInfo, _
                   ByVal context As StreamingContext)
        FirstName = info.GetString("First")
        LastName = info.GetString("Last")
        Department = info.GetString("Dept")
        LastAccessed = info.GetDateTime("AccessDate")
    End Sub

    Private Sub GetObjectData(ByVal info As SerializationInfo, _
                              ByVal context As StreamingContext) _
                              Implements ISerializable.GetObjectData

        info.AddValue("First", FirstName)
        info.AddValue("Last", LastName)
        info.AddValue("Dept", Department)
```

*Example 8-15. Implementing ISerializable, Part II (continued)*

```
        LastAccessed = DateTime.Now
        info.AddValue("AccessDate", LastAccessed)

    End Sub

    Public employeeID As Integer 'Primary key in database
    Public FirstName As String
    Public LastName As String
    Public Department As String
    Public LastAccessed As Date

End Class

Public Class Test

    Public Shared Sub Main()

        Dim empIn As New Employee()
        empIn.employeeID = 19283
        empIn.FirstName = "Lex"
        empIn.LastName = "Luthor"
        empIn.Department = "Operations"

        Dim formatter As New BinaryFormatter()
        Dim stream As New FileStream("employee.bin", _
                         FileMode.Create, _
                         FileAccess.ReadWrite)
        formatter.Serialize(stream, empIn)

        'Position stream back to the beginning
        stream.Seek(0, SeekOrigin.Begin)

        Dim empOut As Employee = _
            CType(formatter.Deserialize(stream), Employee)

        Console.WriteLine(empOut.FirstName)
        Console.WriteLine(empOut.LastName)
        Console.WriteLine(empOut.Department)
        Console.WriteLine("Last Access: {0}", _
                        empOut.LastAccessed.ToShortDateString)
        Console.ReadLine()

    End Sub

End Class
```

## SerializationContext

The `SerializationContext` parameter of `GetObjectData` (and the matching constructor) describes the target or source context for a serialization stream. This class's `State` property can be one or more values from `StreamingContextState`, whose primary values are CrossAppDomain, CrossMachine, CrossProcess, and File. Other values are available, but they do not pertain here.

This *context* parameter is useful because the serialization and deserialization process might have to be altered based on where the serialization stream comes from or where it is headed. This parameter describes the circumstances under which serialization and deserialization take place, providing the opportunity to exclude irrelevant data. For example:

```
Public Sub New (ByVal info As SerializationInfo, _
                ByVal context As StreamingContext)

    If context.State = StreamingContextStates.CrossMachine Then
        'Do not serialize machine specific data
    Else
        'Serialize it
    End If

    If context.State = StreamingContextStates.CrossProcess Then
        'Do not serialize process specific data
    Else
        'Serialize it
    End If
.
.
.
End Sub
```

# NetworkStream

The NetworkStream class abstracts the transfer of data over networks. The underlying mechanism used for transmission is System.Net.Sockets.Socket, which is actually used by all the classes in the System.Net namespace that pertain to network communication. Socket can be used directly, but like Stream, higher-level classes make interaction over the network much simpler. This chapter discusses two of these classes: TcpClient and TcpListener.

## TCP

It is hard to find a machine that doesn't have several TCP-based clients already on it. Most have an email client, a web browser, or maybe even a Napster client (that sadly does not do a thing). TcpClient, which uses the Socket class, makes it easy to connect, send, and receive data over a network, facilitating the creation of these types of clients.

Most Internet applications work as follows: a connection is established to a server on a specified port, data is sent in a specified format, and a response is received. It's as simple as that. The difficult part has always been working with sockets, but .NET abstracts the difficulty away.

By using `TcpClient`, creating a TCP-based client is easy. For instance, Example 8-16 contains the listing for a finger client. Finger used to be more popular than it is today. It associates information with an email address, so someone with a finger client can type

```
finger xyz@mail.com
```

and retrieve all kinds of information—possibly the real name of the person, where the person currently works, and so forth. You can find finger servers running on most *.edu* domains, but they are rare on *.coms*.

RFC 742 describes the finger protocol. To summarize: connect to the domain where the finger will occur on port 79, send the name of the user in question, and wait for the response, which will be the user's finger information.

Here is a testament to .NET. Not knowing anything about finger, reading the RFC document consumed most of the time involved in writing Example 8-16. The entire journey from ignorance to implementation took 28 minutes. Time was wasted because the carriage return and line feeds were originally left off the data being sent to the server. It took a few more minutes of debugging to figure out what was going on. RFCs must be followed to the letter!

In Example 8-16, notice the use of streams. The example uses the same paradigm as that used to read and write to a file.

*Example 8-16. Finger client using TcpClient*

```
'vbc /t:exe /r:system.dll finger.vb

Imports System
Imports System.IO
Imports System.Net
Imports System.Net.Sockets

Public Class Finger

  Public Const Port As Integer = 79  'TCP Port 79

  Public Function Finger(ByVal EmailAddress As String) As String

    Dim params() As String = EmailAddress.Split("@"c)

    Try

      Dim client As New TcpClient()
      client.Connect(params(1), Port)

      'Get NetworkStream
      Dim baseStream As NetworkStream = client.GetStream()
      'Wrap it with a buffered stream
```

*Example 8-16. Finger client using TcpClient (continued)*

```
      Dim stream As New BufferedStream(baseStream)

      Dim writer As StreamWriter = New StreamWriter(stream)
      writer.Write(String.Format("{0}{1}", params(0), Environment.NewLine))
      writer.Flush()

      Dim reader As StreamReader = New StreamReader(stream)
      Dim response As String = reader.ReadToEnd()

      'Close TCP connection and stream
      client.Close()

      Return response

    Catch e As SocketException
      Return e.Message
    Catch e As Exception
      Return e.Message
    End Try

  End Function

End Class

Friend Class FingerClient

  Public Shared Sub Main(ByVal args() As String)
    Dim f As New Finger()
    Console.WriteLine(f.Finger(args(0)))
    Console.ReadLine()
  End Sub

End Class
```

When the program is run, the account being fingered is nabbed from the command line and passed to the `Finger` class. The domain is extracted from the account and passed to the `Connect` method of `TcpClient` along with the port—in this case, 79.

Once the connection is opened, the `TcpClient` object's `GetStream` method is called to retrieve an instance of `NetworkStream`. Although it is overkill in this example, the `NetworkStream` is then wrapped in a `BufferedStream` object. This is really just to demonstrate the buffered stream. While buffered streams are useful in network applications, finger servers typically do not return much data. Thus, providing a buffer is really unnecessary, but it does no harm, either. The buffered stream can be used like any other stream. The fact that data might stream in from halfway around the world is of no consequence. The concept of streams should be familiar to you by now.

The `BufferedStream` is passed to the constructor of a `StreamWriter`, making it possible to easily write a string to the stream. Notice that the account name is written back to the stream first with a call to `StreamWriter.Write`, which just writes the data to the internal buffer. The data is not actually sent to the server until the call to `StreamWriter.Flush`, which occurs on the next line.

Finally, the `BufferedStream` is passed to an instance of `StreamReader`, which reads back the response from the server. `StreamReader.ReadToEnd` gets the response back in one shot in the form of a string. Relying on a single read operation is safe for the most part, because finger does not usually return significant amounts of data. Finally, `TcpClient.Close` is called. It closes not only the client, but also the `BufferedStream`.

Ten lines of code are responsible for the finger. Developers who have done sockets programming in C on Unix systems can surely appreciate this. Otherwise, understand that this fact is pretty amazing. MIT has a really good finger server. After you have compiled the example, check it out:

```
finger help@mit.edu
```

## Writing a Server

Building applications that accept connections from TCP clients is as easy as writing a TCP client. Just use `System.Net.Sockets.TcpListener` to wait for incoming connections. Use the following steps:

1. Create a new `TcpListener`, specifying the port on which to listen.
2. Call `TcpListener.Start` to begin listening.
3. Call `TcpListener.AcceptTcpClient`. This is a blocking call; it causes program execution to halt until a TCP connection request is received and a connection is established. The return value of this call is a `TcpClient` instance.
4. Call the `GetStream` method of the returned `TcpClient` object. The method will return an instance of `NetworkStream`. At this point, it is possible to read from the stream (if accepting data), write back to the stream, or both.
5. Close the stream, the `TcpListener`, and the `TcpClient`.

Actually, Example 8-17 is a little more complicated. It contains the code for a War of the Worlds server. This server provides copies of H.G. Wells' book *War of Worlds* over a network connection. The text is long enough to put the example through its paces, and it is public domain. The book's text can be downloaded from the Gutenberg Project, along with many other classics, at *http://www.gutenberg.org*.

The example demonstrates several important concepts regarding servers and the transfer of data across a network. For one, it is multithreaded, so it can handle multiple requests simultaneously. To provide greater scalability, each thread reads from the data stream asynchronously and writes back to the client asynchronously. The example is several pages long, but that is the price you must pay for reality-based coding. Go over the example, but get ready to step through it afterward for an explanation.

*Example 8-17. War of the Worlds server*

```
'vbc /t:exe /r:system.dll wow.vb

Imports System
Imports System.IO
Imports System.Net
Imports System.Net.Sockets
Imports System.Text
Imports System.Threading

Public Class WarOfTheWorldsServer

  Private port As Integer
  Private listener As TcpListener

  Public Sub New(ByVal port As Integer)
    Me.Port = Port
  End Sub

  'Start listening for incoming requests
  Public Sub Start()

    listener = New TcpListener(Port)
    listener.Start()
    Console.WriteLine("War of the Worlds Server 1.0")

    While (True)
      'If there is a pending request, create a new
      'thread to handle it
      If (listener.Pending()) Then
        Dim requestThread As New Thread( _
            New ThreadStart(AddressOf ThreadProc))
        requestThread.Start()
      End If
      Thread.Sleep(1000)
    End While

  End Sub

  'Handles incoming requests
  Private Sub ThreadProc()

    'Get client
    Dim client As TcpClient = listener.AcceptTcpClient()

    'And pass to handler that will
    'do asynchronous writes back to the client
    Dim handler As New ClientHandler(client)
    handler.SendDataToClient()

  End Sub

  'Provides asynchronous quote support!
```

*Example 8-17. War of the Worlds server (continued)*

```
Private Class ClientHandler

  Private Const BUFFER_SIZE As Integer = 256
  Private buffer(BUFFER_SIZE) As Byte

  Private client As TcpClient
  Private rawClient As NetworkStream
  Private clientStream As BufferedStream
  Private dataStream As FileStream
  Private writeCallback As AsyncCallback
  Private readCallback As AsyncCallback

  Public Sub New(ByVal client As TcpClient)

    'Buffer the client stream
    rawClient = client.GetStream()
    clientStream = New BufferedStream(rawClient)

    'Callback used to handle writing
    writeCallback = New AsyncCallback(AddressOf _
                      Me.OnWriteComplete)
    readCallback = New AsyncCallback(AddressOf _
                     Me.OnReadComplete)

  End Sub

  'Start sending the data to the client
  Public Sub SendDataToClient()
    'Open stream to data and start reading it
    dataStream = New FileStream("war of the worlds.txt", _
                   FileMode.Open, _
                   FileAccess.Read)
    dataStream.BeginRead(buffer, 0, buffer.Length, _
        readCallback, Nothing)
  End Sub

  Private Sub OnReadComplete(ByVal ar As IAsyncResult)
    Dim bytesRead As Integer = dataStream.EndRead(ar)
    If (bytesRead > 0) Then
      clientStream.BeginWrite(buffer, 0, _
          bytesRead, writeCallback, Nothing)
    Else
      dataStream.Close()
      clientStream.Close()
    End If

  End Sub

  Private Sub OnWriteComplete(ByVal ar As IAsyncResult)
    clientStream.EndWrite(ar)
    clientStream.Flush()
    dataStream.BeginRead(buffer, 0, buffer.Length, _
```

*Example 8-17. War of the Worlds server (continued)*

```
            readCallback, Nothing)
    End Sub

  End Class

End Class

Friend Class Application
  Public Shared Sub Main(ByVal args() As String)
    If args.Length < 1 Then
      Console.WriteLine("usage: wow <port number>")
      Return
    End If
    Dim wow As New WarOfTheWorldsServer( _
                  Convert.ToInt32(args(0)))
    wow.Start()
  End Sub
End Class
```

The action begins in `Sub Main`, where the port number the server uses is acquired from the command line. This port number is the input argument to the constructor of the server class, `WarOfTheWorldsServer`. The server starts listing on the supplied port number by creating a new instance of `TcpListener` and calling its `Start` method:

```
listener = New TcpListener(port)
listener.Start()
```

The server sits in an infinite loop until a pending request comes in. This is OK because the server runs in a console window, and everything terminates properly when the window is shut down. A real server would be better implemented as a Windows Service. Implementing it in this way is not hard to do, but it would make the example considerably longer. When a request is received, a new thread is created and the work of handling the request is given to it. If there is not a pending request, the current application thread is put to sleep for one second. This is good behavior on the servers' part that allows the rest of the programs running on the machine to get some work done. The following block of code does this:

```
While (True)
  'If there is a pending request, create a new thread
  'to handle it
  If (listener.Pending()) Then
      Dim requestThread As New Thread( _
          New ThreadStart(AddressOf ThreadProc))
      requestThread.Start()
  End If
  Thread.Sleep(1000)
End While
```

When the thread procedure assumes program control, `TcpListener.AcceptTcpClient` is ordered to get an instance of `TcpClient` that represents the client that currently requests data from the server. It also creates an instance of ClientHandler, which is a private class used to read and the write data to the client:

```
'Handles incoming requests
Private Sub ThreadProc()

    'Get client
    Dim client As TcpClient = listener.AcceptTcpClient()

    'And pass to handler that will
    'do asynchronous writes back to the client
    Dim handler As New ClientHandler(client)
    handler.SendDataToClient()

End Sub
```

ClientHandler reads data asynchronously and then writes it to the client, 256 bytes at a time. This is definitely not optimal. The size of the buffer is purposely small for two reasons:

- To make the server work harder
- To make the server able to work with smaller amounts of data

In the constructor of ClientHandler, a call is made to GetStream on the incoming TcpClient instance. This call returns a NetworkStream to the client, which is then wrapped by a buffered stream. Next, two delegates are declared. The first is the address of a method called OnWriteComplete, which is called whenever a write operation has finished. The second is the address of the OnReadComplete method, which is called when a read operation is completed. The ClientHandler constructor is as follows:

```
Public Sub New(ByVal client As TcpClient)

  'Buffer the client stream
  rawClient = client.GetStream()
  clientStream = New BufferedStream(rawClient)

  'Callback used to handle writing
  writeCallback = New AsyncCallback(AddressOf Me.OnWriteComplete)
  readCallback = New AsyncCallback(AddressOf Me.OnReadComplete)

End Sub
```

Once the handler is initialized, ClientHandler.SendDataToClient is called in order to start the process of sending text to the client. A FileStream object opens the *War of the Worlds* text file, and BeginRead is called to read the first 256 bytes of the file into a buffer. The callback delegate is also passed so that OnReadComplete will be called after the operation is finished. SendDataToClient has the following code:

```
'Start sending the data to the client
Public Sub SendDataToClient()
  'Open stream to data and start reading it
  dataStream = New FileStream("war of the worlds.txt", _
                 FileMode.Open, _
                 FileAccess.Read)
  dataStream.BeginRead(buffer, 0, buffer.Length, _
                     readCallback, Nothing)
End Sub
```

When OnReadComplete is called, an IAsyncResult interface is obtained that allows the number of bytes actually read to be determined (which is done by calling Stream.EndRead). If data was read, then the buffer is written to the client stream. This time, the OnWriteCompleted delegate is used in the call. As soon as the write operation is finished, it is called. If no data is left, the *War of the Worlds* stream is closed along with the client stream. At this point, the process ultimately ends. The code for the OnReadComplete procedure is:

```
Private Sub OnReadComplete(ByVal ar As IAsyncResult)
  Dim bytesRead As Integer = dataStream.EndRead(ar)
  If (bytesRead > 0) Then
    clientStream.BeginWrite(buffer, 0, bytesRead, _
      writeCallback, Nothing)
  Else
    dataStream.Close()
    clientStream.Close()
  End If
End Sub
```

When OnWriteComplete is called, Stream.EndWrite is called on the incoming IAsyncResult interface, ending the write operation. The client stream is flushed, causing the client to receive the first 256 bytes of data. Finally, Stream.BeginRead is called on the data stream in order to fetch the next 256 bytes of data. Then, the read/write process begins again, over and over, until there is no more data:

```
Private Sub OnWriteComplete(ByVal ar As IAsyncResult)
  clientStream.EndWrite(ar)
  clientStream.Flush()
  dataStream.BeginRead(buffer, 0, buffer.Length, readCallback, Nothing)
End Sub
```

## Writing a Client to Test the Server

After the server is compiled, it can be run from the command line along with the desired port:

```
C:\>wow 1969
```

A client is needed to test the server. The one listed in Example 8-18 will work just fine. Open a second console window to run it. It requires the IP address of the server and the port that it listens on. Localhost will work:

```
C:\>wow-client 127.0.0.1 1969
```

The client example uses asynchronous read operations to get the data, which means that other work can be done while the data is retrieved.

*Example 8-18. War of the Worlds client*

```
'vbc /t:exe /r:system.dll get-quote.vb

Imports System
Imports System.IO
Imports System.Net.Sockets
Imports System.Text
Imports System.Threading

Public Class WarOfTheWorldsClient

    Private server As String
    Private port As Integer

    Private client As TcpClient
    Private buffer(256) As Byte
    Private readCallback As AsyncCallback
    Private stream As BufferedStream

    Public Sub New(ByVal Server As String, ByVal Port As String)
        Try
            client = New TcpClient()
            client.Connect(Server, Convert.ToInt32(Port))
            Dim raw As NetworkStream = client.GetStream()
            stream = New BufferedStream(raw)
            readCallback = New AsyncCallback(AddressOf Me.OnReadComplete)
            stream.BeginRead(buffer, 0, buffer.Length, _
                readCallback, Nothing)
        Catch e As Exception
            Console.WriteLine(e.Message)
        End Try
    End Sub

    Private Sub OnReadComplete(ByVal ar As IAsyncResult)
        Dim bytesRead As Integer = stream.EndRead(ar)
        If (bytesRead > 0) Then
            Dim output As String = _
                Encoding.ASCII.GetString(buffer, 0, bytesRead)
            Console.WriteLine(output)
            stream.BeginRead(buffer, 0, buffer.Length, _
                readCallback, Nothing)
```

*Example 8-18. War of the Worlds client (continued)*

```
        Else
            stream.Close()
            client.Close()
        End If
    End Sub

End Class

Friend Class Application
    Public Shared Sub Main()
        Dim args() As String = Environment.GetCommandLineArgs()
        If args.Length < 3 Then
            Console.WriteLine("usage: wow <server> <port>")
            Return
        End If
        Dim client As New WarOfTheWorldsClient(args(1), args(2))
    End Sub
End Class
```

# CHAPTER 9
# Object Remoting

Every program hosted by the Common Language Runtime lives within the confines of an application domain, the fundamental boundary of application isolation within the .NET Framework. When one object wants to communicate with an object in another application domain, *remoting* is what makes it possible.

Each assembly exposes the types it contains, and those types are exactly the same, regardless of the programming language used. Combine this feature with serialization and reflection, and some of the major pieces of the .NET puzzle fall into place. The remoting framework makes heavy use of all these technologies.

There are many choices to consider when remoting objects, including channel, activation model, type of server, and configuration. Each choice is discussed in context throughout the chapter. Rather than a reference to remoting, this chapter represents more of a "code along" story. This story has many twists and turns, so it's better to start at the beginning and enjoy the ride.

## Channels

Channels are objects that help transport messages between objects in a remoting relationship. The .NET Framework comes configured with two channels: one that uses TCP as the transport protocol and another that uses HTTP. Each uses SOAP as its message format, but the TCP channel encodes it into a proprietary binary format, while the HTTP channel uses XML. The HTTP channel is ideal when firewalls must be traversed, but otherwise, it is best to use the TCP channel for its pure speed.

Although .NET is configured to use TCP and HTTP out of the box, the remoting framework is completely extensible. .NET ships with channel objects that implement two of the most popular protocols, but anyone can write a channel using any protocol, and it will plug right into the remoting infrastructure as long as the specifications are adhered to.

## Activation Models

Remote objects fall into two major categories: server-activated objects (SAOs) and client-activated objects (CAOs).

SAOs are also referred to as "well-known" objects, probably because no mechanism for object discovery is inherently built into the remoting architecture. Compare this feature to the TCP/IP "well-known ports," which refer to ports such as 25 (SMTP), 80 (HTTP), and 110 (POP3). Clients using well-known objects have a priori knowledge of the object's location.

When a client requests an SAO, it is initially given a proxy object that resembles the object located on the server. However, the object on the server is not created until the first method call is made on the proxy object. When the remote object's lease has expired, garbage collection occurs.

Server-activated objects come in two forms: Singleton or SingleCall. The properties of each are as follows:

*Singleton*
: Regardless of the number of clients, one instance processes every request in a multithreaded fashion. From one call to the next, the actual instance might be different, but at any given time, there is only one instance. State is shared between all clients and is maintained between calls. Singletons are marshaled by reference.

*SingleCall*
: SingleCall objects are activated once per request. Thus, for every method called (by every client), a new instance is created on the server to process each request. As a result, SingleCall objects do not maintain state of any kind between successive calls. SingleCall objects can be marshaled by value (so that the client has a copy of the object) or by reference.

The term *marshaling* refers to preparing an object to be moved to another application domain.

The choice of whether to use a Singleton or SingleCall object usually involves some compromise between performance and scalability. Singletons are fast because one instance can serve every request. SingleCall objects are inherently slower because a new object is created for every request. However, the object remains active only during the lifetime of the request, so scalability is much higher.

CAOs resemble SAO Singletons in that object state is maintained between calls. The difference is that the state is unique to the particular instance of the object; it is not shared among every instance on every client. Also, when a CAO is activated by the client, an instance of the object is immediately created on the server. The other major difference involves the object's lifetime. With SAOs and CAOs alike, the server determines when a remote object can be garbage collected. However, the CAO can participate in that decision. For instance, if a CAO goes out of scope on the client, it will probably be garbage collected right then. The SAO is not freed until its lease expires—a topic that will be discussed in the section "Lifetime leases" later in this chapter.

## A Remotable Object

This chapter discusses two methods of hosting remote objects. The first method is *Windows Services*, which are background processes that lack a user interface. They are started either manually or automatically when Windows first loads. They are ideal for hosting remote objects because they do not interfere with other users on the machine. All interaction with services is done through the Service Control Manager (SCM), as shown in Figure 9-1. This program is run from the Administrative Tools directory in the Control Panel and is simply called "Services." Typically, Windows Services can be started, stopped, and paused from within the SCM. When these actions occur, a corresponding method within the service is called, allowing reciprocating action to occur.

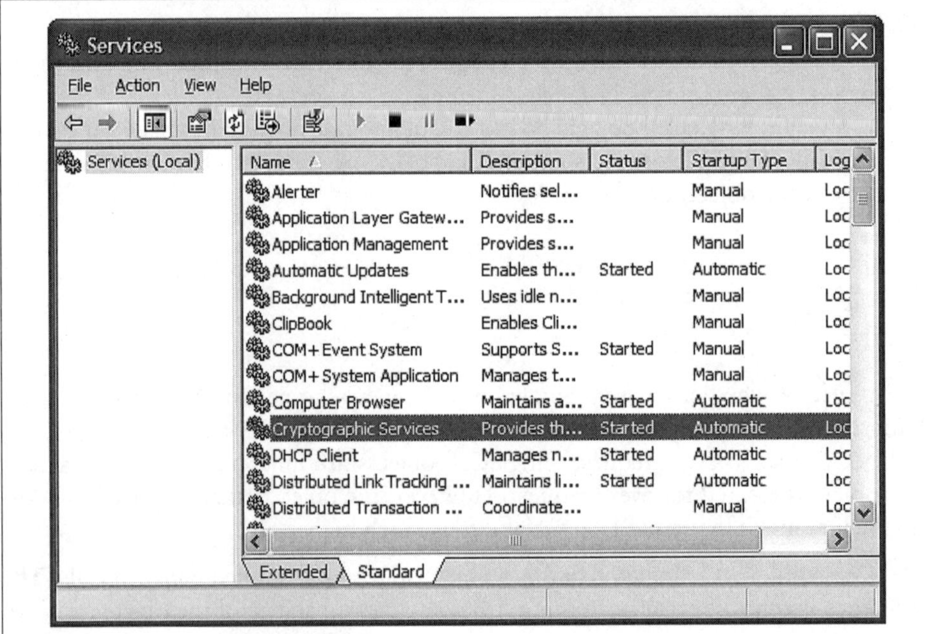


*Figure 9-1. Service Control Manager*

The second method involves the use of an Internet Information Server (IIS) to host remotable objects. The advantages of this method are that no code is required and it only takes a few moments to configure. However, the configuration options are limited, compared to what can be done with a Windows Service, and the only available channel is `HttpChannel`. Windows Services can also use `TcpChannel`, which is considerably faster.

A remotable object is an essential ingredient for hosting a remote object. Example 9-1 contains a remotable version of the `ServerInfo` class from Chapter 7 (minus a few superfluous methods). The class provides rudimentary information regarding a machine, such as IP address and processor utilization. It is used to demonstrate various remoting concepts in this chapter. Compile it to an assembly called *ServerInfo.dll*, which will be used throughout the chapter (but be ready to modify it at a moment's notice).

*Example 9-1. Remotable ServerInfo class*

```
'vbc /t:library /r:System.dll serverinfo.vb

Imports System
Imports System.Diagnostics
Imports System.Net
Imports System.Threading

Namespace ObjectServerSpace

Public Class ServerInfo : Inherits MarshalByRefObject
    Private machine As String
    Private ip As IPAddress
    Private Shared calls As Integer

    Public Sub New()
      'Get machine info when object is created
      machine = Dns.GetHostName()
      Dim ipHost As IPHostEntry = Dns.GetHostByName(machine)
      ip = ipHost.AddressList(0)
      calls = 0
    End Sub

    'Shared method
    Public Function GetMachineTime() As DateTime
      calls += 1
      Return DateTime.Now
    End Function

    'Get % of process currently in use
    Public Function GetProcessorUsed() As Single
      calls += 1
      If PerformanceCounterCategory.Exists("Processor") Then
        Dim pc As New PerformanceCounter("Processor", _
            "% Processor Time", "_Total", True)
        Dim sampleA As CounterSample
```

*Example 9-1. Remotable ServerInfo class (continued)*

```
            Dim sampleB As CounterSample

            sampleA = pc.NextSample()
            Thread.Sleep(1000)
            sampleB = pc.NextSample()
            Return CounterSample.Calculate(sampleA, sampleB)
          End If
        End Function

        'Get MBytes of free memory
        Public Function GetAvailableMemory() As Long
          calls += 1
          If PerformanceCounterCategory.Exists("Memory") Then
            Dim pc As New PerformanceCounter("Memory", "Available MBytes")
            Return pc.RawValue()
          End If
          Return 0
        End Function

        Public ReadOnly Property MachineName() As String
          Get
            calls += 1
            Return machine
          End Get
        End Property

        Public ReadOnly Property IPAddress() As IPAddress
          Get
            calls += 1
            Return ip
          End Get
        End Property

        Public ReadOnly Property CallCount() As Integer
          Get
            Return calls
          End Get
        End Property

      End Class

    End Namespace
```

# Windows Services

It is possible to write a server that runs within a console window in a few lines of code. However, it is neither realistic nor practical because there is no easy way of administering a server running in this environment. Using a Windows Service provides more of a real-world scenario, so considerable time will be spent developing one. The classes in the next few examples form the basis of a service that can be used to host all kinds of objects generically. The code is completely reusable and extensible.

To make building a Windows Service easier, Example 9-2 contains the listing for an abstract base class called `ObjectServer` that is specifically designed to build services that remote objects. Like all Windows Services, it inherits from `System.ServiceProcess.ServiceBase`. The class also provides both an `HttpChannel` and a `TCPChannel` object instance so objects can be remoted with each protocol.

*Example 9-2. Windows Service base class for remotable objects*

```
'Windows Service Base Class for Remoting Objects
'
'Compile:
'vbc /t:library /r:system.dll /r:System.Serviceprocess.dll
'/r:System.Runtime.Remoting.dll objectserver.vb
'
'Install:
'installutil objectserver.exe
'
'Uninstall:
'installutil /u objectserver.exe

Imports System
Imports System.Diagnostics
Imports System.Runtime.Remoting
Imports System.Runtime.Remoting.Channels
Imports System.Runtime.Remoting.Channels.Http
Imports System.Runtime.Remoting.Channels.Tcp
Imports System.ServiceProcess

Namespace ObjectServerSpace

  Public MustInherit Class ObjectServer : Inherits ServiceBase

    Private name As String
    Protected tcp As TcpChannel
    Protected http As HttpChannel
    Protected httpPort As Integer
    Protected tcpPort As Integer

    'This method will be used to register objects
    Public MustOverride Sub RegisterObjects()

    'Configure server properties
    Public Sub New(ByVal ServiceName As String)

      'Save service name
      Me.name = ServiceName

      'Set default service parameters
      ConfigureService()

    End Sub

    Protected Overridable Sub ConfigureService()
```

*Example 9-2. Windows Service base class for remotable objects (continued)*

```
        'Automatically log event on start, stop, pause, and continue
        Me.AutoLog = False
        'Set service name - must match name used in installer class
        Me.ServiceName = name
        'Service can be stopped
        Me.CanStop = True
        'Service can be paused and continued
        Me.CanPauseAndContinue = False
        'Notify when power status changes
        Me.CanHandlePowerEvent = False
        'Notify service on system shut down
        Me.CanShutdown = False
    End Sub

    Protected Overrides Sub OnStart(ByVal args() As String)

        'Register objects that will be served
        RegisterObjects()

        'Default port
        If (args.Length < 2) Then
            tcpPort = 1969
            httpPort = 1970
        Else
            tcpPort = Convert.ToInt32(args(0))
            httpPort = Convert.ToInt32(args(1))
        End If

        'Create and register channel
        tcp = New TcpChannel(tcpPort)
        ChannelServices.RegisterChannel(tcp)
        http = New HttpChannel(httpPort)
        ChannelServices.RegisterChannel(http)

        Dim log As EventLog = New EventLog()
        log.WriteEntry(ServiceName, "Service started")
        Dim sLogEntry As String
        sLogEntry = String.Format("TCP - {0} HTTP - {1}", tcpPort, httpPort)
        log.WriteEntry(ServiceName, sLogEntry)

    End Sub

    Protected Overrides Sub OnStop()
        'Called when service is stopped
        ChannelServices.UnregisterChannel(tcp)
        ChannelServices.UnregisterChannel(http)
    End Sub

    'Protected Overrides Sub OnPause()
    '   CanPauseAndContinue must be True
    'End Sub

    'Protected Overrides Sub OnContinue()
```

*Example 9-2. Windows Service base class for remotable objects (continued)*

```
    '  CanPauseAndContinue must be True
    'End Sub

    'Protected Overrides Function OnPowerEvent _
    '    (ByVal ps As PowerBroadcastStatus) As Boolean
    'CanHandlePowerEvent must be true
    'End Function

    'Protected Overrides Sub OnShutdown()
    ' CanShutdown must be True
    'End Sub

  End Class

End Namespace
```

The constructor to `ObjectServer` takes the name of the service as it should appear in the SCM. In the constructor, a call is made to `ConfigureService`, which initializes the service. The method is overridable, so derived classes can change the behavior if necessary. Table 9-1 summarizes the various properties (inherited from `ServiceBase`) that can be configured here.

*Table 9-1. ServiceBase configuration properties*

| Property | Description |
| --- | --- |
| `AutoLog` | When `True`, a log entry is made every time the service is started, stopped, paused, or continued. |
| `CanStop` | The service can be stopped. The stop button is available in the SCM, and the `OnStop` method is called in the service object when it is clicked. |
| `CanPauseAndContinue` | The service can be paused or continued, causing the `OnPause` and `OnContinue` methods, respectively, to be called within the service object. |
| `CanHandlePowerEvent` | The service can handle power notification events through the `OnPowerEvent` method. |
| `CanShutdown` | The service is notified when the system shuts down. |
| `ServiceName` | The name of the service as it appears in the SCM. |

The `OnStart` method registers a `TcpChannel` and an `HttpChannel`, as well as calls `RegisterObjects`, the method that eventually configures the remotable objects provided by the service. This method has no base implementation and must be overridden by any class that wishes to derive from it.

`OnStart` is called when the service is started from the SCM. If the service is configured to start automatically, it is called when the machine boots. The SCM provides a properties dialog that allows the start parameters to be defined. However, if no arguments are specified, the `TcpChannel` uses port 1969 and the `HttpChannel` defaults to 1970.

The OnStop method merely unregisters each channel, effectively prohibiting any objects from being remoted. If a client tries to attach to the service at this point, a SocketException is thrown.

Note that an object does not own a channel. A server can provide any number of channels that can remote an object. Two incoming requests could ask for the same object but use different channels, one for TCP and another for HTTP. The server handles these requests by using separate threads, so blocking is not an issue.

Example 9-2 should be compiled to a library called *ObjectServer.dll*, which allows the class to be more readily reusable.

## Building the Windows Service

Example 9-3 contains the listing for the RemotingObjectService class that comprises the actual service. It also contains three other classes:

- WindowsServiceInfo
- RemotingObjectInstaller
- Application

WindowsServiceInfo contains a public constant that defines the name of the Windows Service—in this case, "Remoting Object Server." This is done because the service name must be used in the three other classes, and if the name doesn't match, the service won't work.

*Example 9-3. Remote Object Service*

```
'Object Server
'
'Compile:
'vbc /t:exe /r:system.dll /r:System.Serviceprocess.dll
'/r:System.Configuration.Install.dll
'/r:System.Runtime.Remoting.dll
'/r:ObjectServer.dll /r:serverinfo.dll remoteservice.vb
'
'Install:
'installutil remoteservice.exe
'
'Uninstall:
'installutil /u remoteservice.exe

Imports System
Imports System.ComponentModel
Imports System.Configuration
Imports System.Configuration.Install
Imports System.Runtime.Remoting
Imports System.ServiceProcess

Namespace ObjectServerSpace

  Friend Class WindowsServiceInfo
```

*Example 9-3. Remote Object Service (continued)*

```
    Public Const Name As String = "Remoting Object Server"
  End Class

  Public Class RemotingObjectService : Inherits ObjectServer

    Public Sub New()
      MyBase.New(WindowsServiceInfo.Name)
    End Sub

    'This method will be used to register objects
    Public Overrides Sub RegisterObjects()
        'Implementation forthcoming
    End Sub

  End Class

  <RunInstallerAttribute(True)> _
  Public Class RemotingObjectInstaller : Inherits Installer
    Public Sub New()
      Dim pi As New ServiceProcessInstaller()
      pi.Account = ServiceAccount.LocalSystem

      Dim si As New ServiceInstaller()
      si.StartType = ServiceStartMode.Manual
      si.ServiceName = WindowsServiceInfo.Name

      Installers.Add(si)
      Installers.Add(pi)
    End Sub
  End Class

  Public Class Application
    Public Shared Sub Main()
      ServiceBase.Run(New RemotingObjectService())
    End Sub
  End Class

End Namespace
```

### Windows Service installation

The `RemotingObjectInstaller` is a class that is used to install the service. Installer classes are derived from `System.Configuration.Install.Installer`, and, in terms of Windows Services, they define what account the service runs under (services run whether or not someone is logged in) and how the service should be started: disabled, manual, or automatic. The classes used in the installer write the appropriate entries into the registry to make the service available from the SCM.

To install the service from the command line, use *installutil.exe* like this:

```
installutil remoteservice.exe
To uninstall the service, use the /u switch:
installutil /u remoteservice.exe
```

The utility is not located with the .NET Framework SDK; rather, it is in the framework folder located within the *System* directory. The path is similar to this:

*<%windir%>\Microsoft.NET\Framework\<version>*

It is definitely a good idea to add this path to the environment variables of any machine used for .NET development, since it contains several useful utilities.

When *installutil.exe* is run, it scans the assembly looking for the class that has a `RunInstaller` attribute applied (with a `True` value) and creates an instance of it.

The constructor of the installer class should contain everything needed to configure the service. In the case of Example 9-2, `ServiceProcessInstaller` specifies that the service will run under the local system account. If necessary, a specific user account can be used; there are properties for specifying users and passwords.

`ServiceInstaller` declares how the service is started (manually) and the name of the service. This property represents the minimal information that the installer class must supply to get the service up and running.

Finally, after the service is installed, it is loaded. The `Application` class contains the service startup code. This code is just a call to `ServiceBase.Run`, which takes an instance of the service class. The method is overloaded to take an array of `ServiceBase`, which provides the means for one executable to host several services.

### Remote Object Service

There really isn't much to `RemotingObjectService`, the service class. Most of the work is done in the `ObjectServer` base class.

The first point of interest is the constructor. In `ObjectServer`, a default constructor was purposefully not supplied, which forces the derived `RemotingObjectService` class to call `MyBase.New` and pass the name of the service to the base class.

All that remains is the override of `RegisterObjects`. The remote objects provided by the server are configured in this method.

## Registration

You can register well-known objects either programmatically or through the use of a configuration file. This section discusses both methods.

### Programmatic registration

Example 9-4 contains the long-awaited implementation of `RegisterObjects`, the code for which can be incorporated into the source code from Example 9-3. This version of `RegisterObjects` uses the programmatic method for registration. After the application name is defined (think of this as a virtual directory under IIS), an instance of type `WellKnownServiceTypeEntry` is created for each object the service will expose.

*Example 9-4. Registering well-known objects in code*

```
Public Overrides Sub RegisterObjects()

  RemotingConfiguration.ApplicationName = "RemotingTest"

  Dim entry1 As New WellKnownServiceTypeEntry( _
    GetType(ServerInfo), "ServerInfo", WellKnownObjectMode.Singleton)

  RemotingConfiguration.RegisterWellKnownServiceType(entry1)

  Dim entry2 As New WellKnownServiceTypeEntry( _
    GetType(ServerInfo), "ServerInfo2", WellKnownObjectMode.SingleCall)

  RemotingConfiguration.RegisterWellKnownServiceType(entry2)


End Sub
```

The constructor of the `WellKnownServiceTypeEntry` class takes the type of service, the URI of the object, and the activation method (Singleton or SingleCall). Ultimately, two objects are exposed: a Singleton instance of `ServerInfo` and a SingleCall version. The machine name of the service, the application name, and the object URI form the URL where the objects are located. Because the service exposes both a `TCPChannel` and an `HttpChannel`, clients can refer to these objects in several ways:

```
tcp://192.168.1.100/RemotingTest/ServerInfo
tcp:// 192.168.1.100/RemotingTest/ServerInfo2
http:// 192.168.1.100/RemotingTest/ServerInfo
http:// 192.168.1.100/RemotingTest/ServerInfo2
```

#### Using configuration files

Using programmatic configuration is less than ideal. The server must be recompiled every time a new object is exposed. By using configuration files, you can implement `RegisterObjects` in a completely generic fashion. This implementation allows any number of objects (from one or more assemblies) to be exposed without coupling any specific type information to the service.

Example 9-5 contains a version of `RegisterObjects` that uses a configuration file for registration purposes. Normally, configuration files are kept in the same directory as the executable, which is the case here. However, when Windows Services run, their executing directory is *<%windir%>/System32*. To load the configuration file correctly, the current application domain is used to derive a path to the file, which is called *RemoteService.exe.config*. For conventional reasons, configuration files have the same name as the executable, followed by *.config*.

*Example 9-5. Final implementation of RegisterObjects*

```
Public Overrides Sub RegisterObjects()
  Dim ad As AppDomain = AppDomain.CurrentDomain()
```

*Example 9-5. Final implementation of RegisterObjects (continued)*

```
  Dim path As String = _
    String.Format("{0}\RemoteService.exe.config", ad.BaseDirectory)
  RemotingConfiguration.Configure(path)
End Sub
```

This method of configuration has obvious advantages—the primary one being that this version of `RegisterObjects` will never have to be rewritten again; everything is defined in an external file. This advantage makes the `RemotingObjectService` class much more reusable and extensible. To remote new objects, you only need to drop a new assembly in the services directory, add a `<wellknown>` entry for the new class in the configuration file, and restart the server.

The framework documentation contains the full schema for the remoting configuration file. To show it here would detract from the discussion at hand, because only a small portion of the schema pertains to server activated objects. Example 9-6 contains the configuration file, which is basically the XML version of Example 9-4. The type element contains the object's full type name, followed by the assembly name (minus the file extension).

One noticeable difference is the fact that the `objectUri` attribute contains the extension *.rem* (it can also be *.soap*). Theoretically, this configuration file could be reused under IIS. These extensions are for the benefit of the HTTP remoting handlers used in this circumstance.

*Example 9-6. RemoteService.exe.config*

```
<configuration>
  <system.runtime.remoting>
    <application name="RemotingTest">
      <service>
        <wellknown mode="Singleton"
                   type="ObjectServerSpace.ServerInfo,ServerInfo"
                   objectUri="ServerInfo.rem" />
        <wellknown mode="SingleCall"
               type="ObjectServerSpace.ServerInfo,ServerInfo"
               objectUri="ServerInfo2.rem" />
      </service>
    </application>
  </system.runtime.remoting>
</configuration>
```

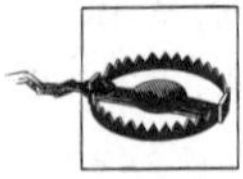

Make sure the service, *ServerInfo.dll*, and the *RemoteService.exe.config* are in the same directory.

The server is complete, so start it up from the SCM. The only things that will ever need to be changed (in terms of this chapter) are the `<wellknown>` entries in the configuration file.

Make sure the server is configured correctly and the remote object is available. You can do this by using a browser. Just enter in the URL of the object (and don't forget to use the port for the registered `HttpChannel`). Also, make sure `?wsdl` (web service description language) is appended to the address, as in the following example:

```
http://192.168.1.100:1970/RemotingTest/ServerInfo.rem?wsdl
```

This should generate a SOAP message similar to the one shown in Figure 9-2.

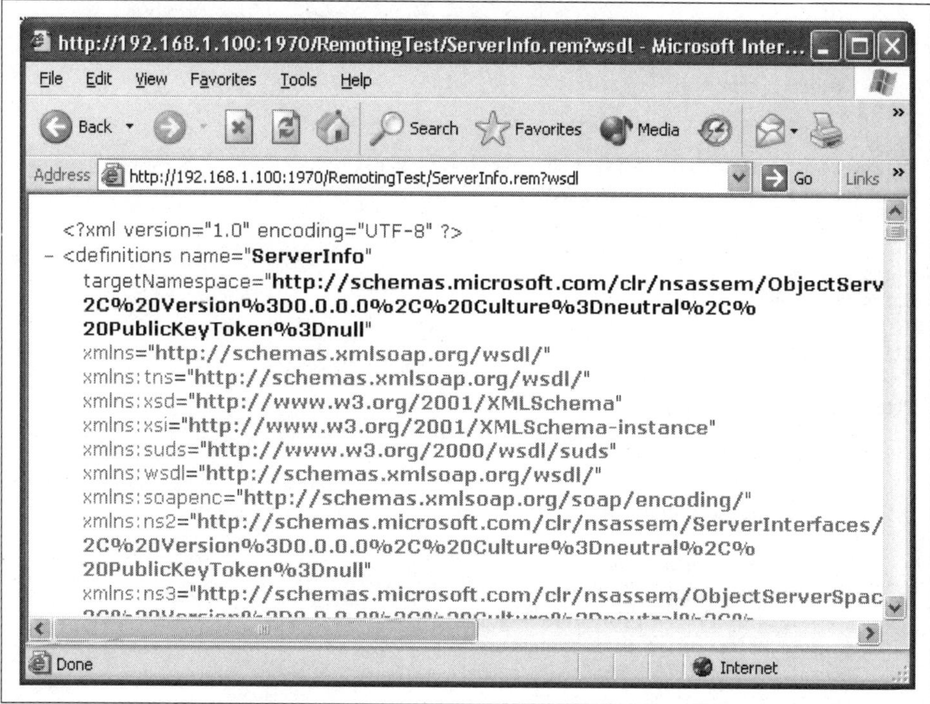


*Figure 9-2. SOAP definition of remote object*

# The Client

Now that the server is running, it's time to talk about building the client. The million dollar question is how the client will get the type information for `ServerInfo`. Directly referencing the *ServerInfo* assembly is one option, but not a realistic one, so it will not be considered. It doesn't take an active imagination to foresee the problems that can occur. Instead, this section examines a few techniques for consuming remote objects that allow the implementation to change without affecting the client.

## SoapSuds

The .NET Framework SDK ships with a utility called *SoapSuds.exe* that can generate a proxy object the client can use. *SoapSuds.exe* will even generate the source code for the proxy (but only in C#). Just point it to the URL of the remote object, link to the client shown in Example 9-7, and run. The `HTTPchannel` must be specified along with the port that was given to the server.

The following command creates a proxy object (with C# source) to the Singleton version of `ServerInfo`:

```
soapsuds -url:http://192.168.1.100:1970/RemotingTest/
ServerInfo.rem?wsdl -oa:ServerInfoProxy.dll -gc
```

*Example 9-7. Client for Remote Object Server*

```
'Remote Object Client
'
'Compile:
'vbc /t:exe /r:system.dll /r:System.Runtime.Remoting.dll
'/r:ServerInfoProxy.dll remoteclient.vb
'


Imports System
Imports ObjectServerSpace

Public Class Client

  Public Shared Sub Main()

    Try

      Dim si As New ServerInfo()

      If Not (si Is Nothing) Then
        Console.WriteLine(si.MachineName)
        Console.WriteLine(si.IPAddress)
        Console.WriteLine(si.GetMachineTime)
        Console.WriteLine("{0}MB Free", si.GetAvailableMemory)
        Console.WriteLine("Processor Used: {0}", si.GetProcessorUsed)
        Console.WriteLine("Calls made: {0}", si.CallCount)
      End If

    Catch e As Exception
      Console.WriteLine("Type: {0}", e.GetType().FullName)
      Console.WriteLine(e.Message)
    End Try

    Console.WriteLine("Hit ENTER to continue...")
    Console.ReadLine()

  End Sub

End Class
```

`si` looks like a local instance of `ServerInfo`. However, when the example is run (as shown in Figure 9-3), the statistics for the server machine are returned. The mystery is solved when the source code output from *SoapSuds* is examined. The namespace, class name, and methods are the same as ServerInfo, but the similarity ends there.

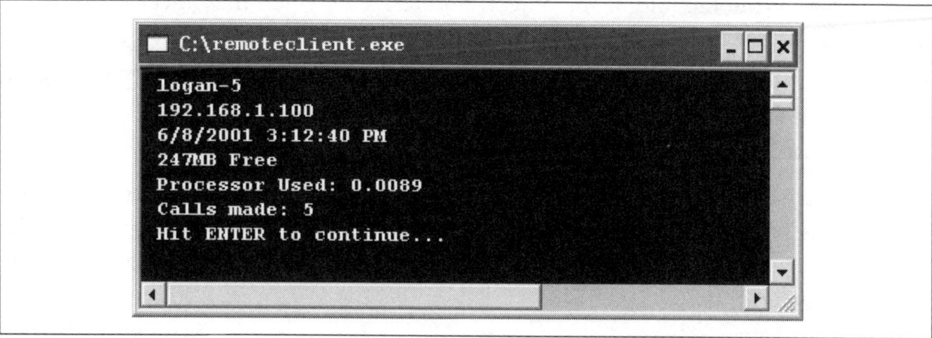


*Figure 9-3. Client output*

### Lifetime leases

If the client is run successively, the call count is steadily incremented, proving that the object is in fact a Singleton. However, Singleton objects do not live forever. When created, server-side objects are associated with a *lease*, which is a countdown to destruction. By default, the lease time is 5 minutes. If a call is not made during this time, the object is garbage collected. Otherwise, when the lease expires, it is renewed, by default, for another 2 minutes.

After running the client, walk away for a while (get a peanut butter and jelly sandwich or something) and come back. When the client is run again, the call count should be back down to 5, indicating that a new instance of the Singleton was activated.

You can change the lease defaults by overriding the InitializeLifetimeService method in the ServerInfo class. To make the Singleton live forever, just return Nothing:

```
'Inherited from MarshalByRefObject
Public Overrides Function InitializeLifetimeService() As Object
  Return Nothing
End Function
```

Optionally, the lease time can be changed. Here, the initial lease is set to 10 minutes, with a renewal time of 20 seconds:

```
Public Overrides Function InitializeLifetimeService() As Object
  Dim lease As ILease = CType(MyBase.GetLifetimeService, ILease)
  If lease.CurrentState = LeaseState.Initial Then
    lease.InitialLeaseTime = TimeSpan.FromMinutes(10)
    lease.RenewOnCallTime = TimeSpan.FromSeconds(20)
  End If
  Return lease
End Function
```

### Server and client activation

In Example 9-7, ServerInfo is a *server-activated* object. This means the server is responsible for the lifetime of the object; it determines when the object is no longer used. Each instance of the client will make calls on the same ServerInfo object.

In contrast, you can specify that a remote object be *client-activated*, meaning the client will have a say in determining an object's lifetime. To illustrate the concept, two changes must be made.

First, the server configuration file must be changed to allow ServerInfo to be client-activated. An <activated> element that supplies the client-activated type and the assembly in which it is located must be added within <service>, as the following code illustrates:

```
'RemoteService.exe.config
<service>
  <wellknown.../>
  <wellknown.../>
  <wellknown.../>
  <activated type="ObjectServerSpace.ServerInfo,ServerInfo"/>
<service>
```

The addition of the <activated> tag does not mean that the server will create client-activated types; it means that a client can now specify what kind of activation it wants (client or server).

The client must also be modified to register the type as client-activated, as follows (registration can occur anywhere, but the *Main* procedure is an obvious possibility):

```
Tmports System.Runtime.Remoting
.
.
.
RemotingConfiguration.RegisterActivatedClientType( _
  GetType(ServerInfo), "tcp://192.168.1.100:1969/RemotingTest")
Dim si As New ServerInfo()
```

RegisterActivatedType takes the client-activated type and a URL to the type's location. Note the location does not contain the object URI, only the path to the object.

The client-activated object is still created on the server, but the reference held is unique to the client. Running multiple instances of the client shows that the call count returned by the object is 5 for each instance. When the client terminates, the object is garbage collected as if it were local. However, the CAO still has a lease. If the client did not terminate (and if the object is still in scope) and the lease expired, the object would be garbage collected just like an SAO.

## Creating an Object Factory

Using *SoapSuds* to generate proxy assemblies has two shortcomings. First, it doesn't work if the object's constructor takes a parameter (it accepts only default constructors). Second, the server address is hardcoded into the proxy, which makes distribution more difficult. Changes on the server side would require the client to regenerate the proxy.

To get around this problem, you can use an object factory on the server. The idea behind this design pattern is that two interfaces are defined; the first interface (the factory) defines a method that returns the second (the object):

```
Public Interface IObjectFactory
    Function CreateObject() As IRemoteObject
End Interface
Public Interface IRemoteObject
    'Interface methods correspond to remote object
End Interface
```

The interfaces are kept in a separate assembly that is then shared between the client and the server. The remote object assembly resides on the server and is implemented like this:

```
Public Class ObjectFactory : Inherits MarshalByRefObject
  Implements IObjectFactory

  Public Function CreateObject() As IRemoteObject _
    Implements IServerInfoFactory.CreateServerInfo
    Return New RemoteObject()
  End Function

End Class

Public Class RemoteObject : Inherits MarshalByRefObject
  Implements IRemoteObject
  'Methods corresponding to IRemoteObject
End Class
```

The server configuration file exposes only the `ObjectFactory` class (which is implemented as a Singleton), preventing clients from establishing a dependency on `RemoteObject`. New functionality (or implementation of existing methods) can be added to the remote assembly without affecting existing clients.

### Factory interfaces

Example 9-8 contains the object factory interfaces for a new version of `ServerInfo`.

*Example 9-8. ServerInfo object factory interfaces*

```
'vbc /t:library /r:system.dll ServerInterfaces.vb
Imports System
Imports System.Net

Namespace ServerInterfaces

  Public Interface IServerInfoFactory
    Function CreateServerInfo() As IServerInfo
```

*Example 9-8. ServerInfo object factory interfaces (continued)*

```
  End Interface

  Public Interface IServerInfo
    Function GetMachineTime() As DateTime
    Function GetProcessorUsed() As Single
    Function GetAvailableMemory() As Long
    ReadOnly Property IPAddress() As IPAddress
    ReadOnly Property MachineName() As String
  End Interface

End Namespace
```

### ServerInfo factory

The ServerInfo class must now be changed in order to implement IServerInfo; the new version is shown in Example 9-9. In addition to referencing *ServerInterfaces.dll*, the object factory class must be implemented to return instances of the ServerInfo class.

*Example 9-9. ServerInfo and object factory*

```
'vbc /t:library /r:System.dll
'/r:ServerInterface.dll ServerInfo.vb

Imports System
Imports System.Diagnostics
Imports System.Net
Imports System.Threading

    'Private Data Members
Imports ServerInterfaces
Namespace ObjectServerSpace

  Public Class ServerInfoFactory : Inherits MarshalByRefObject
    Implements IServerInfoFactory

    Public Function CreateServerInfo() As IServerInfo _
      Implements IServerInfoFactory.CreateServerInfo
      Dim si As New ServerInfo()
      Return si
    End Function

  End Class

  Public Class ServerInfo : Inherits MarshalByRefObject
    Implements IServerInfo
    Public Sub New()
      'Init data members
    End Sub

    'Shared method
    Public Function GetMachineTime() As DateTime _
      Implements IServerInfo.GetMachineTime
```

*Example 9-9. ServerInfo and object factory (continued)*

```
    'Implementation
  End Function

  'Get % of process currently in use
  Public Function GetProcessorUsed() As Single _
    Implements IServerInfo.GetProcessorUsed
    'Implementation
  End Function

  'Get MBytes of free memory
  Public Function GetAvailableMemory() As Long _
    Implements IServerInfo.GetAvailableMemory
    'Implementation
  End Function

  Public ReadOnly Property MachineName() As String _
    Implements IServerInfo.MachineName
    'Implementation
  End Property

  Public ReadOnly Property IPAddress() As IPAddress _
    Implements IServerInfo.IPAddress
    'Implementation
  End Property

 End Class

End Namespace
```

## Using the Object Factory

The Windows Service does not need to be recompiled, because it does not directly reference *ServerInfo.dll* or *ServerInterfaces.dll*. However, the configuration file must be changed to expose a well-known Singleton object entry for the factory class (see Example 9-10). Generally, if there are entries for the object type returned by the factory in the *config* file, they can be removed.

*Example 9-10. Server configuration using object factory*

```
<configuration>
  <system.runtime.remoting>
    <application name="RemotingTest">
      <service>
        <wellknown mode="Singleton"
                   type="ObjectServerSpace.ServerInfoFactory,ServerInfo"
                   objectUri="ServerInfoFactory.rem" />
        <!--not needed
        <wellknown mode="Singleton"
                   type="ObjectServerSpace.ServerInfo,ServerInfo"
                   objectUri="ServerInfo.rem" />
        <wellknown mode="SingleCall"
                   type="ObjectServerSpace.ServerInfo,ServerInfo"
```

*Example 9-10. Server configuration using object factory (continued)*

```
                objectUri="ServerInfo2.rem" />-->
      </service>
    </application>
  </system.runtime.remoting>
</configuration>
```

*ServerInfo.dll* and *ServerInterfaces.dll* should be moved to the same directory as the service.

There are also several small changes to the client. First, add a reference to *ServerInterfaces.dll*. Then, remove the reference to *ServerInfoProxy.dll*.

Getting an interface is the factory's purpose. However, since interfaces cannot be created, another mechanism has to be used to obtain the remote object, which, unfortunately, means no transparent activation (e.g., creating an instance using `Dim` like a normal object).

`Activator.GetObject` can be called to return an interface reference to an existing server-side object. This method can be used in place of the old `ServerInfo` declaration:

```
'Replace this
'Dim si As New ServerInfo()

'with this
Dim factoryObj As Object = _
  Activator.GetObject(GetType(IServerInfoFactory), _
  "tcp://192.168.1.100:1969/RemotingTest/ServerInfoFactory.rem")

Dim factory As IServerInfoFactory = CType(factoryObj, IServerInfoFactory)
Dim si As IServerInfo = factory.CreateServerInfo()
```

The first parameter is the interface type—in this case, `IServerInfoFactory`. The second is the URL of the object as defined in the server *config* file, including the object URI. The returned `Object` can be typecast to the factory interface. Note, though, that the proxy does not transmit anything over the network until a method is called. Here, that is during `CreateServerInfo`.

## Designing for Remoting

Designing an object that lives in distributed environments almost runs counter to traditional OOP, in which public interfaces are kept lean and mean. Here are some general guidelines for remotable objects:

- Avoid "chatty" objects. These objects contain numerous properties that generate unnecessary traffic over the wire. Remember, each time a property is set, a round-trip on the network occurs.
- Make "chunky" calls. This means passing as much data as possible when making a method call.

- The method on a remote object should be Herculean. Normally, a method performs one specific task. In a remoting situation, a method should perform as many tasks as possible before returning.
- Return as much data as possible from a remote method. When you can, try to use structures containing only value types (but only if you know that boxing and unboxing will be kept to a minimum once the data is across).

The "GC allocations and collections" item in the Performance Monitor tells you how much boxing and unboxing is occurring.

Here are some general guidelines for the various activation models:

- Singletons are ideal for providing and maintaining data that is static or updated very infrequently. The services provided by a Singleton are not specific to any client.
- SingleCall objects are stateless and best used in high-traffic situations (for reasons of scalability) when data is specific to a client and is updated frequently.
- Client-activated objects are used when maintaining state (specific to one client) is necessary.

The `ServerInfo` class that was used throughout this chapter is very poorly (but purposefully) designed to make a point: objects that will live in a distributed environment should be designed with that environment in mind. `ServerInfo` was definitely not built with any such consideration.

In Example 9-7, it takes quite a few round-trips on the network to get all of the information because the object must be queried for each distinct piece of information it provides. It's not possible to marshal the current version of `ServerInfo` by value because the idea is to get machine information at a remote location. What is needed is a way to get all the information at one time and return it to the client in one call.

The idea behind this, of course, is to minimize travel across the wire. There is no reason why `ServerInfo` could not return all the required information at once. The point emphasized here is to design with distribution in mind. Don't expect to retrofit existing objects for dispersed locales and gain any benefits.

# Marshal by Value (MBV)

Example 9-11 contains yet another version of `ServerInfo`. There are only two differences between this version and the last:

- The class is marked `<Serializable>` instead of derived from `MarshalByRefObj`, which is required to marshal an object by value.
- All data that is provided by the class is obtained in the constructor instead of at call time.

When ServerInfoFactory.CreateServerInfo is called, all remote machine properties are ascertained immediately. This is necessary because next, the entire class is marshaled by value back to the client; that is, a complete copy is transferred to the client. If the machine values were not obtained in the constructor, the class would return values relative to the client machine (because the object will be local to the client).

Example 9-11 is not meant to be presented as the optimal method for the ServerInfo case. The purpose is to demonstrate the flexibility of the remoting framework and to present some of the issues that are faced in real-world development. Remember, when remoting, use what works and is really fast.

*Example 9-11. MBV version of ServerInfo*

```
<Serializable()> _
Public Class ServerInfo
  Implements IServerInfo

  Private machineTime As DateTime
  Private processorUsed As Single
  Private availableMemory As Long
  Private machine As String
  Private ip As IPAddress

  Public Sub New()

    'Get machine info when object is created
    machine = Dns.GetHostName()
    Dim ipHost As IPHostEntry = Dns.GetHostByName(machine)
    ip = ipHost.AddressList(0)

    'Machine date
    machineTime = DateTime.Now

    'Processor used
    If PerformanceCounterCategory.Exists("Processor") Then
      Dim pc As New PerformanceCounter("Processor", _
          "% Processor Time", "_Total", True)
      Dim sampleA As CounterSample
      Dim sampleB As CounterSample
      sampleA = pc.NextSample()
      Thread.Sleep(1000)
      sampleB = pc.NextSample()
      processorUsed = CounterSample.Calculate(sampleA, sampleB)
    End If

    'Available memory
    If PerformanceCounterCategory.Exists("Memory") Then
      Dim pc As New PerformanceCounter("Memory", "Available MBytes")
      availableMemory = pc.RawValue()
    End If
```

*Example 9-11. MBV version of ServerInfo (continued)*

```
End Sub

'Shared method
Public Function GetMachineTime() As DateTime _
  Implements IServerInfo.GetMachineTime
  Return machineTime
End Function

'Get % of process currently in use
Public Function GetProcessorUsed() As Single _
  Implements IServerInfo.GetProcessorUsed
  Return processorUsed
End Function

'Get MBytes of free memory
Public Function GetAvailableMemory() As Long _
  Implements IServerInfo.GetAvailableMemory
  Return availableMemory
End Function

Public ReadOnly Property MachineName() As String _
  Implements IServerInfo.MachineName
  Get
    Return machine
  End Get
End Property

Public ReadOnly Property IPAddress() As IPAddress _
  Implements IServerInfo.IPAddress
  Get
    Return ip
  End Get
End Property
```

Other than these two changes, everything is the same on the server side—even the configuration file (which contains one well-known entry that exposes the object factory). Just stop the service, copy the assembly to the appropriate location, and restart.

Some interesting architectural changes must be made to accommodate the fact that `ServerInfo` is now an MBV object. The client must have access to the *ServerInfo* assembly to use the object, which raises several questions.

Can the client get the type information from the *ServerInfo* assembly without linking to it? Thankfully, yes. The client does not need to reference the object directly. Otherwise, the object factory concept would be rendered useless. *ServerInfo* just needs to be in the same directory as the client executable.

This still presents some problems, though. The client is not linked to the assembly, but what about distribution? If changes are made to the remote assembly, how is the client going to get it? Also, the source to the remote assembly will be on the client machine, where it can be disassembled by money-hungry corporate spies! IL is not difficult to pick up, and reverse engineering has never been easier.

One solution is to move the entire Windows Service into a virtual directory on the web server. The service can still provide the objects over TCP, and the client can now use a few lines of code to download the *ServerInfo* assembly to its location at runtime. This way, the client always has the latest version of the object. The assembly can be loaded into the client `AppDomain`, making the `ServerInfo` type available. Once this has occurred, the downloaded file can be deleted from the client directory, leaving no trace of its existence.

## Configuring IIS

To make the *ServerInfo* assembly available from IIS, set up a directory called *ServerInfo* for the component under *wwwroot* (it can be set up anywhere local to the web server if a different location is desired):

```
Inetpub
  wwwroot
    ServerInfo
      bin          <- server, assemblies, service .config file
```

In IIS, configure *ServerInfo* as a virtual directory. Make sure that the *ServerInfo* and *bin* directories use the following settings:

- Execute Permissions = "Scripts Only"
- Application Protection = "Low (IIS Process)"
- Read Permission
- Anonymous and Integrated Windows authentication (IWA)

If Execute Permissions are not set to "Scripts Only," the *ServerInfo* assembly will not download.

All server files should be placed in the *bin* directory, while the upper-level *ServerInfo* directory contains nothing. The server should be started with everything configured as before. Remember that this configuration also applies when using IIS (versus a server) to remote objects.

## Custom Application Settings

On the client side, the location of the virtual directory and the object name can be stored in the client configuration file, which is shown in Example 9-12. For the .NET configuration class to find the file, it must have the same name (with file extension) as the client assembly, followed by *.config* (i.e., *remoteclient.exe.config*). Custom settings can be added in `<appSettings>`, as illustrated in Example 9-12.

*Example 9-12. Client-side configuration settings*

```
<configuration>
  <appSettings>
    <add key="location" value="http://192.168.1.100/ServerInfo/bin/" />
    <add key="assembly" value="ServerInfo" />
  </appSettings>
  <system.runtime.remoting>
    <!--
    client side remoting settings are here
    -->
  </system.runtime.remoting>
</configuration>
```

At runtime, these values can be retrieved (rather than hardcoded in the source) by using the `System.Configuration.ConfigurationSettings` class:

```
Dim location As String
Dim remoteAssembly As String
Dim fileName As String

location = ConfigurationSettings.AppSettings("location")
remoteAssembly = ConfigurationSettings.AppSettings("assembly")
fileName = remoteAssembly + ".dll"
```

Example 9-13 contains the listing for the revised client that uses the MBV `ServerInfo` object. The *ServerInfo* assembly is downloaded to the client by calling `WebClient.DownloadFile`, which conveniently provides just what is needed here. The first parameter to the method is the remote file's URL, while the second is the name it should be saved to locally.

Once the file is downloaded, a call is made to `AppDomain.SetShadowCopyFiles` (for the current domain). This call is necessary to prevent *ServerInfo.dll* from being locked when the assembly is loaded into the AppDomain. After calling `AppDomain.Load` to inject the assembly into the current AppDomain, the file is deleted using `File.Delete`. However, the `ServerInfo` type is now available to the client. The rest of the client code behaves as it did previously, using `Activator.GetObject` to get the object factory interface. This time, when `CreateServerInfo` is called, the factory returns an MBV instance of the remote object.

*Example 9-13. Revised client*

```
Imports System
Imports System.Configuration
Imports System.IO
Imports System.Net
Imports System.Reflection
Imports System.Runtime.Remoting

Imports ServerInterfaces

Public Class Client
```

*Example 9-13. Revised client (continued)*

```
  Public Shared Sub Main()

    Try

     '----- Download ServerInfo.dll
      Dim location As String
      Dim remoteAssembly As String
      Dim fileName As String

      location = ConfigurationSettings.AppSettings("location")
      remoteAssembly = ConfigurationSettings.AppSettings("assembly")
      fileName = remoteAssembly + ".dll"

      Dim wc As New WebClient()
      wc.DownloadFile(location + fileName, fileName)

      AppDomain.CurrentDomain.SetShadowCopyFiles()
      AppDomain.CurrentDomain.Load(remoteAssembly)
      File.Delete(fileName)
      '----------------------------

      Dim factoryObj As Object = _
      Activator.GetObject(GetType(IServerInfoFactory), _
        "tcp://192.168.1.100:1969/RemotingTest/ServerInfoFactory.rem")

      Dim factory As IServerInfoFactory = _
        CType(factoryObj, IServerInfoFactory)
      Dim si As IServerInfo = factory.CreateServerInfo()

      If Not (si Is Nothing) Then
        Console.WriteLine(si.MachineName)
        Console.WriteLine(si.IPAddress)
        Console.WriteLine(si.GetMachineTime)
        Console.WriteLine("{0}MB Free", si.GetAvailableMemory)
        Console.WriteLine("Processor Used: {0}", si.GetProcessorUsed)
      End If


    Catch e As Exception
      Console.WriteLine(e.GetType().FullName)
      Console.WriteLine(e.Message)
    End Try

    Console.WriteLine("Hit ENTER to continue...")
    Console.ReadLine()

  End Sub

End Class
```

## Hosting Objects in IIS

One of the biggest benefits of using IIS over a Windows Service is security. It is trivial to configure the remote object to use Windows Authentication to validate an incoming call. Drawbacks include limited configuration options and communication that is restricted to the `HttpChannel` (which means slower performance). However, you can configure the channel to use binary formatting (versus SOAP), which is somewhat better, performance-wise. The only other requirement is that the hosted object be derived from `MarshalByRefObject`.

IIS should already be configured at this point. All the necessary assemblies should be in place. If not, review the "Configuring IIS" section earlier in the chapter and configure accordingly. Only one addition should be made; a configuration file containing the appropriate entries must be placed in the *ServerInfo* virtual directory.

### Web.config

The good news is that the configuration file from Example 9-10 can be used as a starting point; just copy it and rename the copy to *Web.config*. Before placing it in the *ServerInfo* virtual directory, make these two important changes:

- Remove the `name` attribute from the `<application>` element. The application name is determined by the name of the virtual directory defined in IIS, not the configuration file. An exception will be thrown otherwise.
- Make sure the `objectUri` is unique. If the Windows Service is still used concurrently with this example, change the `objectUri` value to something that denotes that it is served from IIS.

When all is said and done, *Web.config* should look similar to this:

```
<configuration>
  <system.runtime.remoting>
    <application> <!-- cannot define application name -->
      <service>
        <wellknown mode="Singleton"
          type="ObjectServerSpace.ServerInfoFactory, ServerInfo"
          objectUri="ServerInfoFactoryWeb.rem" />
      </service>
    </application>
  </system.runtime.remoting>
</configuration>
```

That's all there is to it. Copy the file to *ServerInfo* and make sure the *bin* directory contains a version of `ServerInfo` that is derived from `MarshalByRefObject`. To be safe, restart the web server. Many sources say that restarting the server is not necessary, but testing indicates otherwise.

## Client for IIS-Hosted Remote Object

To work, the client configuration file from Example 9-12 needs a few modifications. First, an `HttpChannel` must be added that uses the binary formatter (*slightly* better performance). The formatter does not have to be specified on the server side because the `HttpChannel` is set up to use both. The client decides which one to use. The modified configuration file is as follows:

```
<!-- remoteclient.exe.config -->
<configuration>
  <!-- No longer used
  <appSettings>
    <add key="location" value="http://192.168.1.100/ServerInfo/bin/" />
    <add key="assembly" value="ServerInfo" />
  </appSettings> -->
  <system.runtime.remoting>
    <application>
      <channels>
        <channel ref="http">
        <clientProviders>
          <formatter ref="binary"/>
        </clientProviders>
        </channel>
      </channels>
    </application>
  </system.runtime.remoting>
</configuration>
```

Until now, the client has used its configuration file only for custom application settings. Now that there are remoting settings, the client must be modified in order to use them. This modification is done in exactly the same manner as the server, by calling `RemotingConfiguration.Configure`.

The client from Example 9-13 can be modified easily to accommodate these changes. Remove the block marked "Download ServerInfo.dll" and replace it with the following line of code:

```
RemotingConfiguration.Configure("remoteclient.exe.config")
```

The only other mandatory change is the call to `Activator.GetObject`. The URL needs to be changed to point to the `<wellknown>` object exposed from IIS:

```
Dim factoryObj As Object = _
      Activator.GetObject(GetType(IServerInfoFactory), _
        "http://192.168.1.100/ServerInfo/ServerInfoFactoryWeb.rem")
Example 9-14 contains the final client listing.
Example 9-14: Client for IIS-hosted object

'vbc /t:exe /r:system.dll /r:system.runtime.remoting.dll
'/r:ServerInterfaces.dll remoteclient.vb

Imports System
Imports System.Net
```

```
Imports System.Runtime.Remoting
Imports System.Threading

Imports ServerInterfaces

Public Class Client

  Public Shared Sub Main()

    Try

      RemotingConfiguration.Configure("remoteclient.exe.config")

      Dim factoryObj As Object = _
      Activator.GetObject(GetType(IServerInfoFactory), _
        "http://192.168.1.100/ServerInfo/ServerInfoFactoryWeb.rem")

      Dim factory As IServerInfoFactory = _
        CType(factoryObj, IServerInfoFactory)

      Dim si As IServerInfo = factory.CreateServerInfo()

      If Not (si Is Nothing) Then
        Console.WriteLine(si.MachineName)
        Console.WriteLine(si.IPAddress)
        Console.WriteLine(si.GetMachineTime)
        Console.WriteLine("{0}MB Free", si.GetAvailableMemory)
        Console.WriteLine("Processor Used: {0}", si.GetProcessorUsed)
      End If


    Catch e As Exception
      Console.WriteLine(e.GetType().FullName)
      Console.WriteLine(e.Message)
    End Try

    Console.WriteLine("Hit ENTER to continue...")
    Console.ReadLine()

  End Sub

End Class
```

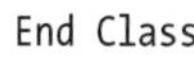

Rewriting the Windows Service to accept the application name as a custom configuration setting would be better than specifying it in the <application> element. The application name could be retrieved from the *config* file and registered programmatically. This would allow the server *config* file to be used interchangeably as a *Web.config* file.

## Windows Service Versus IIS

As it stands now, `ServerInfo` is hosted concurrently from a Windows Service and Internet Information Server. Each has its advantages. In terms of raw speed and configurability, nothing beats the Windows Service. On the other hand, any object derived from `MarshalByRefObject` takes only a few minutes to set up for remoting in IIS. However, this alone shouldn't determine which scenario is appropriate. After all, the server code in this chapter only requires the remote object to be in the same directory and have a `<wellknown>` entry in the configuration file, which takes about a minute for a fast typist.

The Windows Service can easily accommodate Singleton and SingleCall objects (as can IIS), but unlike IIS, it allows objects to be marshaled by value. Also, while both the service and IIS can use SAOs and CAOs, using CAOs from IIS is generally unwise. The ASP.NET worker process, which handles this process for IIS, can be recycled beyond a client's control, causing the CAO to be destroyed unexpectedly.

One of the most tangible benefits of using IIS over a Windows Service is security. There is also another option, XML web services, which is discussed in Chapter 10.

IIS also stands out in the client arena. Essentially, a remote object hosted under IIS is a web application managed by ASP.NET. Even though there are no visual elements (and the existing client runs in a console window), don't be fooled. Drop the *ServerInfo.aspx* file shown in Example 9-14 into the *ServerInfo* directory.

*Example 9-14. ServerInfo.aspx*

```
<%@ Page Language="VB" %>
<%@ Import Namespace="ObjectServerSpace" %>

<html>
<head>
  <script language="VB" runat="server">
    Sub Page_Load(ByVal obj As Object, ByVal e As EventArgs)
      Dim si As New ServerInfo()
      machine.Text = si.MachineName.ToUpper
      ip.Text = si.IPAddress.ToString
      dt.Text = si.GetMachineTime
      freeMem.Text = si.GetAvailableMemory.ToString + "MB Free"
      procUsed.Text = "Processor Used: " + _
        si.GetProcessorUsed.ToString + "%"
    End Sub
  </script>
</head>
<body>
<form runat="server">
  <asp:label id="machine" runat="server"
    style="font-size: 14pt;"/></br>
  <asp:label id="ip" runat="server"/></br>
  <asp:label id="dt" runat="server"/></br>
  <asp:label id="freemem" runat="server"/></br>
  <asp:label id="procUsed" runat="server"/></br>
```

*Example 9-14. ServerInfo.aspx (continued)*

```
</form>
</body>
</html>
```

Once in place, the page (shown in Figure 9-4) can be hit from the following URL using any browser: *http://192.168.1.100/ServerInfo/ServerInfo.aspx*.

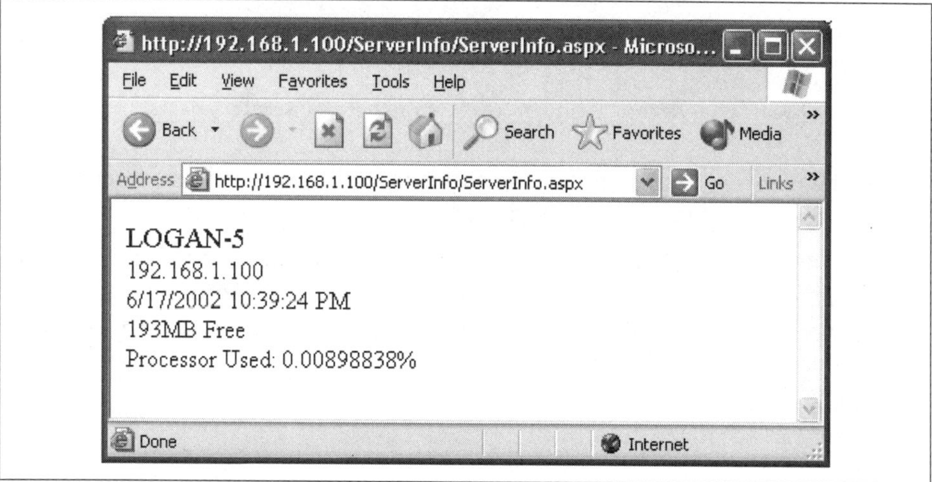


*Figure 9-4. Using a browser with remote objects hosted in IIS*

# Authentication

Currently, the *ServerInfo* virtual directory is configured to allow anonymous access and Integrated Windows authentication (IWA). In spite of this configuration, no authentication takes place because the anonymous connection is always attempted first (which explains why things happen relatively quickly).

To authenticate users, leave IIS in its current configuration ( with anonymous access and IWA turned on) and use the *Web.config* file to control who has access to the resource.

To prevent anonymous users from accessing the assembly, use:

```
<configuration>
<system.runtime.remoting>
  <!-remoting settings are up here
</system.runtime.remoting>
<system.web>
  <authentication mode="Windows" />
  <authorization>
    <deny users="?" />
  </authorization>
</system.web>
</configuration>
```

Specific users can be granted access by initially denying everyone and then specifying who has permission:

```
<authorization>
  <deny users="*" />
  <allow users="Administrator, ServerInfoClient" />
</authorization>
```

Or, permissions can be assigned based on roles (or a permutation of all of the above):

```
<authorization>
  <deny users="*" />
  <allow users="ServerInfoClient" roles="Administrators, Remote Objects" />
</authorization>
```

To avoid confusion, the ? represents unauthenticated users, while the * refers to all users, whether or not they are authenticated.

Typically, when an application accesses restricted resources, it does so through an account created specifically for that purpose (rather than by creating accounts for every user). Therefore, go ahead and modify *Web.config* to restrict access to a single user named `ServerInfoClient`:

```
<authorization>
  <deny users="*" />
  <allow users="ServerInfoClient" />
</authorization>
```

This account fulfills that purpose for the rest of the chapter. No specific rights need to be assigned; just create the user on the domain (or the local machine, if testing is done there) and assign it a password.

## Credentials

If everything is configured correctly, the client from Example 9-14 will no longer work. Instead of receiving server information, the output looks something like this:

```
System.Net.WebException
The remote server returned an error: (401) Unauthorized.
```

This output occurs because the client must now provide the appropriate credentials to access the remote object. Creating the appropriate credentials is easy with the `System.Net.NetworkCredential` class; the constructor takes a user name, password, and domain—just what is needed. But getting the credential to IIS is the trick.

Calling `ChannelServices.GetChannelSinkProperties` returns an `IDictionary` interface that allows various properties associated with the proxy object to be set or retrieved.

The properties are:

`username`
: Username for basic and digest authentication

`password`
: Password for basic and digest authentication

`domain`
: Domain name for basic and digest authentication

`preauthenticate`
: Indicates whether preauthentication of requests is enabled

`credentials`
: Security credentials for web service client authentication

`clientcertificates`
: Collection of client certificates

`proxyname`
: The name of the proxy server to use for requests

`proxyport`
: The port number of the proxy server to use for requests

`timeout`
: The timeout (in milliseconds) for synchronous calls

`allowautoredirect`
: Indicates whether automatic handling of server redirects is enabled

The property of interest is `credentials`. The following fragment demonstrates how this property is set using the `NetworkCredential` class. Notice that the credentials must be set for the factory object as well as the `ServerInfo` proxy instance:

```
Dim factory As IServerInfoFactory = _
Activator.GetObject(GetType(IServerInfoFactory), _
  "http://192.168.1.100:80/ServerInfo/ServerInfoFactoryWeb.rem")

Dim dictionary As IDictionary = _
  ChannelServices.GetChannelSinkProperties(factory)

'Set the cedentials for factory object
Dim nc As NetworkCredential = _
  New NetworkCredential("RemoteUserWithRights", "pass", "MYDOMAIN")
dictionary("credentials") = nc

'Get object from factory
Dim si As IServerInfo = factory.CreateServerInfo()

'Use credentials for ServerInfo, too
dictionary = ChannelServices.GetChannelSinkProperties(si)
dictionary("credentials") = nc

'Make calls on IServerInfo here
```

## CHAPTER 10

# Web Services

XML web services represent the next evolution (revolution?) of distributed computing. Web services are a testament to the fact that often in computing, simplicity can be elegant.

Essentially, a web service is a specialized web server that listens and responds to SOAP messages (of a particular type) over HTTP. The implementation of web services and clients is irrelevant: the client sends a request to a known URL in a predetermined format. A web service only needs to process that message and send back a response. It is as simple as that. As long as an Internet connection is available, the client can be a browser or a background process, or it can have a feature-rich GUI—and it can exist on any platform that supports the HTTP, SOAP, and XML protocols.

The use of industry-standard protocols is not accidental. XML web services are not a Microsoft-centric technology, but rather a global effort involving just about every major player in computing. The driving force behind web services is the need to provide cross-platform services over the Internet

.NET brings encapsulation to XML web services. The communication details are completely hidden, making it possible to write a web service without any knowledge of HTTP, SOAP, or XML. This feature allows the developer to shift focus toward the application itself and providing services, rather than being caught up in what some would consider tedious implementation details.

For the most part, writing an XML web service under .NET is just like writing any other class. The same can be said for consuming an XML web service. A component that contains web services looks and feels just like any other component to the .NET developer. It just so happens that the method calls are invoked over the Internet. However, web service class design is constrained because web services are inherently stateless, much like a SingleCall object under .NET remoting.

## Writing a Web Service

Zip code verification is a simple but useful example of a service that can be provided over the Web. The sole purpose of this web service is to confirm that a zip code for a given city is valid. Imagine it as just one of several services offered to online businesses to authenticate shipping and billing addresses and minimize fraud. It also solves a real-world problem: someone in California makes an online purchase from a web site in California, provides a California address, but uses a zip code from Texas. Chances are that the order will arrive, albeit late, to the intended address. However, by specifying an improper zip code, the purchaser has circumvented paying sales tax.

### The Web Service Class

Any class that wishes to become a web service must have at least one method that is decorated with a `WebMethod` attribute. This is the bare minimum requirement for running a web service.

There is also a `WebService` attribute that is used at the class level, as in:

```
<WebService(Namespace:="http://www.mydomainhere.com/")> _
Public Class ZipService
```

Although the `WebService` attribute is not a runtime requirement, it should be used nonetheless to provide a namespace that uniquely identifies the web service on the Internet. Usually, a company uses its domain to form the namespace. However, the namespace itself does not have to conform to a site that can be reached over the Internet. If a namespace is not given, *http://tempuri.org/* is used by default. (This stands for "temp URI" and has nothing to do with Japanese food.) Additionally, the attribute provides properties that allow the name of the service to be specified as well as the service to be described.

Example 10-1 contains the list for the zip code validation web service. The class contains a single method, `IsValid`, which simply returns `True`. The actual method implementation is delayed until the end of the chapter, for those who are interested. The goal here is to get the web service to work. Compile it to an assembly named *ZipService*, since it will be used throughout the rest of the chapter.

*Example 10-1. Zip code validation web service (shell)*

```
'vbc /t:library /r:System.dll
'/r:System.Web.Services.dll ZipService.vb

Imports System
Imports System.Web.Services

<WebService(Namespace:="http://www.mydomainhere.com/")> _
Public Class ZipService
```

*Example 10-1. Zip code validation web service (shell) (continued)*

```
  <WebMethod()> _
  Public Function IsValid(ByVal City As String, _
                          ByVal Zip As String) As Boolean
    Return True
  End Function

End Class
```

The web service class can optionally inherit from `System.Web.Services.WebService`:

```
Imports System
Imports System.Web.Services
<WebService(Namespace:="http://me.com")> _
Public Class ZipService : Inherits WebService
```

This inheritance gives the class access to intrinsic ASP.NET objects such as `Session`, `Application`, `Context`, and `Server`.

Several interesting properties can be used with the `WebMethod` attribute:

`BufferResponse`
: This Boolean indicates whether the response should be buffered before it is sent to the client. When `True`, the response is buffered first and then sent to the client in its entirety. This is beneficial when a large amount of data is passed. If `False`, data is sent to the client as it is serialized. This is ideal when small amounts of data are sent. If the `BufferedResponse` property is not provided, its value defaults to `True`; the response to the client is buffered.

`CacheDuration`
: This property specifies the number of seconds a response should be held in the cache. A value of `0` (the default) indicates that the response is not cached. Setting this property would not be appropriate for a web service like `ZipService` because of the variance in the requests (hundreds of different zip codes and cities, with very few identical requests).

`Description`
: This property associates descriptive text with the method.

`EnableSession`
: If `True`, this property indicates that session state is maintained for the web method. Its default value is `False`; session state is disabled. Maintaining session state causes poor performance and requires that the web service inherit from the `WebService` class.

`MessageName`
: This property allows a different name to be associated with a method. It is particularly useful when a web service has several overloaded methods.

## Hosting Under IIS

To deploy the web service, create a virtual directory called *ZipService* (see "Configuring IIS" in Chapter 9) and place its DLL in the */bin* subdirectory, as follows:

```
Inetpub
  wwwroot
    ZipService   <-- ZipService.asmx
      bin        <-- Web service assembly
```

Once the assembly is in place, a way is needed to find it. To access the web service from a browser, place an *.asmx* file (*ZipService.asmx*) describing the service in the *ZipService* virtual directory. The file contains this single line:

```
<%@ WebService Class="ZipService" %>
```

As long as the class specified in the `WebService` entry is in the */bin* directory, it will be found.

### Web Services from ASP.NET

Rather than compiling the web service to a separate assembly, the entire web service can be defined within an *.asmx* file such as the following, named *ZipService.asmx*:

```
<%@ WebService Language="VB" Class="ZipService" %>

Imports System
Imports System.Web.Services

<WebService( _
  Namespace:="http://www.mydomainhere.com/")> _
Public Class ZipService

  <WebMethod()> _
  Public Function IsValid(ByVal City As String, _
    ByVal Zip As String) As Boolean
    Return True
  End Function

End Class
```

In this case, a `Language` directive is required to specify the language used. This directive allows ASP.NET to compile the web service on the fly. The assembly that is generated will be in the ASP.NET cache rather than the */bin* directory. Its path is *<%windir%>/Microsoft.NET/Framework/<%version%>/Temporary ASP.NET Files/<%assembly%>*.

## Testing the Web Service

As for testing, ASP.NET does most of the work by generating the necessary pages to test the web service. Navigating to the URL of *ZipService.asmx* brings up the page shown in Figure 10-1.

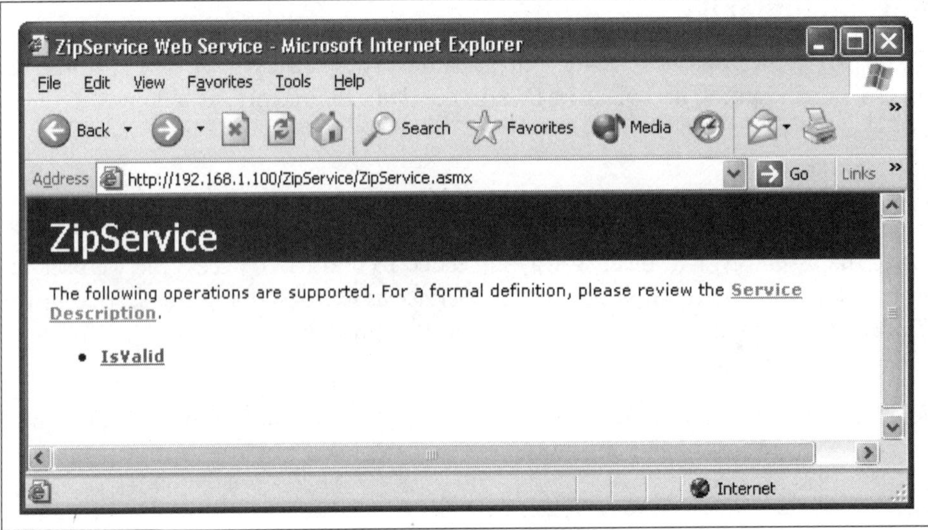


*Figure 10-1. ZipService gateway*

Clicking on the Service Description link brings up a description of the web service in Web Service Description Language (WSDL), as Figure 10-2 illustrates. WSDL is a specification that describes a web service by using XML. Notice that the URL shown in Figure 10-2 has `?WSDL` appended to it. This is similar to the way a URL is specified for *SoapSuds* (see Chapter 9). The resulting output is different, though. Remoting uses RPC-encoded SOAP, while ASP.NET web services use what is known as the Document/literal format.

Essentially, *SoapSuds* expects RPC-encoded SOAP, so `ZipService` is not available within the remoting framework (yet). However, the WSDL that is produced serves the same purpose. It is used to create a proxy class that allows clients to access the service.

Clicking on the IsValid link shown in Figure 10-1 brings up a test harness for the web method. A test form, shown in Figure 10-3, is generated automatically. It allows individual parameters of the method to be specified and provides a button to invoke the method. At this point, regardless of the parameters passed, the following XML containing the result of the call is returned in the browser:

```
<?xml version="1.0" encoding="utf-8" ?>
<boolean xmlns="http://192.168.1.100/">true</boolean>
```

## The Client

Creating a client for a web service is similar to creating one for remoting. The difference is the tool that is used. Attempting to use *SoapSuds* returns the following error (because it expects a different encoding than that provided by ASP.NET):

```
Error: Invalid schema data., No Bindings with Soap, Rpc and
Encoded elements.
```

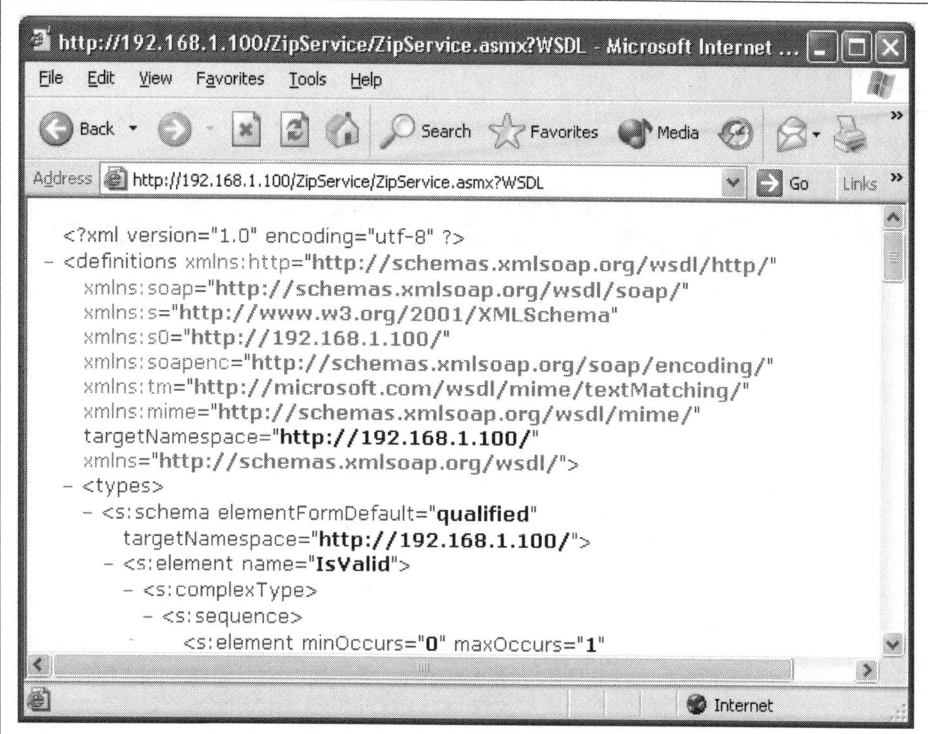


*Figure 10-2. WSDL for ZipService*

Another available utility, *wsdl.exe*, can generate the proxy instead. The program provides all the options necessary to reach a web server from the command line. It has switches to specify a username, password, domain, and proxy server. To get a complete list of options, run the utility with the `/?` switch. Unlike *SoapSuds*, the output can be generated in VB by entering the following code at the command line:

```
wsdl /language:VB /out:ZipServiceProxy.vb
  http://192.168.1.100/ZipService/ZipService.asmx?wsdl
```

This example produces a file called *ZipServiceProxy.vb* that contains a class called `ZipService`. But instead of one method, this version has three: `IsValid`, `BeginIsValid`, and `EndIsValid`. For every web method exposed in the class, two additional methods, with the `Begin`*<webmethod>* and `End`*<webmethod>* format, are generated in the proxy.

These methods are provided for calling the method asynchronously (a nonblocking call). While using these methods with the zip validation service is unnecessary, an asynchronous client example will be presented anyway. First, though, look at Example 10-2, which contains a synchronous version of the client. It's pretty much a nonevent; it's not even possible to tell that a web service is called by looking at the code.

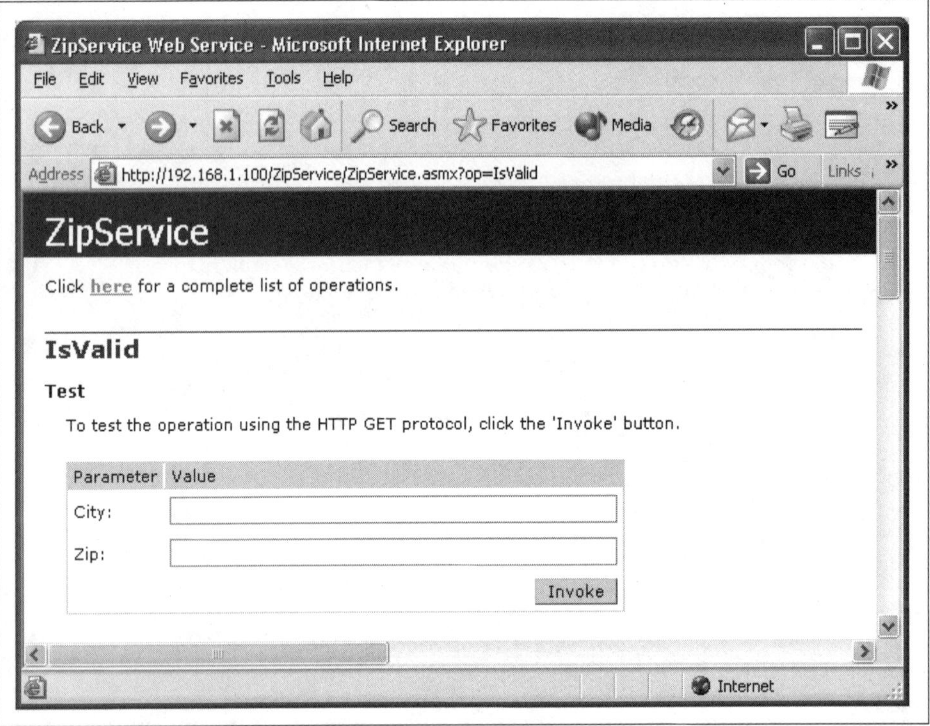


*Figure 10-3. Testing ZipService*

When compiling, the proxy class is also specified. This class requires three assemblies to be referenced: *System*, *System.Web.Services*, and *System.Xml*.

*Example 10-2. Synchronous client*

```
'vbc /t:exe /r:system.dll /r:system.web.services.dll
'/r:system.xml.dll zipclient.vb zipserviceproxy.vb

Imports System

Public Class Test
  Public Shared Sub Main()
    Dim zs As New ZipService()
    Dim result As Boolean = zs.IsValid("Houston", "77006")
    Console.WriteLine(result)
  End Sub
End Class
```

Example 10-3 is a little more involved, since it contains the listing for an asynchronous client. The code is similar, in many ways, to the War of the Worlds server that was presented in Chapter 8 (see Example 8-17). When the client is initially run, a new thread is created, along with an instance of ZipServiceHandler.

*Example 10-3. Asynchronous web service client*

```
'vbc /t:exe /r:system.dll /r:system.web.services.dll
'/r:system.xml.dll zipclient.vb zipserviceproxy.vb

Imports System
Imports System.Threading

Public Class ZipServiceHandler

  Public Sub New()
    Dim zs As ZipService = New ZipService()
    Dim callback As New AsyncCallback(AddressOf ZipServiceCallback)
    Dim ar As IAsyncResult = _
      zs.BeginIsValid("Houston", "77006", callback, zs)
    While (ar.IsCompleted = False)
      'Do work here while service is running
    End While
  End Sub

  Private Sub ZipServiceCallback(ByVal ar As IAsyncResult)
    Dim zs As ZipService = CType(ar.AsyncState, ZipService)
    'Write the results to the console
    Console.WriteLine(zs.EndIsValid(ar))
    Console.WriteLine("Press ENTER to continue...")
  End Sub

End Class

Public Class Client

  Public Shared Sub Main()
    Dim t As New Thread(New ThreadStart(AddressOf ThreadProc))
    t.Start()
    Console.ReadLine()
  End Sub

  Private Shared Sub ThreadProc()
    Dim zipHandler As New ZipServiceHandler()
  End Sub

End Class
```

In the constructor of `ZipServiceHandler`, an instance of the web service is created first, followed by an `AsyncCallback` delegate. The callback delegate refers to the method that is called once the web service finishes executing. A client calling a web service and using an asynchronous callback is different from the War of the Worlds server in Chapter 8, in that data is not sent in chunks when calling a web service asynchronously. There is only one SOAP request and one SOAP response. The proxy class uses a different thread than the client to handle the SOAP response.

Next, `BeginIsValid` is invoked. The `Begin`*`<webmethod>`* methods have the same parameters as the original web method. Additionally, two parameters are appended to the signature. The first is the callback delegate, and the second is an `Object` parameter that can pass information to the callback method. In the example, the web service class is passed to `ZipServiceCallback` in this way. The call returns an `IAsyncResult` interface that can determine when the web method has completed. Additional processing can occur while waiting for the web method to return.

The callback function takes an `IAsyncResult` as its only parameter. `IAsyncResult.AsyncState` is called to retrieve the instance of the web service that was passed during the `BeginIsValid` call. Processing is stopped by calling `EndIsValid` and passing it the incoming `IAsyncResult` interface.

## Web Services Versus Remoting

Performance considerations make it just as important to know when to use web services as when not to use them. In this race, as shown in Figure 10-4, web services come in dead last every time.*

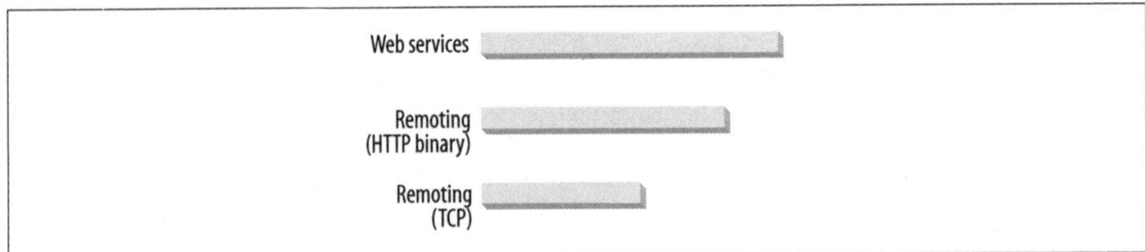


*Figure 10-4. Mean relative method call duration*

There seem to be several misconceptions about when to use web services. One common fallacy is that web services should be used when the client must traverse a firewall. Another myth is that if the client makes method calls over the Internet, web services must be used. Both assumptions are plainly false because these tasks can be accomplished easily with remoting.

The question of when to use web services over .NET remoting is answered by looking at the endpoints of the application. If the client is .NET, use remoting: it's just faster and more configurable. You can use binary and XML-based protocols. If security is an issue, use IIS to host the object, as shown in Chapter 9. In most cases, using binary over HTTP is faster than using a web service. Also, the client experience has the potential to be richer because events and callbacks can be used.

If the client is on a non-.NET platform or is unknown, use web services. The benefit is cross-platform activation, but at the expense of performance.

* The results differ depending on the size of the objects used. When very small objects are used, web services actually perform slightly better than HTTP binary. This conclusion is based on information (and source code) published at *www.dotnetremoting.cc*. My tests mirror these results.

## Using Web Services from .NET Remoting

To get the best of both worlds—that is, cross-platform compatibility and performance—you can access web services from .NET remoting. Imagine a scenario in which a service is not only provided to the world at large, but internally—within the company providing it. There is no reason why the internal clients should suffer from potential performance problems and implementation limitations because the objects they need are web services.

Achieving this compatibility takes little effort. Just add an additional attribute to the web method to let it know that RPC-encoding is needed. The attribute is called `SoapRpcMethodAttribute`, and it is applied like this:

```
<SoapRpcMethod(), _
 WebService(Namespace:="http://www.mydomainhere.com/")> _
Public Class ZipService : Inherits MarshalByRefObject
```

Additionally, the class needs to derive from `MarshalByRefObject`. If not, *SoapSuds* generates the wrong type of proxy.

### Configuration

A *Web.config* file must be provided for the web service (placed into the *ZipService* virtual directory) to register any channels that might be needed and to define well-known object entries. In Example 10-4, a TCP channel is configured to listen on port 1969 and a Singleton that is accessible at *ZipService.soap* is specified for `ZipService`.

*Example 10-4. Web.config for ZipService*

```
<configuration>
  <system.runtime.remoting>
    <application>
      <channels>
        <channel ref="tcp" port="1969" />
      </channels>
      <service>
        <wellknown mode="Singleton"
                   type="ZipService,ZipService"
                   objectUri="ZipService.soap" />
      </service>
    </application>
  </system.runtime.remoting>
</configuration>
```

### Creating the Proxy

Now that the *Web.config* is place, *SoapSuds* can be used to generate a proxy. Do not use the URL to *ZipService.asmx*. Instead, use the URL that includes the `objectUri` attribute from *Web.config*. Remember, the URL is formed from the machine name (or IP address), the virtual directory, and the objectUri attribute from the well-known entry in the configuration file, with ?wsdl appended:

```
soapsuds -url:http://192.168.1.100/ZipService/
ZipService.soap?wsdl -oa:ZipServiceProxy2.dll
```

## The Client

The client, shown in Example 10-5, is similar to most clients from Chapter 9, but with a small variation. Rather than using a configuration file to specify a channel, the channel is registered programmatically.

*Example 10-5. Remoting client to web service*

```
'vbc /t:exe /r:System.Runtime.Remoting.dll
'/r:ZipServiceProxy2.dll remoteclient.vb

Imports System
Imports System.Runtime.Remoting
Imports System.Runtime.Remoting.Channels

Public Class RemotingClient

  Public Shared Sub Main()

    Try

      Dim tcp As New Tcp.TcpChannel(1969)
      ChannelServices.RegisterChannel(tcp)

      Dim zs As New ZipService()
      'Or
      'Dim zsObj As Object = Activator.GetObject(GetType(ZipService), _
      '  "tcp://192.168.1.100:1969/ZipService/ZipService.soap")
      'Dim zs As ZipService = CType(zsObj, ZipService)

      Console.WriteLine(zs.IsValid("Houston", "77002"))

    Catch e As Exception
      Console.WriteLine(e.ToString)
      Console.WriteLine(e.Message)
    End Try

    Console.WriteLine("Press ENTER to continue...")
    Console.ReadLine()

  End Sub

End Class
```

To verify that the TCP channel is in fact used, forgo transparent activation and test it by using Activator.GetObject with "tcp."

# Compatibility

Document/literal and RPC-encoded SOAP were already briefly discussed. The terms themselves mean that the SOAP body can be either RPC-based or Document-based, and the method parameters described within the SOAP body are either `Literal` or `Encoded`.

`Literal` maps method parameters to an XSD schema for each parameter. Each parameter has an element that contains a literal string describing type. These types are mapped to the `xsd` namespace defined in the SOAP envelope:

```
<!-- Used by ASP.NET Web services -->

<?xml version="1.0" encoding="utf-8"?>
<soap:Envelope xmlns:xsi=http://www.w3.org/2001/XMLSchema-instance
               xmlns:xsd=http://www.w3.org/2001/XMLSchema
               xmlns:soap=http://schemas.xmlsoap.org/soap/envelope/ >
  <soap:Body>
    <IsValid xmlns="http://192.168.1.100/">
      <City>string</City>
      <Zip>string</Zip>
    </IsValid>
  </soap:Body>
</soap:Envelope>
```

`Encoded` means that the parameters are encoded as described in Section 5 of the SOAP specification.* A complex type is defined for each parameter:

```
<!-- Used by remoting and other non-.NET SOAP clients -->

<?xml version="1.0" encoding="utf-8"?>
<soap:Envelope xmlns:xsi=http://www.w3.org/2001/XMLSchema-instance
               xmlns:xsd=http://www.w3.org/2001/XMLSchema
               xmlns:soapenc=http://schemas.xmlsoap.org/soap/encoding/
               xmlns:tns=http://192.168.1.100/
               xmlns:types=http://192.168.1.100/encodedTypes
               xmlns:soap=http://schemas.xmlsoap.org/soap/envelope/ >
<soap:Body soap:encodingStyle="http://schemas.xmlsoap.org/soap/encoding/">
<tns:IsValidRPC>
    <City xsi:type="xsd:string">string</City>
    <Zip xsi:type="xsd:string">string</Zip>
  </tns:IsValidRPC>
</soap:Body>
</soap:Envelope>
```

While Document can use `Literal` or `Encoded` parameters, RPC-style SOAP is limited to encoded parameters. To create Document/encoded SOAP, use the `SoapDocumentMethod` attribute on the web method:

* This specification can be found at *http://www.w3c.org*.

```
<WebMethod(), SoapDocumentMethod(Use:=SoapBindingUse.Encoded)> _
  Public Function IsValidEncoded(ByVal City As String, ByVal Zip As String) As
Boolean
```

Example 10-6 contains a listing of `ZipService` that provides methods using all three styles.

*Example 10-6. ZipService encoding test*

```
'vbc /t:library /r:System.dll
'/r:System.Web.Services.dll ZipService.vb

Imports System
Imports System.Web.Services
Imports System.Web.Services.Description
Imports System.Web.Services.Protocols

'Inherits from MarshalByRefObject for .NET Remoting

<WebService(Namespace:="http://192.168.1.100/")> _
Public Class ZipService : Inherits MarshalByRefObject

  <WebMethod()> _
  Public Function IsValid(ByVal City As String, _
                          ByVal Zip As String) As Boolean
    Return True
  End Function

  <WebMethod(), SoapRpcMethod()> _
  Public Function IsValidRPC(ByVal City As String, _
                             ByVal Zip As String) As Boolean
    Return True
  End Function

  <WebMethod(), SoapDocumentMethod(Use:=SoapBindingUse.Encoded)> _
  Public Function IsValidEncoded(ByVal City As String, _
                                 ByVal Zip As String) As Boolean
    Return True
  End Function

End Class
```

The service description pages generated by ASP.NET allow inspection of the SOAP for each method.

Even if using a web service from remoting is not desired, it is still a good idea to use the `SoapRpcMethod` attribute for interoperability. There are quite a few SOAP clients out there that expect RPC-encoded SOAP. Supplying the attribute doesn't hurt because ASP.NET supports both encoding styles.

Also, a few SOAP toolkits do not know how to deal with the `HTTP/Post` and `HTTP/Get` bindings generated by ASP.NET. For these SOAP clients to use the web service, you might need to disable these bindings by placing the following entries in *Web.config*:

```
<system.web>
  <webServices>
    <protocols>
      <remove name="HttpPost" />
      <remove name="HttpGet" />
    </protocols>
  </webServices>
</system.web>
```

There is an upside and a downside to doing this. While the web service is now potentially available to many more SOAP clients, ASP.NET uses the `HTTP/Get` to create the testing form for the web method. As shown in Figure 10-5, it will no longer be available when the bindings are removed.

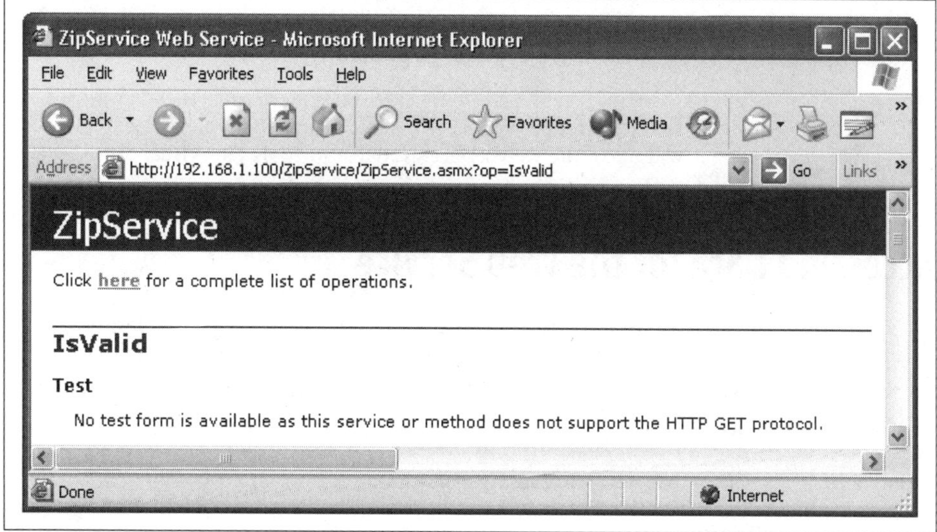


*Figure 10-5. Web method test is no longer available when HTTP bindings are removed*

# UDDI

For web services to work, a mechanism must allow their discovery. That's where Universal Description, Discovery, and Integration (UDDI) comes in. Initially, the UDDI project was started by Ariba, IBM, and Microsoft, but currently, over 220 companies are involved in the effort. The primary goal behind UDDI is to enable companies to find one another on the Web and make their systems available to one another. Think of UDDI as an online yellow pages for web services.

Registering with UDDI is not only easy, it's free. Go to *http://www.uddi.org* to get started. The registration process takes only a few minutes. Currently, you can register with either Microsoft or IBM. However, SAP and Hewlett-Packard have registries in beta, so it shouldn't be long before additional options are available.

Select Microsoft as a registrar to be directed to *http://uddi.microsoft.com*. The registration requirements are simple: a valid email or a Passport account and the usual address information. From the administration menu, one or more businesses can be configured under the account, each with as many web services as needed.

The great thing is that one company's services are on equal footing with the others (name recognition aside). The factors that make a difference, of course, are not only the features offered, but performance and scalability. Chances are that a company running `ZipService` over a cable modem from the garage will not fare well against another provider that has serious fire power on its side.

Each web service is described by a *tModel*, which is a data structure that represents an abstract service type in UDDI. UDDI is not specifically made for web services, although that is what it is primarily known for. The registry is more generic than that. UDDI is really about describing services in general.

A tModel that describes a web service should have the type `wsdlspec`. Having it will make the web service available to tools like Visual Studio .NET.

## Accessing Data for the Web Service

A production version of the `ZipService` would probably use a database like SQL Server or Oracle to provide data for the service. To keep the example self-contained, an XML file (shown in Example 10-7) containing zip code information is used. The file contains only partial data for two cities, but can easily be extended if desired.

*Example 10-7. Partial zip code data for Houston and Austin*

```
<?xml version="1.0" ?>
<cities>
    <city name="Houston">
        <zip>77002</zip>
        <zip>77003</zip>
        <zip>77004</zip>
        <zip>77005</zip>
        <zip>77006</zip>
    </city>
    <city name="Austin">
      <zip>78742</zip>
      <zip>78744</zip>
      <zip>78746</zip>
      <zip>78748</zip>
      <zip>78750</zip>
    </city>
</cities>
```

## Typed DataSet

The implementation does not use the XML directly. Instead, a typed DataSet is created to handle data access. A DataSet provides a consistent relational programming model that is independent of a data source. This means that, once a DataSet is populated, where the data came from is irrelevant. By coding against a DataSet, the data source can be changed at a later time without negatively impacting the web service

The XML Schema Definition Tool that ships with the .NET Framework SDK (*xsd.exe*) does most of the work. This tool can generate an XSD schema that describes the XML in Example 10-7. In turn, that schema can build a derived DataSet class that allows the XML to be manipulated programmatically.

Building a DataSet with this tool is a three-phase process. The first step is to generate a schema from the XML. To do this, run xsd from the command line and pass the name of the XML file as an argument:

```
xsd zipcodes.xml
```

This produces a file called *zipcodes.xsd* that contains the schema shown in Example 10-8.

*Example 10-8. zipcodes.xsd*

```
<?xml version="1.0" encoding="utf-8"?>
<xs:schema id="cities"
          xmlns=""
          xmlns:xs="http://www.w3.org/2001/XMLSchema"
          xmlns:msdata="urn:schemas-microsoft-com:xml-msdata">
  <xs:element name="cities" msdata:IsDataSet="true">
    <xs:complexType>
      <xs:choice maxOccurs="unbounded">
        <xs:element name="city">
          <xs:complexType>
            <xs:sequence>
              <xs:element name="zip"
                          nillable="true"
                          minOccurs="0"
                          maxOccurs="unbounded">
                <xs:complexType>
                  <xs:simpleContent msdata:ColumnName="zip_Text"
                                    msdata:Ordinal="0">
                    <xs:extension base="xs:string">
                    </xs:extension>
                  </xs:simpleContent>
                </xs:complexType>
              </xs:element>
            </xs:sequence>
            <xs:attribute name="name"
                          type="xs:string" />
          </xs:complexType>
        </xs:element>
```

*Example 10-8. zipcodes.xsd (continued)*

```
      </xs:choice>
    </xs:complexType>
  </xs:element>
</xs:schema>
```

If the DataSet were created directly from the schema, the following classes would be created: cities (the DataSet), cityDataTable, cityRow, zipDataTable, and zipRow. Two event classes are also created, zipRowChangeEvent and zipRowChangeEvent. In essence, a class is created that represents a table in a database along with a corresponding class that represents a row of data from that table. Two events are defined that will be fired when data in those rows change. Internally, a parent-child relationship is defined between the two tables.

Because the zip is defined by an XML element, it gets the moniker zip_Text. The city name is described by the name attribute (as opposed to an element). So, to get a zip code, a call to zipRow.zip_Text is used, compared to getting a city name by calling cityRow.name. Very inconsistent!

Using the schema at this point to create a DataSet results in the generation of some very ugly source code, as the following testifies:

```
Dim city As cities.cityRow
Dim row As System.Data.DataRow
For Each row In cityZipDS.city.Rows
  city = CType(row, cities.cityRow)
  If city.name = "Houston" Then
    Dim zipRow As cities.zipRow
    Dim zipRows() As cities.zipRow = city.GetzipRows
    For Each zipRow In zipRows
      If zipRow.zip_Text = "77004" Then
        Return True
      End If
    Next zipRow
  End If
Next row
```

The XSD really needs to be tweaked before the DataSet is created. Rather than thinking of the data in terms of data or a row, a collection analogy is much better—a Cities class that contains a collection of City that, in turn, contains a collection of Zipcode. Getting the city name and zip code through a consistent Text property would also be nice.

The second phase modifies the XSD output by the tool. Before anything can happen, an additional namespace must be added to the schema:

```
xmlns:codegen="urn:schemas-microsoft-com:xml-msprop"
```

This namespace makes several annotations available to the schema. Table 10-1 lists the ones that are pertinent to the discussion.

*Table 10-1. DataSet annotations*

| Annotation | Description |
| --- | --- |
| typedName | Object name |
| typedPlural | Object collection name |
| typedParent | Name of the object when used in a parent relationship |
| typedChildren | Name of the method to return child objects |

Consider the city element here:

```
<xs:element name="city"
            codegen:typedName="City"
            codegen:typedPlural="Cities">
```

By using the typedName and typedPlural annotations with this element, the cityRow class becomes the City class and the Rows property of the primary DataSet class becomes Cities.

Now, when a city is used in a singular context, whether it is a property name or a class name, "City" is used. In the plural, "Cities" is used:

```
Dim cityZipDataSet As cities
.
.
.
Dim city As cities.City
For Each city In cityZipDS.Cities
  'Do something city-like here
Next city
```

Example 10-9 contains the complete listing for the modified XSD that uses the typedName and typedPlural annotations.

*Example 10-9. Schema for annotated DataSet*

```
<?xml version="1.0" encoding="utf-8"?>
<xs:schema id="cities"
   xmlns=""
   xmlns:xs="http://www.w3.org/2001/XMLSchema"
   xmlns:msdata="urn:schemas-microsoft-com:xml-msdata"
   xmlns:codegen="urn:schemas-microsoft-com:xml-msprop">
  <xs:element name="cities" msdata:IsDataSet="true">
   <xs:complexType>
     <xs:choice maxOccurs="unbounded">
       <xs:element name="city"
                   codegen:typedName="City"
                   codegen:typedPlural="Cities">
         <xs:complexType>
           <xs:sequence>
             <xs:element name="zip"
                         nillable="true"
                         minOccurs="0"
                         maxOccurs="unbounded"
```

*Example 10-9. Schema for annotated DataSet (continued)*

```
                        codegen:typedName="Zip"
                        codegen:typedPlural="Zipcodes">
          <xs:complexType>
            <xs:simpleContent msdata:ColumnName="zip_Text"
                              msdata:Ordinal="0"
                              codegen:typedName="Text">
              <xs:extension base="xs:string">
              </xs:extension>
            </xs:simpleContent>
          </xs:complexType>
        </xs:element>
      </xs:sequence>
      <xs:attribute name="name" type="xs:string"
         codegen:typedName="Text" />
    </xs:complexType>
  </xs:element>
 </xs:choice>
</xs:complexType>
</xs:element>
</xs:schema>
```

Once the XSD has been modified to produce aesthetic output, the last phase is the creation of the DataSet. This is done by feeding the schema back to *xsd.exe*. This time, a few additional command-line parameters are necessary:

```
xsd /dataset /language:VB zipcodes.xsd
```

/dataset tells xsd to build a DataSet. An alternative switch is /classes, which causes a set of collection classes to be created. /language determines what language the output file will be written in. This will produce a file called *zipcodes.vb* that can be compiled with the web service.

To get a better feel for what annotations actually accomplish, try creating a DataSet from Example 10-8 and then another from Example 10-9. Do some comparative analysis.

## ZipService.IsValid

Now that a typed DataSet exists, IsValid can finally be implemented. To get the XML into the cities dataset, an instance of StreamReader is used to create a file stream to the XML. The StreamReader is then used to create an XMLTextReader that reads the XML from the stream:

```
Dim cityZipDS As cities

Dim xmlFile As String = AppDomain.CurrentDomain.BaseDirectory & _
  "/bin/zipcodes.xml"

Dim reader As New XmlTextReader(New StreamReader(xmlFile))
```

Finally, an XMLSerializer serializes the XML from the reader into cities, and the reader is closed:

```
Dim serializer As New XmlSerializer(GetType(cities))
cityZipDS = CType(serializer.Deserialize(reader), cities)
reader.Close()
```

At this point, navigating the data is similar to navigating a collection:

```
Dim city As cities.City
For Each city In cityZipDS.Cities
  If city.Text = "Austin " Then
    Dim zipcode As cities.Zip
    Dim zipcodes() = city.GetZipcodes
    For Each zipcode In zipcodes
      If zipcode.Text = "78756" Then
        Return True
      End If
    Next zipcode
  End If
Next ct
```

The final listing for ZipService is in Example 10-10. However, there is a major problem with the implementation. The data is reloaded into cities every time IsValid is called. Remember, calling a web method is just like SingleCall in remoting. The entire object is created and destroyed with every call. The challenge here is finding a way to cache the data so that performance will not be hindered. This implementation actually works well with a few simultaneous callers, but overall, it lacks scalability. There are probably several ways to fix this, but one suggestion is to move the implementation to a Singleton and make the web service a client of that object. The data is fairly static; new zip codes are not created every day. This way, the data would be loaded as needed. The ZipService class would really become a wrapper class to the Singleton implementation.

*Example 10-10. The final version of ZipService.vb*

```
'vbc /t:library /r:System.dll
'/r:System.Web.Services.dll ZipService.vb

Imports System
Imports System.Diagnostics
Imports System.IO
Imports System.Web.Services
Imports System.Web.Services.Description
Imports System.Web.Services.Protocols
Imports System.Xml
Imports System.Xml.Serialization

<WebService(Namespace:="http://192.168.1.100/", _
Description:="This service provides city/zipcode authentication")> _
Public Class ZipService
```

*Example 10-10. The final version of ZipService.vb (continued)*

```
  <WebMethod(), SoapRpcMethod()> _
  Public Function IsValid(ByVal City As String, _
                          ByVal Zip As String) As Boolean

    Dim cityZipDS As cities

    Dim xmlFile As String = AppDomain.CurrentDomain.BaseDirectory + _
      "/bin/zipcodes.xml"

    Dim reader As New XmlTextReader(New StreamReader(xmlFile))

    Dim serializer As New XmlSerializer(GetType(cities))
    cityZipDS = CType(serializer.Deserialize(reader), cities)
    reader.Close()

    Dim ct As cities.City
    For Each ct In cityZipDS.Cities
      If ct.Text = City Then
        Dim zipcode As cities.Zip
        Dim zipcodes() = ct.GetZipcodes
        For Each zipcode In zipcodes
          If zipcode.Text = Zip Then
            Return True
          End If
        Next zipcode
      End If
    Next ct

    Return False

  End Function

End Class
```

# Bibliography


Cheesman, John and John Daniels. *UML Components: A Simple Process for Specifying Component-Based Software*. Addison-Wesley, 2001.

Cline, Marshall P. and Greg A. Lomow. *C++ FAQs*. Addison-Wesley, 1994.

Coad, Peter. *Object Models: Strategies, Patterns, & Applications*. Prentice Hall, 1996.

Gamma, Erich, et al. *Design Patterns: Elements of Reusable Object-Oriented Software*. Addison Wesley, 1995.

Grimes, Richard. ".NET Data I/O." *CodeGuru*, December 2000.

Klipstein, Donald L. Jr. *The Great Internet Light Bulb Book, Part I.* available from *http://www.misty.com/~don/bulb1.html*, 1996.

Knuth, Donald E. "Structured Programming with goto Statements." *Computing Surveys*, December 1974.

Lange, Sebastian, et al. *.NET Framework Security*. Addison-Wesley, 2002.

Lau, Yun-Tung, Ph.D. *The Art of Objects: Object-Oriented Design and Architecture*. Addison-Wesley, 2001.

Liskov, Barbara. "Data Abstraction and Hierarchy,." *SIGPLAN Notices*, May 1988.

Martin, Robert C. "The Open Closed Principle." *C++ Report*, January 1996.

Martin, Robert C. "The Liskov Substitution Principle." *C++ Report*, March 1996.

Martin, Robert C. "The Dependency Inversion Principle," *C++ Report* , May 1996.

Martin, Robert C. "Stability—the Stable Dependencies and Stable Abstractions Principles." *C++ Report*, February 1997.

Meyer, Bertrand. *Object-Oriented Software Construction*. Prentice Hall, 1998.

Rammer, Ingo. *Advanced .NET Remoting*. APress, 2002.

Richter, Jeffrey. "Overview of the BCL Collection Types." *CodeGuru*, November 2000.

Riel, Arthur J. *Object-Oriented Design Heuristics*. Addison-Wesley, 1996.

Synder, Alan. "Encapsulation and Inheritance in Object-Oriented Languages." *Object-Oriented Programming Systems, Languages, and Applications Conference Proceedings*, 1986.

# Index

## A



We'd like to hear your suggestions for improving our indexes. Send email to *index@oreilly.com*.

## H



## I



## J



## K



## L



## M

## R



## S

## T



## U



## V



## W



## X

## About the Author

**J.P. Hamilton** is an independent software developer who lives and works in Houston, Texas. He was born and raised on the 6502 processor (long live Atari) and punk rock, but now devotes most of his time to the .NET Framework. He is also the author of *Visual Basic Shell Programming* (O'Reilly).

## Colophon

Our look is the result of reader comments, our own experimentation, and feedback from distribution channels. Distinctive covers complement our distinctive approach to technical topics, breathing personality and life into potentially dry subjects.

The animal on the cover of *Object-Oriented Programming with Visual Basic .NET* is a double-crested cormorant. Double-crested cormorants (*Phalacrocorax auritus*) are goose-sized birds with dark plumage, webbed feet, long necks, and hooked bills. Though males are usually larger than females, they are otherwise similar in appearance. Immature cormorants are browner, with pale necks and breasts. Cormorants live in marine and inland waters throughout North America. Their diet consists primarily of fish, which they usually hunt in moderately shallow waters.

Cormorants spend much of their time perching on land with their wings outstretched. This behavior may help eliminate parasites, realign feathers, or serve a number of other purposes, but it is most commonly attributed to the drying of feathers. The feathers of cormorants are not waterproof. This decreases their buoyancy and assists their hunting of fish, but requires them to dry their feathers after leaving the water. On particularly hot days, cormorants can also be seen with their mouths open, fluttering their distensible, orange throat pouches. Known as gular fluttering, this behavior helps reduce body temperature.

Derived from the Latin words *corvus* (raven) and *marinus* (of the sea), the name "cormorant" literally means "sea raven." During breeding season, adults have a short, white tuft of feathers over each eye, giving them the "double-crested" appearance for which they are named. The scientific name also refers to these crests; *Phalacrocorax auritus* is Latin for "eared" (*auritus*) "cormorant" (*phalacrocorax*). The word "cormorant" is also used to describe a person who is rapacious or greedy.

Brian Sawyer was the production editor, and Ann Schirmer was the copyeditor for *Object-Oriented Programming with Visual Basic .NET*. Catherine Morris was the proofreader. Claire Cloutier provided quality control. Lynda d'Arcangelo wrote the index.

Emma Colby designed the cover of this book, based on a series design by Edie Freedman. The cover image is a 19th-century engraving from Grosvenor Prints in London. Emma Colby produced the cover layout with QuarkXPress 4.1 using Adobe's ITC Garamond font.

David Futato designed the interior layout. This book was converted to FrameMaker 5.5.6 by Joe Wizda with a format conversion tool created by Erik Ray, Jason McIntosh, Neil Walls, and Mike Sierra that uses Perl and XML technologies. The text font is Linotype Birka; the heading font is Adobe Myriad Condensed; and the code font is LucasFont's TheSans Mono Condensed. The illustrations that appear in the book were produced by Robert Romano and Jessamyn Read using Macromedia FreeHand 9 and Adobe Photoshop 6. The tip and warning icons were drawn by Christopher Bing. This colophon was written by Brian Sawyer.

# Other Titles Available from O'Reilly

## Microsoft .NET Programming

### VB.NET Language in a Nutshell, 2nd Edition

*By Steven Roman, Ron Petrusha & Paul Lomax*
*2nd Edition May 2002*
*682 pages, ISBN 0-596-00308-0*

The documentation that comes with VB typically provides only the bare details for each language element; left out is the valuable inside information that a programmer really needs to know in order to solve programming problems or to use a particular language element effectively. *VB .NET Language in a Nutshell*, 2nd Edition documents the undocumented and presents the kind of wisdom that comes from the authors' many years of experience with the language. Bonus CD ingegrates the book's reference section with Visual Studio .NET.

### Programming C#, 2nd Edition

*By Jesse Liberty*
*2nd Edition February 2002*
*650 pages, ISBN 0-596-00309-9*

The first part of *Programming C#*, 2nd Edition introduces C# fundamentals, then goes on to explain the development of desktop and Internet applications, including Windows Forms, ADO.NET, ASP.NET (including Web Forms), and Web Services. Next, this book gets to the heart of the .NET Framework, focusing on attributes and reflection, remoting, threads and synchronization, streams, and finally, it illustrates how to interoperate with COM objects.

### Programming Visual Basic .NET

*By Dave Grudgeiger*
*1st Edition December 2001*
*460 pages, ISBN 0-596-00093-6*

*Programming Visual Basic .NET* will give you an idea of where the various parts of .NET fit with VB .NET. Ensuing chapters break down and present the language, the common language runtime, Windows Forms, ASP.NET and Web Forms, Web Services, and ADO.NET. The book then moves into topics on developing transactional applications, internationalization, security, and debugging.

### Programming ASP.NET

*By Jesse Liberty & Dan Hurwitz*
*1st Edition February 2002*
*960 pages, ISBN 0-596-00171-1*

The ASP.NET technologies are so complete and flexible; your main difficulty may lie simply in weaving the pieces together for maximum efficiency. *Programming ASP.NET* shows you how to do just that. Jesse Liberty and Dan Hurwitz teach everything you need to know to write web applications and web services using both C# and Visual Basic .NET.

### C# in a Nutshell

*By Peter Drayton & Ben Albarhari*
*1st Edition March 2002*
*856 pages, ISBN 0-596-00181-9*

C# is likely to become one of the most widely used languages for building .NET applications. *C# in a Nutshell* contains a concise introduction to the language and its syntax, plus brief tutorials used to accomplish common programming tasks. It also includes O'Reilly's classic-style, quick-reference material for all the types and members in core .NET namespaces, including System, System.Text, System.IO, and System.Collections.

### ASP.NET in a Nutshell

*By G. Andrew Duthie & Matthew MacDonald*
*1st Edition June 2002*
*816 pages, ISBN 0-596-00116-9*

As a quick reference and tutorial in one, *ASP.NET in a Nutshell* goes beyond the published documentation to highlight little-known details, stress practical uses for particular features, and provide real-world examples that show how features can be used in a working application. This book covers application and web service development, custom controls, data access, security, deployment, and error handling. There is also an overview of web-related class libraries.